CALLSIGN
HADES

CALLSIGN
HADES

PATRICK BURY

**SIMON &
SCHUSTER**

London · New York · Sydney · Toronto

A CBS COMPANY

First published in Great Britain by Simon & Schuster UK Ltd, 2010
A CBS COMPANY

1 3 5 7 9 10 8 6 4 2

Simon & Schuster UK Ltd
1st Floor
222 Gray's Inn Road
London
WC1X 8HB

www.simonandschuster.co.uk

Simon & Schuster Australia
Sydney

The publishers have made every effort to contact those holding rights
in the material reproduced in this book. Where this has not been possible, the publishers
will be glad to hear from those who recognise their material.

End paper images provided courtesy of the author and Richard Pohle, 2008.

Pictures provided courtesy of the author, excluding pictures 3,
Crown copyright, and 10, 13, 15 and 16 which are provided courtesy
of Richard Pohle, 2008.

A CIP catalogue for this book is available
from the British Library.

ISBN: 978-1-84737-859-0 (hardback)
ISBN : 978-1-84737-860-6 (trade paperback)

Typeset by M Rules
Printed in the UK by CPI Mackays, Chatham ME5 8TD

Dedicated to Ranger Justin James Cupples

7 Platoon, Ranger Company, The Royal Irish Regiment

Killed in Action, Sangin, 4 September 2008

And to 7 Platoon

'Get A Fire Goin''

CONTENTS

PART 4: A STORM IS THREATENING

PART 5: THE LONGEST MONTH

O shining Odysseus, never try to console me for dying.
I would rather follow the plough as thrall to another man,
one with no land allotted to him and not much to live on,
than be a king over all the perished dead.

Achilles' soul to Odysseus, Homer's Odyssey

PROLOGUE

This book is not a 'Who's Who of Helmand 2008'. Nor is it history, strategy, politics or an analysis of foreign policy.

It is not meant to glorify 7 Platoon, Ranger Company or myself, nor denigrate anyone. I have tried to be honest to every character I have seen through my own, imperfect eyes.

It is not meant as a statement of fact; more, these are my thoughts and feelings as they happened.

It is not meant for those who serve bravely in the infantry, for I fear my observations are too soft for men who need to remain hard.

Please do not think that any frictions or mishaps portrayed in this book were unique to Ranger Company. I guarantee they are being played out in other FOBs, in other units, in other armies across Afghanistan as you read this. They are what happen when men go to war.

For this is simply a story of war and men. About what men do in war and what war does to men.

That is all.

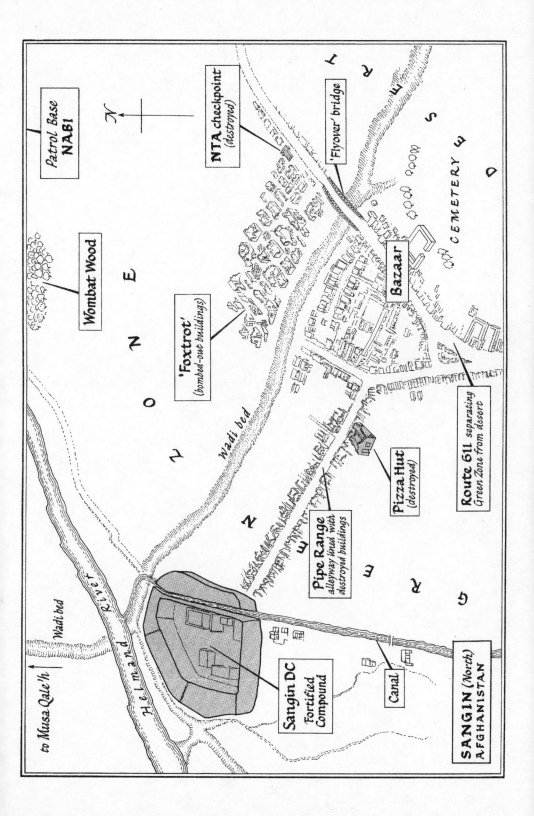

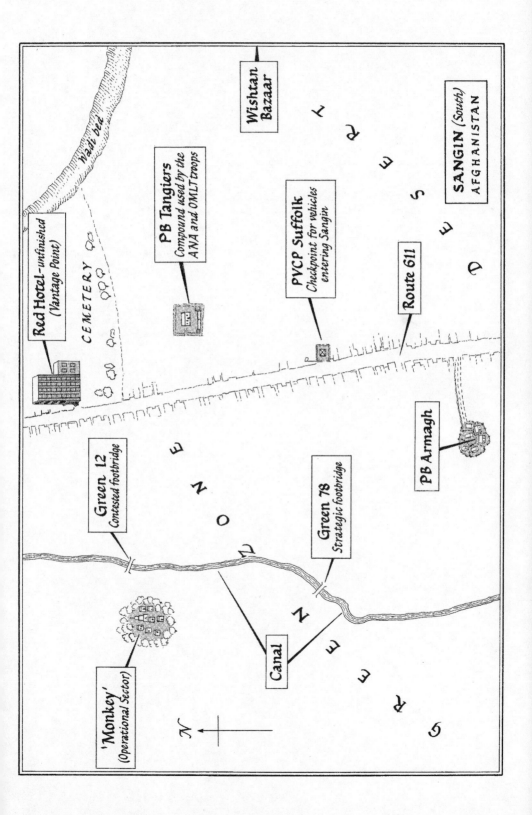

Wishtan
Bazaar

Red Hotel –unfinished
(Vantage Point)

CEMETERY

Wadi bed

PB Tangiers
Compound used by the
ANA and OMLT troops

PVCP Suffolk
Checkpoint for vehicles
entering Sangin

SANGIN (South)
AFGHANISTAN

Route 611

Green 12
Contested footbridge

Green 78
Strategic footbridge

PB Armagh

Canal

'Monkey'
(Operational Sector)

N

Part 1

CHASING THE DRAGON

BROOKWOOD

I know that I shall meet my fate
Somewhere among the clouds above;
Those that I fight I do not hate,
Those that I guard I do not love.

'An Irish Airman Foresees His Death'
W. B. Yeats

I stared at the rows of flagstones standing grey against the large conifers. Shadows fell across them. In other places sunlight lit the graves. Chance had played its part even here. Under the pines and firs of the dark evergreens, weathered and mouldy headstones glared enviously at their bright, clean neighbours in the sun. Did the dead really mind where they were buried? I thought so. I wanted a clean, bright stone that a schoolchild might tend perhaps once a year. They might remember me for the rest of their long lives. I'd be their personal link to the past. Their contribution and mine linked for ever in a veil of understanding. For them my flagstone would signify a real person, alive. But dead.

The Brookwood Necropolis train line delivered London's dead to their final resting place in the countryside. A sombre, macabre train dressed with dark curtains to keep grief in and awkward

3

compassion out. It left the private station beside Waterloo, and made a strange spectacle; mourners packed on the platform as caskets were loaded on to one of the eight separate carriages. As the engine built up steam, pistons working and wheels creaking, the eleven-thirty would pull out of its terminal to arrive an hour later at its special passengers' final destination.

Almost every day, for nearly a hundred years, this ritual was obediently followed, an administrative answer to the Victorian problem of death, space and the ever-expanding city. A whole industry sprang up in the village of Brookwood, Surrey. At its height it had numerous funeral homes, undertakers, florists, stonemasons, all in a village of a thousand inhabitants. Soon the army saw the attraction and began burying its dead there too. Brookwood became the largest cemetery in the world. By 1918 it was the capital of death. A one-stop shop for the grim reaper. Until chance again intervened.

It was only right that war, having profited Brookwood so much, would lead to its downfall. In the early hours of 17 April 1941, a German Heinkel bomber, intent on flattening London, dropped its lethal load on Waterloo Station and destroyed the Necropolis terminal. It was never revived. Now all that remains is a small stretch of track between today's Brookwood railway station and the cemetery. It was this piece of track I stepped across in my crisp camouflage, gleaming black boots and blue beret of a Sandhurst Officer Cadet. I didn't know it at the time, but I may as well have been crossing the Styx.

We visited some time in the first five weeks of training, a whirlwind of sleep-deprived stress and information intake. While we learned how to work our weapons and trained with blank ammunition, our masters had rightly determined that the real cost of war needed to be hammered home to us. It would awaken us to the ultimate sacrifice our chosen profession could call on us to make. And yet as I whiled away my time through the rows and rows of flagstones, looking for anyone with the same name as me, or, when that failed, anyone from an Irish regiment or even Ireland, death still seemed distant, cool, still part of the game that was Sandhurst and training with blanks. War was clean, fun. Everyone came back to life at the end.

Not that I was ignorant of the implications of what I was getting myself into. Since I was a boy I had been enthralled by the army and war. I had read, watched and studied at the altar of war all my life. I had seen and thought I understood the tears of veterans. I knew, I thought, the horror, the bleakness, the pain and the dirt. In fact, I was in awe of it. Transfixed. And maybe I could understand it. But I hadn't felt it. Just like you haven't. And that made all the difference.

I couldn't find any Bury. I couldn't even find anyone from the Royal Irish Regiment. In a way it felt that some emotional link had been stumped.

But I found many dead Irishmen. And there would be many more.

GREEN SEVEN EIGHT

Lightning flashes
Across the sky,
You're only young,
But you're gonna die . . .

'Hell's Bells'
AC/DC

I see the explosion before I hear it. A dark, black vortex spewing out spiralling, deadly chunks of rock. Mud. Dark brown dust
encircles the blackness, screaming out, shooting upwards, out-
wards, sucking and searching and enveloping its victims. Finally
the light brown dust, high, weak, diluted in the uninterested blue
sky. And then a leg. Arching slowly up and falling. Raggedly. Bits
of clothing and flesh separating lazily and falling off it as it tumbles towards the ground.

And then the blast. CRRRUUUUUUMMMPPPPHHHH.

This is it! Here we go!

'Get down! Get down!'

The boys don't need to be told. They are already down on
their knees and bellies in the mud, watching, breathing. Hearts
beat and heads think. Fast. Just above them the pink, white and

purple poppies sway gently in the breeze. We have a panoramic view of the scene ahead of us. Through the poplar trees glistening gently in the wind which line the irrigation ditches separating the plentiful poppy fields from one another. Along the blue-green canal that is flowing speedily south, dissecting the landscape and giving water to the irrigation ditches that nourish the fields. Up the baked white mud tracks that line the canal and lead on to a concrete slab footbridge. It has been destroyed by some forgotten bomb and haphazardly repaired. Now it just clears the water and points skywards and downwards like a concrete Toblerone bar hovering over the water beneath. And finally to the vortex, dissipating into a gentle dust cloud that reveals the outline of a dry mud-walled compound. Across an opium sea of pink, white and green, other, identical compound walls jut out from behind a treeline a hundred metres away from the explosion.

Tom speaks hurriedly down the radio: 'Contact! Wait out!'

Already we can hear the small-arms fire beginning to chatter across the fields. It's too far away for us to worry about. Pitter-patter. Pitter-patter.

My mind races. Tactics. Threats. But, beneath it all, there is the awareness that this is it. Combat. The experience I have sought all my life. Now I will know if I have what it takes. Now I will know if I can do it.

What is going on?

I look at Ronnie; he's already away, moving his section from the exposed field to the safer irrigation ditch.

'Get into cover! Get into cover!' I shout as we start following him, running, bent double in single file towards the ditch.

Ditches equal IEDs.

'Check for IEDs, check for IEDS! Spread out!'

We clamber into the channel, sweating, panting and crawling, snaking forwards until we are level with Tom's platoon. Reports

bounce over the canal: Zip. Crack. Zipzip. Crackcrack . . .
Duhduhduh. Duhduh. Taliban bullets are zinging over our heads
as they try to hit 9 Platoon, who are between us and them on the
other side of the canal. 9 Platoon are firing back.

*Close the door. Close the door. Don't let a suicide bomber jump out and
blow the lads away.*

'Close the door! Close the back door!' I shout anxiously into
the radio.

'Already done, boss,' comes the calm reply from P.J. at the
rear.

Keep the arcs. Maintain security.

'Three-sixty! Three-sixty, lads! Remember three-sixty.
Maintain those arcs. Look out!'

'Williams! Get a fucking grip! Look out that way, not in at me!
That way!'

It's understandable. The young fella is in his first contact and
the bullets are coming from one direction, and I'm telling him to
ignore them and look in the other. And he's been on the ground
for six hours. Six hours in the boiling, exhausting, sapping heat.

More bullets. Over our heads.

What was that?

'Get down! Get down!'

We hug the clay.

The long bursts of our light machine guns and Jimpys are
instantly familiar.

Brrbrrbrr. Duhduhduhduh. Brrbrrbrr.

Our side of the canal.

'Matt! Matt! What the fuck is going on up there?'

He's only a few metres in front of me, watching the canal path.
In the din it may as well be a mile.

More long, lazy roars.

'Matt! Matt! What's happening?'

His reply comes in staccato bursts of a man under intense pressure.

'Boss! Boss! Two blokes just came tearing up on a motorbike, saw us, jumped off, fired at us and ran away. We missed them.'

'Which way, Matt? Which way?'

'East, boss! East!'

'Roger. Listen in. Watch and shoot. Watch and shoot. Anything moves to the east, waste it!'

Crackcrack.

Thatwasclose!

'There! At the wall!' shouts Dev.

The platoon unleashes with everything it has. Finally we are released from those tense, charged moments where we have been scared and confused. It feels good. Everybody bar myself and P.J. are firing. Bullets scream towards the wall, exploding, dancing across it and sending mushrooms of dust into the air.

'Hello, Hades Four Zero, this is Hades Four One. Now in contact too! Repeat . . . now in contact from the east as well.'

'Roger, clear the net . . . Hades Four Three, Hades Four Three, do you have any casualties?'

'Cease fire! Cease fire!' I wrestle with the platoon's destructive urges.

Nobody wants to. Firing has given them back power in this deadly, random situation. But they must.

I tap Williams's shoulder and roar down the radio. We quieten down, content, like a spent lover.

'Hades Four Zero, Hades Four Zero, this is Hades Four Three. We have no friendly casualties. No friendly casualties.'

The drowning, plummeting weight we have all felt since the blast is lifted in an instant.

'Thank fuck for that, boss. Now let's kill the bastards,' P.J. natters into the radio.

By now all hell is breaking loose on the far side of the canal. Tom's platoon has turned away from us and is using every rifle, machine gun and grenade launcher they have to kill the Taliban. The noise is deafening. Radios are rendered useless. Shouting is the only method.

I scream at Sam across the canal. He's standing behind the compound wall, shouting fire control orders to his section smashing the Taliban.

'Sam! SAAAM!'

'What? WHAT?'

'What happened? WHAT HAPPENED?'

'SUICIDE BOMBER, BOSS! Suicide bomber! Blew up in front of Panky's section. Five metres from the point, man! Only blew them on their arses! CAN'T FUCKEN' BELIEVE IT, BOSS!'

I listen carefully as the situation report comes in from Tom.

'Roger, suicide bomber detonated against 1 Section at Green Seven Eight. 2 Section then saw armed men moving on compound roofs across the field. They are engaging and taking incoming. Think we foiled an ambush, probably meant to be initiated by the bomber.'

The boss acknowledges his message on the radio.

'Roger that, Hades Four Three. I want you to assault that position now. Start with compound five one and work north. Move ASAP. I will bring in Hades Four One to echelon through you when you're done. Acknowledge, Hades Four One.'

'Hades Four One, roger. Out.'

'Fellas, we're gonna move across that bridge and echelon through Nine if they need us. Wait for the rate of fire to pick up and then get across. Happy, Matt? Get across as quick as possible; it's bare-arsed out there.'

'Roger, boss.'

The covering fire starts.

There is no incoming now, only outgoing.

'Let's go!'

We rip out of the ditch and race for the baked path. It is completely exposed, the only thing protecting us now the rate of fire pummelling the Taliban compounds.

'Space out! Space out! Keep moving! Fuuucking move!' I pass a struggling ranger. It's not surprising. He is carrying a machine gun, a thousand rounds of ammunition, twenty kilos of body armour, helmet, four litres of water and his rations. Almost forty kilos of kit. He is slowing but does not understand just how dangerous this situation is. Otherwise he'd be sprinting.

Behind me I can hear P.J.: 'Conboy, if you don't get that arse movin' I'll kick you across the fucken' canal meself! FUCKEN' MOOOOVE!'

We reach the bridge. I am waiting for someone down the canal to open up on us as we cross. Bated breath. Up, down. Up, down.

Don't fall in don't trip don't get shot.

We get across.

We reach the safe wall of the compound, melting, heaving. Bungle is there, controlling the fire support guns and waiting to see if there are any casualties in the assault.

'Sergeant Harrison.'

He gives me a wide grin and speaks calmly.

'Boss, good to see ya. Platoon commander's taken two sections across the field and assaulted those two compounds. Both clear. Get over there and get a brief off him.'

'Roger. 7 Platoon, move now! P.J. moving now!'

'Roger, boss. Right behind ye.'

We cross the field and come up into a dry mud alley leading to the compounds. On either side, backs resting against the low walls, sit exhausted soldiers, drawing on cigarettes or staring blankly. At the end, sentries look out, alert. I reach Tom, who's hunkered down, dripping large salty drops of sweat on to his map.

'What's up?'

He grins back, cheeks flustered red, brown banks of dust containing little rivers of sweat running down them.

'Right, Paddy. We blew a hole in the wall and went in red. Cleared the building. No enemy, found an RPG [rocket-propelled grenade], though, and a manual. That one's clear too. But the one round there on the right isn't. We're fucked, mate. The OC wants you to take that one.'

'Roger dodge. Get that, Matt?'

'Yeah, boss. I'm goin' in red, not takin' any chances. Give us a minute to brief the boys.'

'Yeah, no worries. I'll be right behind you with 2 Section if you need us.'

We move up the alley, Matt's point man ahead of him, then him. His section follows behind.

Here we go. Just like training . . .

The point man fires a couple of rounds through the door. Matt kicks it. It crashes in, swinging wildly on its only hinge. The two men charge into the dusty blackness. Bullets seek the corners of the room.

'Room clear!'

The rest of the section sweep in and spread out. I can hear wailing somewhere in the compound.

Matt comes back out.

'Go green, Matt. Go green. Think they've all legged it. It's just kids in there now.'

Soon the compound is clear. The wailing women and children are starting to calm down. Overhead, an Apache is circling in its whirring whocka-whocka, looking for the fleeing enemy. Further above a B52 bomber is watching, spying, for us.

We clear two more compounds 'green' and discover families locked in rooms that the Taliban have been firing from the roofs of. *Sneaky bastards.*

An old man comes out to speak to us. His weathered face, hard hands and white beard indicate he's an elder. He wants compensation for blowing the hole in his wall. I send him to the boss.

We move back to the scene of the blast while 9 Platoon covers us. We find the wheat where the bomber blew himself up pushed flat in a three-metre circular swathe. We find his leg, dirty, bloody and already being eaten by an army of ants. His kidney is still attached. Chunks of torn flesh litter the ground, like raw bloody strips of chicken meat. His scalp rests on the roof of the compound. His tongue near a wall. An iron, bloody smell lingers, mixed with the burned cordite particles that hover around us.

Today we have been very lucky.

The sergeant major is busy packing what is left of the suicide bomber into clear plastic bags and loading them on to a quad motorbike. The boys joke and take pictures with the leg while maintaining a watchful eye on their surroundings. We replenish our empty water packs, sucking, guzzling at our suck straws like babies at the teat.

I am shocked by the suddenness of it, by the immediacy. It looks like the bomber was about my age. Angry, indoctrinated and then wheeled out by the Taliban to blow himself apart harmlessly in an Afghan field. What a waste of a life. Was he brought into the world only to do that? Created in an act of love, of hope, only to destroy himself in an act of hatred?

As we trudge back through the waterlogged fields, feet stinging in our boots, heads and backs baking in the sun, we still try to maintain some semblance of vigilance. Ten hours on the ground has all but killed us. We are at our most vulnerable now. Tired and dehydrated, myself and P.J. urge the platoon on. 'Stay alert, boys, stay focused. There could be another one of those fuckers waiting for us here. Stay sharp.'

The sergeant major drives the quad slowly along the canal path. Out to his flank we patrol through the beautiful fields. Sometimes this place feels like Tuscany.

As we near the gate my mind is wandering. *What a waste.*

I still have my compassion.

SANDHURST

Rejoice, O young man, in thy youth, and let thy
heart cheer thee in the days of thy youth.

Ecclesiastes 11, 9

*Turn back. What are you doing? What are you getting yourself into? This
is crazy . . .*

The battered, Dublin-registered Toyota keeps rolling towards
the gate despite my inner objections. There are many other cars,
all full of bags and ironing boards, driven by other young men and
heading for the same place. I follow suit. Pulling up in the courtyard of a beautiful square of sandstone Victorian houses, fronted
by pristine lawns and tidy trees, I join the busy throng of other
military hopefuls unloading their wares. Here I am.

My first day in Sandhurst is organized chaos, like many things
in the military, I subsequently learn. Cadets dash around, unpacking their cars so they can get more time to do whatever it is they
will be told to do next. With my heart thundering in my chest,
I begin clambering up the red linoleum stairs with my ironing
board under arm. I am greeted by the stern face of the British
military. There, standing straight backed and straighter faced, is

17

a figure that immediately fills me with fear. The man peers at me from under the rim of his peaked cap, head tilted back so he can see me, piercing eyes glaring wildly. Across his smart khaki jacket stands not only a row of imposing medals but the red sash of a colour sergeant. Clenched in his fist, a black and brass pacing stick reaches to the floor. Shining out from under his pressed khaki trousers is a pair of glinting black shoes that immediately catch the eye. This man looks mean.

Oh, feck.

'Name?'

'Bury, colour sergeant.'

'Yeah. Mr Bury. You're 27 Platoon, alright. Down the corridor on the left. Second last room.'

'Yes, colour sergeant.'

That night we are kept very busy. At some stage Colour Sergeant Collins assembles the embryonic platoon for a briefing. He outlines his military experience, which leaves us aspiring wannabes wide-mouthed. He tells us about his family. And he explains his work ethic:

'Work hard for me and I'll work hard for you.'

That's reasonable, mature, even . . . Maybe he's trying to lull us into a false sense of security?

'And if that fails, CLF.'

'CLF, colour sergeant?'

'CLF, Mr Shenton: Cheat. Like. Fuck!'

And that was my first introduction to both British military acronyms and British military humour. My relationship with both would continue throughout my year at Sandhurst.

Why does an Irishman serve as an officer in the British army? It's a question I am asked almost every time I return to Ireland, sometimes with varying degrees of accusation or incredulity.

Certainly, there are big contradictions in serving the Queen as an Irishman. But even the fact that I can admit I served in the British army is a testament to how much attitudes in Ireland have changed in the last five years. I joined the British army for two simple reasons. One: I always wanted to be a soldier. And two: I didn't get into the Irish Defence Forces.

I was born in Dublin to an Irish father and an English mother, both of whom, I can say with affection, were old hippies. From an early age I was fascinated by all things military; by guns, by tanks, but most especially by the Second World War. For me it captured everything that was interesting about war: the clash of good and evil, the power of the Nazis' black uniforms and swastikas, the importance of generals' personal ability, the technological advances that still required a high level of individual skill by their controllers. In short, it had it all, and I dedicated much of my time as a seven-year-old to reading and watching, exploring, what I could. I collected magazines about Vietnam, about weapons of the SAS, and paid my full pocket money every fortnight to subscribe to a Second World War magazine that ran to sixty volumes by the time it finished three years later. To me it was alive. So not only did I study war; I started to live it.

Unfortunately for my parents, I became interested in toy guns from an early age. Unfortunately for me, being the liberal parents they were, they operated a strict arms control policy. Concerned with the mounting arms cache in their home, they implemented a 'one-in, one-out' policy that immediately scrapped my plans of being the most heavily and realistically armed kid on my estate. But, like any soldier, I would not be deterred. Useless red and yellow water pistols, obviously given as gifts, were handed in for decommissioning. In their place, and at considerable cost to myself, were bought the most lethal-looking toy weapons I could find: M16s, sub-machine guns, pistols, anything that looked real and deadly. I wanted to be a real soldier, and I knew enough about it to know what was genuine and what was not. Or so I thought.

Armed with this collection of lethal-looking toys that my friends would borrow when they came over, we set about re-creating battles in the hedgerows and on the lawns of my housing estate. Sloped hills covered in bushes became fortresses for storming, hedges became perfect fire support positions and, best of all, the small clusters of mud that dried at the bottom of these hedges were perfect 'muck bombs' that disintegrated like a grenade when hurled at an opposing fighter. For me it was paradise, and as much of my time as possible was spent trying to find militaristic eight-year-olds who were up for chasing glory in the streets.

And I was attracted to the glory of war. The fantasy. The heroes with their citations and medals were almost other-worldly, untouchable. I relished any stories of heroism as most children relish bedtime tales. I was in awe of their actions, their courage and bravery. And I was aware of the deep bonds of comradeship that drove them to commit such acts. As a lonely child I yearned for that emotional connection. Later, such emotions would come to represent to me the essence of what being a man was, and I would deeply seek war's experience to prove to myself I was a man.

My interest in military history and the army in particular continued throughout school. My parents and our growing family left the city for the space of the Irish countryside. My on-call band of brothers was promptly disbanded and now I had to organize friends' visits and paintball games. My primary school was multi-denominational, which gave me a balanced world view that aided me in Afghanistan later. When adolescence came, my warrior urges were replaced by other urges, but I still found time for war. My secondary school was the closest to home, a local Protestant school where I had great craic, though I managed to underachieve in most people's view.

By the time I was nineteen I was in a bad space and had dropped out of college. Most of this was due to my inability to maintain a relationship with a girl, my first love and best friend at the time. Things fell horribly apart and I was left adrift, trying to discover myself and work things out in my head. I had experimented heavily with ecstasy in the past, but had begun to turn over a new leaf in my attempts to join the Irish army as a private. However, on the way to a party I was stopped and searched by the Gardai; the search revealed some ecstasy pills and I was thrown in jail for the night.

My world was rightly turned upside down. Not only was I a little shit, but I was a naive little shit to boot. But this was exactly the kick in the arse I needed to get my life going. Seeing my future slipping away, I immediately set about voluntary drug testing. The charge was serious, but my lawyers were confident that if they could put enough time between the crime and the court date they could perhaps save me from a criminal record, which would end any chance of my serving in the Irish army.

So for the next two years I worked hard at college. I read history and took any modules even remotely related to conflict and war. I got myself fit. I joined clubs and societies. I got involved and I ended up in positions of responsibility. Another romantic relationship I desperately wanted to succeed fell apart because of my emotional immaturity. Again I was sent reeling, trying to work out who I was. But this time, at least outwardly, I kept it together. By the time of the final court case I was a changed young man. The aspiration and practicalities of getting into the army had brought about this change. It had motivated me to succeed where I had once so obviously failed. I wanted to be an officer more than anything else in the world, and, in striving for it, I had assimilated it; it had become part of my identity.

I stood bolt upright in the dock. Everyone in the court was silent, and there weren't many people, as all the less serious cases had already been dealt with. The prosecution had said their bit. My barrister, expertly chosen by my solicitor not only for her legal skills but also for her beauty and eye-catchingly low-cut blouse, had said her bit. This was it. Complete silence. Outside, the bells of the local church rang high noon.

'Mr Bury, the scourge of ecstasy ruins many families in a particularly heinous way . . .

Oh, Jesus.

. . . and those who use these drugs must understand that they face the full wrath of the law when they commit these crimes.'

Christ, this is bad. I thought they said he was a lenient judge.

'However . . . it is clear to me that you have been clear of drugs for the last two years, and that you have taken the considerable step of volunteering for drug testing at your own expense. I also note that you are now in college and are doing well. . .

This is more like it.

. . . and that you have not come to the attention of the Gardai since the incident in question. Moreover, I understand that a criminal conviction would disqualify you from serving your country, which your solicitor informs me is your goal upon leaving university. While I do not seek to diminish the seriousness of the crime you committed. . .

Here we go . . .

. . . I am prepared to take into account the advice of the probation officer and your conduct since the crime was committed. Therefore I am imposing the Probation Act for two years and a fine of four hundred pounds plus costs. You must understand that if you come to the attention of the Gardai within this time for any matter relating to drugs, you will not only be charged with that offence but with this one as well.'

'I understand, your honour.'

And I was free. I couldn't apply to join the army until a year after finishing college but that wasn't an insurmountable problem. The thing was I could still apply, and that was what mattered. I'd been lucky, I knew that, and I had a second chance.

It was around this time that I began to seek out the somewhat clandestine lives of Southern Irishmen I knew of in the British army. Mick was a brother of a friend in school. He had joined the Defence Forces, won the Sword of Honour there and had been sent to Sandhurst as the Irish army's representative. He won a Sword there as well. He was later poached by Tim Collins's Royal Irish Regiment, just in time for the invasion of Iraq. In my eyes he was a hero.

And another fella from my school, Wes, was in the Paras and loving it. The word was that both got no hassle for being Irish and were having a really good time. They had travelled and they had been to war. I was determined to prove to myself I could be a soldier, an officer. I wanted that life. I had the calling. I decided to run applications to both armies concurrently.

So, with some reservations, an expression-of-interest form went north. Quickly and somewhat unexpectedly I was offered an initial interview. A grumpy colonel interviewed me and was obviously hoping for more than a keen student with no military background. The interview went all right but no better, and I was put off by the way he rapidly fired arithmetic questions at me from across his desk. He did, however, ask me which branch of the army I intended to join – if I was successful.

'I was thinking of the infantry, sir.'

'I see. And who in particular were you thinking of joining in the infantry?'

Now I didn't know much about the regiments of the British army, but I had looked up the Irish Guards' website, so I ventured this as an answer.

'The Irish Guards?' he replied incredulously.

'Yes, if I'm going to serve I want to serve in an Irish regiment, sir.'

'Well, how much land does your family own?'

'None, sir.'

'Well, you wouldn't fit in there then . . . Have you heard of the Royal Irish Regiment? They are full of Southern and Northern Irishmen, and I think that might be the place for you.'

The situation in the north had dramatically improved, so I didn't feel that security would be too much of an issue, but it was an issue nonetheless. As a safety measure, I told only close friends about my plans to join the British army. Whereas I valued their support and also their opinions, I was so set on being a soldier that it didn't really matter to me what anyone thought of my future employers. The same was true of my parents, who realized this was all I wanted to do and were very supportive. However, they obviously had reservations about any army, and my father in particular about the British army. My parents had marched in London against the actions of the army on Bloody Sunday, October 1972. If I was old enough I would have been there too. Thirty-five years later I was attached to the same regiment that opened fire on that crowd of protesters.

Soon I found out that I wasn't going to get in to the Irish army. It hurt, but I could see why. Many of us Southern Irishmen in the British army have experienced the same feeling for varying reasons. The lack of places, the very stringent eye, ear and colour-blindness tests. You can say that some of those who join the British army are therefore the Irish army's rejects, and perhaps they are. But that does not make them any worse soldiers than their compatriots at home. Many others go straight for the British army, with its greater resources, opportunities and deployments. Indeed, those who do take the considerable step of joining the British army have risked more to be a soldier than those lucky enough to be in the Defence Forces. This often makes them more motivated, tougher and better than their peers in the British army. Moreover, we are nothing new. We are an export from our island that is as old as Ireland itself.

Tony Blair also influenced my decision to join. The high-profile 'Force for Good' interventions in Kosovo and Sierra Leone showed the British army as robust peacekeepers who had learned the lessons of Northern Ireland and applied them globally. They also encouraged my more altruistic ideals of military service. Blair's small, successful crusades for justice, democracy and equality were exactly what I wanted to be involved in. These were optimistic times for politicians and military planners alike, and I was persuaded by the idealism of the 'we can fix it' interventionists. When I was joining, Northern Ireland was safe and the Second Gulf War had just been 'won'.

Some ask, 'Well, why didn't you join the Foreign Legion? The Yanks? Anyone but the Brits.' And I can understand that. I did consider them. But I'm not French and the Legion isn't that great. And you can't command in La Légion. Neither am I American, and I would have no idea where I might be sent, with even less of an idea why. So I, like many before me, joined the army closest to home that was not my own.

Still, as I drove towards the gate in Sandhurst, I was having my doubts.

Colour Sergeant Collins screams at me from across the hot asphalt.

'Mr Bury! You look like an epileptic orang-utan!'

'Colour sergeant.'

'Stay in fucking step. It's not fucking hard. Jesus Christ.'

'Colour sergeant.'

My life is a misery. The first weeks of Sandhurst are proving more testing than I had predicted, mainly due to the one activity for which I had failed to prepare myself: drill. I am the most uncoordinated person in my new platoon, and it is starting to piss me, my colour sergeant and, most importantly, my platoon off. Endless lessons of marching, marking time, follow: 'RIIIIIIIGH' TURN, LEEEEEEEFFFF' TURN, INWAAAAAARD WHEEL, ABOUUUUUUUT TURN, MAAAAAARK TIME.' 'KNEES HIGH! KNEES HIGH! MR MONK, THAT MEANS YOU. GET THOSE FUCKING KNEES WAIST HEIGHT. MR HUXFORD, I'M WATCHING YOU . . . MR FUCKING BURY, SORT IT OUT. YOU'RE OUT OF STEP AGAIN . . . 27 PLA-TOOOOOON, QUUUUUIIIICK MARCH! A LEF', A LEF', A LEF', RIGH', LEF', A LEF' . . .'

My life thus far has evaporated into insignificance when compared with the vital matter of moving arms and legs in time with the platoon. I am an outcast, an idiot, and there isn't much I can do about it. No one in the platoon wants to know me. In only the first week I am already not meeting the standard. That elusive omnipresent standard, the guillotine we all fear desperately. I am terrified. Terrified of failure, terrified that I am not good enough. In this early stage, drill is the army, and I am not liking the army one bit. And it isn't liking me either.

Drill was the perfect method with which Sandhurst started its programme of 'socialization'. Throw the new platoon together in an alien environment. Deny them sleep. Change their terms of reference and benchmarks of self-worth. Replace societal and language norms with an alien culture and vocabulary. Deny them wristwatches. Put them together and dress them identically. Scream commands at them and watch as they respond without question, without thought, moving as one body, united.

Not that we don't realize. Or care. We all want to succeed above everything, and we will swallow whatever our instructors tell us in these early weeks. I find it hard. Each time I go out on that parade square I am rightly singled out and screamed at. It becomes confidence shattering, as do the remarks of, and avoidance by, my platoon after drill. Even though I have warned my parents to expect a distressed phone call in the first weeks, when I ring home I really do want out. It is hell. Normally I'm as good as the next person at most things. Now I'm shit at everything. And as the Queen is meant to visit soon for a special display, there is more drill than usual to contend with. We spend hours melting under our thick woven uniforms in the scorching July sun, the Union Jack's shadow rippling on the parade square in front of us. Cadets collapse and are dragged away. I hang in there.

We average about four hours' sleep a night for those first weeks. The days begin with gut-wrenching water parades followed by a light breakfast that is inhaled rather than eaten. Everything is timed to the second; too long a queue in the canteen means that breakfast is sacrificed to arrive five minutes before the first lesson begins. This is typically PT – physical training, of some sort; running, tabbing with your bergen, an assault course. Our instructor is an army physical training staff sergeant by day and DJ'ing maestro by night. A London wide boy, he often confuses himself and us with his instructions, which give us all a lift: 'Form half a semi-circle around me' denotes the beginning of our stretching routine. Or once, delightfully: 'Mr Reed, as I said before, I'm not going to repeat myself.' Thus sometimes the hardest thing about PT is not laughing for fear of the threatened 'beasting' we will get if we do. And our forced marches in the woods often have unexpected infiltrators. The paparazzi leap out from the undergrowth and startle us, cameras clicking wildly. They are after the juiciest of targets in our midst, our celebrity cadet, Prince Harry.

PT is followed by a rushed shower and a change into another order of dress. Fear reigns here too. As we stand outside ready to be marched to our next lesson by Colour Sergeant Collins, he inspects us, one of his five or so inspections a day. Have I remembered everything? Is something ironed incorrectly, not up to standard? The endless changes of uniform create laundry. Laundry equals ironing. Ironing equals inspections. Inspections equal fear. Fear. Am I late? Are the rest of the platoon waiting on me? Usually not, but this pervasive fear runs right through my every day. Through the tactics lessons I try desperately not to sleep through. Through the weapons-handling lessons. Through the endless information being fired at us on first aid, drill, weapons systems, leadership. When someone does succumb I feel better than them. I can fight through. But what will happen to him? Will he get seen? Will he get bollocked? Fear.

It was our first fitness test since being accepted. It had been a torrid week, but fitness was one of my strengths. I ran as fast as my Irish legs would carry me and finished first in my platoon. 'You're a bit of a dark horse aren't you, Paddy?' Welsh Reedy grinned at me afterwards. At this stage I wasn't sure if people actually knew my name was Paddy or just called me that for obvious reasons. 'Jesus Christ, mate, how much training did you do before you turned up?' asked Hux next door. Suddenly I had my confidence back. Suddenly I was good at something the army recognized. Suddenly, it seemed, the instructors were off my back. Actually they weren't, but their criticisms on the parade square did not bite nearly as deep. I even got picked to meet the Queen, something which shocked me and the other members of the platoon who were far more interested in meeting her than I was. In the end she couldn't make it.

The late nights stretched us to the limit. Once lessons finished at about nine, we were free to conduct our own 'administration'. Maps had to be marked and laminated. Uniforms had to be tailored, boots bulled. This was the time for ironing, for folding, for stacking, for polishing, cleaning, sweeping. Communal jobs in our block kept us busy until midnight before the next morning's daily inspection. Then it was into our rooms to measure the gaps between stacks of regulatory folded T-shirts and the cupboard, to check that all our socks were in the correct drawer and folded the correct way, *showing an inch of ankle material front*. Sometimes we slept on the floor for fear of creasing our beds. It was endless, it was pedantic and it was stupid. But together we laughed through it. And because we laughed, as a team, it was very important. We became a platoon.

The desert stretches out in front of me, the platoon around me in desert fatigues, spaced out and cautious as we patrol down a desert track. To my right and above us a walled town of traditional flat-roofed mud buildings and the odd aerial looms over us, turning orange in the ruby dusk light.

Bullets kick up in front of me. No sound, just small explosions of sand and mud, right in front of me. One a few feet away, the second closer, the third closer still. I know what to do but I can't move. I'm helpless. Clay. It's too quick.

Pure, pitch blackness.

I awake with a bang, my body pumping. I know exactly what has happened. I have just been shot in the head.

Our days continue with navigation lessons and orienteering tests. Back bearings, triangulations and route selection are our new gods, maps our bible. On the hot days we run around the beautifully maintained Sandhurst lawns, woods and lakes looking for hidden markers and sweating ourselves fit while the summer sun shines down.

By the end of the fifth week we are fully competent on our weapons, can sustain ourselves in the field and can navigate. We are about to be released for our first weekend of freedom since we rolled through the gates. There is only one last test to pass.

The week five pass-off involves marching out alone, in front of not only all the other platoons lined up on the vast tarmac expanse front of house but also all the college brass. Any mistake in drill, or failure to answer questions when tested by the brass, spells failure and therefore embarrassment.

'Mr Bury!' the adjutant yells across the square.

'Sir!'

In a blur of straight arms and legs I venture out alone on to the square.

Getting closer . . . halt, check . . . Shit I messed that up. I slam my steel-heeled boots hard into the tarmac and stand as straight backed as I can. The adjutant is dressed in the green tartan trousers and Garryowen cap of a Scottish Division officer.

'Who is the new college adjutant?'

'Captain Alderwood, sir.'

'Correct. Who is the old college commander?'

'Colonel Woods, sir.'

'Yes. And who is the Academy sergeant major?'

'Academy Sergeant Major Gaunt, sir.'

'Correct. Off you go.'

I march back, knowing I have messed up, thinking I have failed the drill. The other cadets continue to be called out. Then silence.

'Mr Bury. Again!'

Oh, no.

This time I bang my tabs in perfectly. The adjutant eyes me again.

'In the film *Return of the Jedi* Luke Skywalker, Princess Leia and Han Solo all get medals at the end. Why doesn't Chewbacca?'

'I have no idea, sir.'

'Just checking. Off you go again.'

Having managed to somehow display the required competency in front of the whole intake, I subsequently found out I had passed and was now the proud owner of a belt denoting such competency. I also got that weekend off. I slept through most of it.

The training continues at a whirlwind pace, but we are more experienced and hence get more sleep. Tactics lessons take place out on 'the area', a military playground of tracks, forests and hills behind Sandhurst. Here we formulate our plans to stop a Russian motor rifle company from seizing the local town. Or attack a valley held by a platoon of rebels who have declared their own protectorate of Berkshire-Herzegovina. It is basic stuff, but there is still much to take in. We learn by the time-honoured principle of repetition and debriefing. Each lesson, some unfortunate is singled out to brief his plan and then gets it shredded by our instructors, known as the Directing Staff (DS). But we all learn from each other's mistakes, and especially learn from our own. They are the ones that bring the sting of criticism, the fear of failure. They are the mistakes you do not forget.

We spend hours battling sleep in lecture halls as instructors brief us on the phases of war, the combat estimate, morality in war, British defence policy . . . It never ends and we fight heavy eyelids with as much willpower as our keen but exhausted minds can muster. Often officers visit to share their experiences of commanding in Iraq, Sierra Leone, Kosovo. These visits captivate me. Here is the real deal, away from the bullshit epitomized in the glasshouse that is Sandhurst. We listen intently, like sailors listen to an explorer recently returned from their impending destination. I wonder if I have what it takes to get there.

The morality lectures interest me. Apparently we should all have our own integral moral compasses to be a leader. 'Well, if that's the case,' I ponder, 'why are you ramming it down our necks?' 'Do what is right,' they say. *Whose concept of right?* I wonder. I treat some of what they teach with a healthy degree of liberal scepticism. At the time they were just another bunch of lectures to fight sleep through. Later, they would ring true.

The week-long manoeuvres in the field, 'exercises', are designed to test our developing command and control. Command appointments rotate and dictate who is in command and when. I fear and yet seek them in an uneasy paradox, just as I do combat. My first appointment comes at the end of our first major exercise. The waiting and wondering is over.

Thrust into the limelight, I nervously plan and rehearse and consult before the final attack. I deliver my orders. Lying in my sleeping bag, I go through the plan over and over in my head. Maybe I can get an hour's sleep. The rest of the platoon have been asleep since eleven. Not so the commanders. I awake and pull myself out of my olive-green cocoon. Kit is packed away, weapons loaded and faces smeared with camouflage paint. As the platoon makes its way to the forming-up point, the only things visible are the yellow blast reducers for blank-firing at the end of our weapons.

We creep silently along the track in the blackness, the tops of trees silhouetted against the sky our only guide. The platoon snakes in hushed single file as we move, slither, towards the objective. Around us, other platoons in other snakes are slipping towards the same goal. We cross ditches that flow deep with icy Welsh water and trip through recently deforested blocks that contradict our maps. My lead section commander is an excellent navigator, yet there are moments of sheer panic when I think we are lost. As dawn nears in the valley we are enveloped, not by the enemy, but by a thick, creeping fog. Myself, my navigator and the DS inch forward to confirm we are in the right position, a position that will allow us to suppress the farmhouse another platoon are to attack.

'So, Mr Bury . . .' Captain Jackson whispers in a low tone as he lays himself down by a hedgerow, '. . . where do you think we are then?'

I look intently at my map and point to the pre-marked dot. 'We're here, sir, just east of the fire support position.'

'Well, then, let's see . . . Have you heard of a GPS, Mr Bury?'

'Yes, sir.'

'And do you know what it stands for?'

'Global Positioning System, sir,' I say as I watch him switch it on and the device start to track the satellites spinning miles above us. *If only we could use them . . .*

'Nearly, but not quite . . . It's actually a Gentleman's Positioning System. But well done, you're right where you should be.'

I cast a devilish grin at my navigator and we chuckle our way back to collect the platoon.

The final attack went well. I screamed a lot. I ran around a lot. I moved the platoon as best I could, given the ground. We killed all our Gurkha enemies. And I thoroughly enjoyed it. I could do it. And the DS thought I could do it as well. So did the platoon. It was one of the most rewarding, wholesome experiences of my life to that date.

For my part, I couldn't understand why anyone would join the army and not join the infantry. That was what it was about, and unless you had a real desire to drive tanks, fly helicopters or fire big guns, there was no other choice. No one with the warrior calling joined the army to be a logistician, administrator or educator.

Perhaps more sensible people did, but that was missing the point. Either way, those of us baying for the infantry at the top of the platoon were generally fitter, more capable in command and more resilient to sleep deprivation than those at the bottom.

We are on another night attack, hunched low and close together on a track in a wood. The enemy are close. Captain Jackson walks down our single file of camouflage whispering at us to keep quiet. We peel around into attack formation, all eyes fixed on the small fire that marks the enemy position. Light and noise erupt. The stutter-stutter of rapid rifle fire. Everything is illuminated in flashes. Black. Yellow. Black. Yellow. Yellow. Black. We charge forward through the din and strobe light flashes, closing on the fire.

'Delta drop here, fire base!' someone screams.

The four inky figures to my left drop and start hammering the position. I hit the soft pine needles and start crawling, the muddy boot of the man in front catching my nose. We are close now. I stop moving and start firing on to the position from a different angle. There are now only two attackers crawling towards the enemy. The rate of fire increases. A grenade is flung, bouncing right on to the enemy hunkered down behind a large fallen tree.

The bang is puny, as dummy grenades are. The last attackers storm the position, blanks chattering continuously. The Gurkhas jump, roll over and squeal hilariously. We laugh and close in. All that is left to do is collect the spent brass and find the parts of the dummy grenade. Another training attack over. Everybody back to life.

We wind our way over the Welsh hills, struggling to keep steady as we are blasted by the wind, the judging eyes of our DS ever present. Tonight is an ambush. We break down into the 'killing group' and two 'cut-off groups' to stop the enemy escaping. We sit in a wood and listen to the wind howl. The Gurkha truck comes.

'Ambush sprung.'

Noise and light.

Everything goes silent. The wind still howls, tearing through the trees, seeking out every hole in our uniforms. We fight sleep. Unsuccessfully.

'What was that?'

Silence.

'Hey, J.C., what was that?'

'Huh . . . I don't know, man. I must've fallen asleep.'

'Me too. Listen, what the hell is that?'

'. . . Sounds like someone loading a truck . . .'

'Oh, shite. How long have we been asleep for?'

'God knows. I can't even see my watch it's so black in here.'

'They've forgotten about us, J.C.! They're getting on that truck and leaving us here, man.'

'You could be right. Tell you what, you crawl out there and see if you can get a better look. I'll go and see if I can find the platoon commander. See you back here in figures ten.'

I begin crawling out of the forest and into a rush-covered field, still half asleep. As I move closer, I can hear, despite the wind, the noise of soldiers loading up on to a truck. The rear gate is pulled closed, the distinctive clang of metal on metal echoing out from the road. The engine guns.

They're leaving us! They've forgotten us!

Still confused from sleep and cold, I stand up all alone in that field and roar: '27 PLATOOOON, IS THAT YOU GETTING ON THE BUS?'

From behind me, where the platoon is still shivering in the forestry block, comes a swift reply. It is in a Scottish accent I both recognize and fear.

'Mista' Buraaay! Shu' tha fuck up! Wha' tha fuck are yu dooin'?'

Suddenly reality crashes around me. The ambush is complete. That was the dead Gurkhas driving off. The whole platoon is still here in position. I have just made a complete tit of myself.

'Er . . . just checking the trip flares, colour sergeant.'

'Yeah, righ' yer were. Get tha' fuck back in here now, yu mad mun.'

There were other elements to Sandhurst I enjoyed too. Socially, it was a whole new world to me. While most cadets were middle-class graduates, there were some pretty serious social anomalies. Both royal princes were at Sandhurst. In our platoon we had an extremely friendly and down-to-earth son of an earl. This was not the norm, as I noticed that although the public-school-educated cadets were generally more confident, the state-schooled bunch had better people skills. We had a prince of Bahrain. We had a Senegalese cadet. The platoon was a mixed bag of fit and motivated young men who were enjoying themselves and enjoying the company of like-minded individuals. It was good craic.

We partied like confident young men do, and we were intensely, arrogantly, proud of our militaristic achievements. Most of us were single or newly single due to the demands on our time, and I was no exception, being dumped because I could barely stay awake in her company at weekends. Too much partying could land yourself in hot water, though, and we had to be careful not to overdo things, especially on the Academy social nights. These consisted of formal dinners, held deep in the old innards of Sandhurst, lit by glowing candles. All along the stretched mahogany dining tables were lines of cadets, pristine and robot-like in their constricting yet elegant Number 1's dress uniform. Old silver pieces decorated the tables and glinted in the dark, warm candlelight. We had guests to host and toasts to remember, so getting too drunk was not advised. We still felt the possible wrath of the omnipresent DS, even on these relatively relaxed occasions where we enjoyed silver service and free-flowing alcohol. The pipers played their reels. And, always at the end, the toast to the Queen. And though I neither understood nor felt any affinity with the British monarchy, I joined in, as I felt an Irishman in the British army should. After all, the British army had offered me a way of realizing my dream. It had accepted me as one of their own and had not discriminated against me because of my nationality. But it was still strange.

Just as it feels strange singing the British national anthem at the end of church on Sundays. The red-bricked church is one of the most beautiful I have seen. Inside, in the array of arches and columns, old regimental colours hang from the ceiling. Each column, rising high into the roof above, bears the golden names of a given regiment's dead officers. This is the spiritual home of the British army's officer class.

I have never been religious, so our weekly trip to church is curious. I sing 'God Save the Queen', once I have learned the words, but always with the detached feeling like I am watching myself in a movie. *How did I end up singing this when I've never even been taught my own national anthem? And why haven't I been taught it?* My eye catches an inscription above me. It is emblazoned for all to see; black stencils on grey marble: Horace's 'Dulce Et Decorum Est Pro Patria Mori'. The 'old lie', as Owen had said, with words that I had learned in primary school that contained a bitterness, a final, furious rejection of British society's misplaced norms. Yet here was the original, arching over my head as I sang, trying to convince me otherwise.

Strange.

As we neared the end of our time in Sandhurst the momentous Regimental Selection Boards loomed over us. These boards determined who would be your family for the next three years. Both my choices were infantry, the Royal Irish and the Royal Anglians. I found myself in a dilemma: I didn't know which to choose. I had visited the Anglians and I knew I would fit in there. As a local English regiment they were very welcoming to me. The young officers were professional and relaxed and I could see I would get on with the soldiers. My Irishness simply was not an issue. I was being judged solely on competency and character. I hadn't met any Royal Irish officers because they were in Iraq, but I still figured I'd get on with the soldiers. Most of this certainty was down to a Lance Corporal Coult whom we had met in a bar in Inverness. Capable and outspoken, 'Speedy' gave me a big warning across a pint-laden table. 'Sir, you know, you may be commissioned but you're nothing until you pass Brecon. That's when you get the respect of the boys.' He made sense. Brecon was the specialist infantry training school after commissioning. Meanwhile, I still had to choose whom I would commission with.

The next day, as I stress and seek advice, an email arrives from Mick, the friend who had swapped the Irish army for the British. He is in Iraq with the Royal Irish. He says that there is no other place for an Irishman in the British army than in the Royal Irish. I am sold. I accept a commission in the 1st Battalion, the Royal Irish Regiment. It feels great.

The final Sandhurst exercise takes place in Cyprus. It's like being part of our own war movie, in which we direct and star. We stand, swaying in the landing craft as it approaches the red smoke rising from the shoreline. The enemy guns chatter at us, the ramp is dropped and we storm ashore on our first seaborne invasion, assaulting bunkers, throwing dummy grenades and generally having a whale of a time. Our own interactive *Saving Private Ryan* paid for by the British taxpayer. We move inland and drive rebels out of the mountains. We dig into the hard hills and spend mornings shaving from our tin mugs in the beautiful yellow-red dawn of a Cypriot spring. Dream realized.

And everyone comes back to life at the end.

Friends and family gather in the lush and impressive Sandhurst buildings, and the champagne flows freely all night. Long luxurious drapes decorate the rooms filled with cocktail bars, vodka ice statues and chocolate fountains. Beautiful young women sweep by in elegant dresses as we are crammed uncomfortably into the red waistcoats of our respective regimental mess dress uniforms. A royal prince, girlfriend on arm, stumbles by, all eyes excitedly following them. In their wake come the anecdotes. Harry has recently been in the papers for falling out of a strip joint in Slough. During dinner Prince Charles turns to Harry: 'I don't mind you going to strip joints, but for heaven's sake, Slough?'

The Union Jack flutters proudly above the magnificent Victorian building. As midnight chimes, a spectacular firework display heralds our commissioning. I tear off cloth pieces to reveal a single silver pip on each green shoulder board. *All that hard work for these?*

Our night ends with Wes, the eternal Para, shouting at my guests to jump out of my window on to the ground five feet below. 'Red on. Green on. Jump! Jump! Jump!'

'Maintain momentum! Maintain momentum!' he shouts as girls disappear in a flurry of silver frocks, to be reunited a second later with terra firma. The next day I leave Sandhurst with a killer hangover and my new mess dress torn to shreds. I roll out of the gates in a new car thinking what a great experience that was. *Like school with guns.* But I know things are about to get a lot more serious.

BRECON

The aim of military training is not just to prepare
men for battle, but to make them long for it.

Louis Simpson

As I prepared for the platoon commander's course in Brecon,
things were getting very serious indeed for a select group of men
from the Royal Irish Regiment. Spring 2006 saw Speedy, and
many other characters I had yet to meet, fighting for their lives
in the same towns in Afghanistan that would soon be etched on
my psyche. A select Royal Irish platoon, known as Ranger
Platoon and including hand-picked soldiers from the battalion,
had been quickly formed to reinforce 3 Para's deployment. They
were led by Sean and Richie.

The platoon finds itself operating in myriad duties from escorting medical-response teams that swoop down extracting
casualties to close-quarter combat. In the summer of 2006
Helmand is in flames as NATO tries to crush the Taliban strongholds that dominate the province. The Rangers find themselves
in the midst of a complex ambush in what had seemed the dreary
little village of Zumbelay. They conduct a fighting retreat for four

hours without air support against a pressing enemy. Later, they 'liberate' the strategic town of Sangin from a Taliban force that all but melts away in their presence. For a time Sangin is deemed safe enough for the Rangers to patrol the streets in desert hats, in a tactic that has echoes of the latter-period Northern Ireland, low-key approach. Things soon change.

For six weeks the Royal Irish and the Paras defend Sangin in the face of ever-mounting attacks by the Taliban. While I learn the infantry trade in Brecon, these men practise it in the daily fight for their lives. During one attack, Lance Corporal Luke McCulloch is struck by mortar shrapnel in the head and subsequently dies. Others, like Richie, are badly injured. Still they hold out.

As Helmand begins to spiral out of control, it becomes increasingly clear that we have bitten off more than we can chew. Reserve platoons are called up, trawled for across an already overstretched army. The Royal Irish answers the call again in July. Two more platoons, Somme and Barossa, are formed of volunteers and led by Mick and Paul. They deploy to the besieged town of Musa Qaleh. The struggle there deteriorates into a battle of epic proportions as the Taliban mount daily human wave attacks against the beleaguered Royal Irish defending it. The fighting comes to the walls; grenades have to be dropped from the parapets. Suddenly things are very serious, very real and very close. I endeavour to listen intently to the advice of my new DS at the infantry school.

The course starts with a tough two-miler around the hilly camp with twenty kilos of kit strapped to our backs. I have trained and trained, heeding Speedy's earlier advice and knowing how much first impressions count. I tear off the start line and settle into third place. Those ahead of me are seriously fit young officers. I complete the first mile in under seven minutes. And

then it begins to hit me, halfway through the second lap. First my
ears pop. Then I feel dizzy. My back gives out. I slow to a walk,
furious yet helpless as the lesser fit pass me. I turn the final corner
before the finish line, vision now only in patches and drooling like
a baby. I cross the finish line and collapse in a heap. Unbeknown
to me in my semi-conscious state, another sergeant major rushes
to help. Suddenly there is someone else shaking me, shouting in
my face. I recognize the face of the only Royal Irish instructor in
the school.

Oh, no.

'Sir! What the fuck! Get a grip on yourself! You're fucking
Royal Irish, sir. Sort it out. Sir! Sir! For fuck's sake! Get some
pride!'

His thick Dublin accent is the last thing I hear before I pass out.
Disaster. Absolute. Disaster.

I awake in the hospital, tubes in forearms connected to drips.
They tell me I have just taken two litres of saline solution and am
on a third. *What?*

With the extra fluids, I recover quickly enough to find out that
I have actually passed the race with thirty seconds to spare.
Relief. But this does not save me any embarrassment in front of
the course, or from the Royal Irish instructor, the fearsome
Colour Sergeant Connors. Not only am I dismayed at my loss of
face in front of him, but I know he is to be my new company sergeant major back in battalion. This is a terrible start. Soon I
realize it's the anti-malarial drugs I am on. I stop taking them and
fight through.

The school has an edge to it that Sandhurst does not. A serious edge. A hard edge. A killing edge. The instructors are not the
polished career-oriented colour sergeants of Sandhurst, but
tough, aggressive and rough men who ooze bloody combat experience. They instruct us on the new weapons now available to us

infanteers. They are more deadly, more murderous than anything we have seen before.

'The General Purpose Machine Gun. Or Jimpy. 7.62 millimetre. Maximum Range Light Role 800 metres. Maximum Range Sustained Fire 1,800 metres. Tracer Burnout 1,100 metres. Map Predicted Fire out to 2,400 metres. Remember the lethal beaten zone widens with range. The Light Machine Gun. 5.56 millimetre. Maximum Range 800 metres, effective to about 400 metres. An excellent close-quarter weapon system. The 51-millimetre Mortar. Maximum Range 800 metres. Minimum Range 50 metres. Lethal blast radius 20 metres. Let me tell you the fucking Taliban don't like this one bit. Fifty years old and still producing the fucking goods. I fucking love it. Excellent piece of kit. The Underslung Grenade Launcher. Maximum Range 350 metres. Fires 40-millimetre grenades in a variety of natures. Fellas, it's a new system to replace the 51, but I'd take the 51 any day. Still, it's great for keeping the ragheads pinned.'

Magnified sights to shoot the enemy. Phosphorus grenades to smoke him out. The bayonet to kill him. This is closer, more personal. This is not Sandhurst. It is extreme violence. It is killing. Those who excel are straightforward, common-sense young officers compared with the more reflective, analytical mind that did well in Sandhurst. Over-analysis is indecisiveness. I am merely average in this new practical and earthy world of the infanteer.

The exercises are harder, the sleep non-existent and expectations higher when in command. Other young officers learn to drive tanks or study soldiers' pay matters. We learn to attack, defend, ambush, reconnaissance (recce), raid and patrol with every minute detail and experience our DS can impart to us. The infantry mission becomes our mantra: 'To close with and kill the enemy, in all weather conditions, in all terrain by day or by night.' We relish that word, kill. KILL. We are the sharp end. The bayonet. We are the warriors. We are proud of our role. Who the fuck are the rest of the army? What the fuck do they do? We fight. We kill. We are the infantry. The warriors. The God of fucking war.

A platoon attack, we learn, is maximum aggression, momentum and violence concentrated on a particular place in space and time. We need to be quiet to maintain surprise. Don't make any noise. Don't shout out commands. 'You wouldn't walk up to an old granny in the street and say, "Excuse me but I'm going to mug you in a minute," would you? No, you fucking wouldn't. You'd walk up and kick her fucking head in and take her purse and fuck off. That's what you'd fucking do.' If silence is needed before the attack, music is needed for it: 'A symphony of violence unleashed on the enemy,' our commander imbues. 'At any point in the attack you should be able to know what stage it is at by the rate of fire. The final assault must be conducted in a deafening crescendo of violence.' We like the analogy. And so we conduct our own symphonies on the hills of Wales and in the bushes of Malawi. We attack with live bullets and grenades and mortars. And we destroy. We destroy bunkers, mock villages and targets indiscriminately. Adrenalin pumping, we toss grenades, wait for the crump and storm bunker positions screaming, firing rapidly and finally thrusting our bayonets into the limp, shrapnel-peppered dummies.

'Position clear! Two enemy dead! Enemy depth position 300 metres left of arc!'

Africa tests us further. The burning tracer rounds ignite the Malawian bush around us. The flames burn in the breeze, driving towards the rebel base in the distance. Smoke everywhere. Charred black, hot ground singes our knees and hands. *Hell*. The Jimpys come up and hammer the dummy village, tearing chunks of wood and wattle from the frames of the huts. The mortars pop, followed seconds later by the dull crrruuump as they explode in a cloud of black, brown and grey dust. Another hut bursts into flames. Destruction. It feels good.

I sit contentedly on the huge basalt rock, savouring the view. The covert observation patrol is nestled into the black-red rock face commanding the ground for miles around. Two of the guys are asleep, another on radio watch listening to crackle. Dusk comes and the bush below morphs into red and green waves of jungle, lapping at our rock, beneath the pink-purple sky. My stomach pitches and groans. We ran out of rations a day ago.

The beautiful view heartens me. Somewhere beyond is the border. I am looking straight into Zambia. People would pay to see this. And I'm getting paid. It doesn't get better than this.

Part 2

BAILIFF

FORT GEORGE

We're the Irish Rangers,
The boys who fear no danger,
We're the boys from Paddy's land
YO!
So get off your horse and fight!

Killaloe
Royal Irish Regimental March

The bodhrán beats steadily through the dim orange light. Men huddle low around the tables, eyes on the players, pints in hands. The guitar joins in. Then the whistle. A cheer, a yo! And they're off.

I glance around the snug at the cheery faces absorbed in stories, anecdotes, craic. Near the band, actively encouraging his comrade musicians in his thick Northern Irish accent, is the quartermaster, the longest-serving soldier in the battalion. Lined beside him sit the old hands of the regiment, the officers commissioned from the ranks who now run the vehicle fleet, the welfare office, the careers office. A burst of laughter pulls me to the next table, where a group of sergeant majors, Guinness sloshing in their pint glasses, are cackling at an account of the day's adventures. Then to my new boss, who sits chatting to the young officers with a happy grin on his face. Somebody clocks me.

'Wahhhey! Here he is! Got the three-five-two?'

Much laughter follows. Alerted, the commanding officer (CO), in charge of the whole battalion, spots me. He manages to announce to no one in particular and the whole of the officers' and sergeants' mess at the same time:

'Ah. Young Bury. Well done today! Well done.'

Thank Christ.

I release the heavy radio-filled daysack from my back and join the throng. Hours later, warmed by whisky and traditional reels, I am stumbling back to my hostel in a liquor-fuelled total blackness that can only be experienced in the most isolated place in the British Isles.

I know I have joined the right family.

Days earlier I had arrived like an adopted child meeting his new family for the first time. Again, I had pulled up into a pristine, princely army barracks with a car full of kit and a body full of nerves. The pressure to prove myself, much of it self-inflicted, was immense. Luckily, I was well shepherded.

Steve greeted me and showed me my new room. I knew him from Sandhurst as a Royal Irish cadet from Dublin. He did his best to look after me during my early days in battalion, an onerous task he always endured with great humility and watchfulness. He would grow to become a great friend.

'You're lucky. I arrived six months ago and had to share a room for a while; you've got your own. You're coming to C Company. I'm in it too. Any questions or problems, give me a shout. I'm just upstairs. Don't forget to tip your hat to the OC when you're done unpacking. Oh yeah, and we're off hiking in Knoydart tomorrow. It's in the middle of nowhere, should be good craic, no hassle at all . . . Right, see you 'round.'

During the evening, other young officers take the time to come and introduce themselves to me in my room. One of them is Paul, a friendly, confident Northerner, both hugely competent and committed. In two years he will be serving his second tour of Afghanistan, running our busy operations room in Sangin with a focus and eye for detail that puts most of us to shame. But he doesn't know this as he tells me to be on the bus at 0800 and to bring 'the usual'. Meanwhile the signals officer collars me and tells me I need to sign out a 352 radio to man a safety net back to base. Suspicious, I query the range.

'Oh, don't worry. This thing can bounce to Germany if it has to. And here, take the ancills too,' a wry smile replies.

The radio is nestled safely in the overhead compartment of the coach. I sit self-consciously as we pick up the sergeant majors from the married quarters. Sergeant Major Connors trundles past.

'Alroigh', sir,' he utters gruffly.

He doesn't like me.

As we straddle Loch Ness, the operations officer hands out pieces of paper. To my abject horror, I hear him calling out groups and then the names of young officers to lead them. And then, like a waking nightmare, he comes to the commanding officer's group. I will be leading it. My world shatters. In this close community, impression and perception are everything, and first impressions are crucial. Even I understand that. I am about to lead the feared commanding officer around the highest peaks in Britain in an area I have no knowledge or experience of and which is higher than I have ever been before. And I have no map case, compass, GPS, first-aid kit, torch or whistle. Which the piece of paper now clenched in my shaking hand assures me I should have.

What develops is something like a TV ad for MasterCard. The

coach pulls up in a tiny village on a peninsula in north-west Scotland that reeks of fish. Officers lazily disembark and look for boat. Young officer dashes around and finds adventure shop. Young officer stocks up on every trekking item under the sun, most of which he owns already. Young officer, cashless, hopefully produces MasterCard. Most isolated shop in Britain accepts. Young officer nonchalantly walks back to waiting boat, remarking village 'looks nice'. No one else the wiser. First impression saved. Thank you, MasterCard.

The next day we set out to 'bag a couple of Munros', 3,000-foot peaks in the serene Scottish Highlands. The radio on my back proves a great source of amusement to everybody bar myself as I lug it around despite knowing it's just dead weight. But I'm aware that taking it in my stride is a sign of good character, and, coupled with the CO's words of encouragement that night and the craic and the music, when we return to base I am already beginning to feel at home in my new, old, Irish family.

My new home is one of the most impressive fortifications in Europe. Fort George sits on a natural spit that juts out into the Moray Firth, the deep-water entrance to the port of Inverness, the capital of the Scottish Highlands. For over 250 years, British and Irish soldiers have been stationed here watching out over the ramparts towards the sea, lest a French galleon fancied her chances of stirring up insurrection in the Highlands.

Entrance to this behemoth of British power is under a twenty-five-foot thick defensive rampart that rings the fort in its entirety, around the thick grey stone armoury and casements. Above, a vast array of cannons guards the watery pass through the hills. Home is the old governor's house within this living museum. A gentry house ensconced in a sea of masonry that's battered by the harsh Highlands weather and salty sea spray. Our rooms are massive Georgian affairs, complete with iron fireplaces that the winter winds whistle through and rattle the windows. Ghosts haunt the corridors. Outside, swarms of seagulls squawk and shit on our cars while Japanese tourists laugh at our blackthorn walking sticks and ask us why we wear our distinctive green caubeens – sloped, sock-shaped hats that have been the mark of Irish regiments for centuries.

I love the Irishness of the regiment. The pipers practising the traditional tunes as we start a run in the morning. The banter of the soldiers, always ribbing, slagging, laughing, irrespective of rank. The storytelling, recounting tales of mishaps, adventures, close calls. The green champagne breakfasts on St Patrick's Day followed by a chariot race and a parade. And the adjutant's choir practices, where upstairs in our own bar the young officers sing 'Whisky in the Jar' or 'The Fields of Athenry' or 'Wild Rover' at the top of their Guinness-filled lungs. More often than not when we gathered, the topic would turn to the famous Colonel Tim Collins, the last CO, and tales of his bold character and charisma. A regimental legend told he once dropped a grenade beside a sergeant to see if he could still run fast. His legacy lingered in the battalion like the ghosts in the corridors.

On my first day in the fort, I venture out to a coniferous wood to meet my new platoon. It's a bright summer's day. They are practising tactical living, digging concealed positions to fight from. 7 Platoon, C Company, is at least fourteen years old. For hundreds of years before that it can trace its ancestry back through amalgamations and cutbacks. As I approach the woods I am aware that this platoon has been here before me, and will be here after me. I am just transiting through. So are the other members. But it's the other members I must now get to know and earn the respect of. All eyes follow me as I cross into a glade and watch as the boys dig shell scrapes into the soft pine-laden earth.

And boys they are. Despite some old hands and experienced corporals, whose faces wind and wet have weathered, I am struck by the number of baby faces observing me from under their helmets. Most of them are nineteen or twenty, some only sixteen. They seem timid. They are from towns and villages I've never heard of, yet will become part of our collective psyche: Carrickfergus, Portrush, Tandragee. As I walk the outskirts of the position, stopping to chat with each occupier of a foxhole, I am aware that for me this is a momentous occasion, but for most of the Rangers it is only a moment of mild interest.

Most young platoon commanders want to be liked by their men, and I was no exception. Although it ran against the Sandhurst line – that soldiers 'don't want a friend; they want a leader' – I always knew that my style of leadership would be largely based on my character and personality rather than rank and rules. I didn't want to be their friend, but I wanted them to like me. Most of all, at some unconscious level, as a combat leader, as a man, I sought their respect, which I knew could only ever be truly earned on the battlefield. I was also aware that love was a greater motivator than fear, and a psychotic regimental sergeant major in Sandhurst had confirmed as much. Fear, rules, the threat of punishment, worked only when the threat of punishment exceeded that involved in completing the task. From my understanding of war, I reasoned that there would be no rules, and no punishment greater than the very real threat of death. Thus, leading and motivating people in war were essentially about love and respect. The army knew this and stuck soldiers together in foxholes in 'buddy' pairs so soldiers formed tight bonds and often performed above and beyond the call of duty, not for the army or the cause, but for their mates. I would do all I could for these men, and in return I hoped they would trust my judgement, respect me and do what I said, even if they didn't want to. I saw these introductions as the first step in building relationships and a team that would keep us alive in war.

I stepped forward to a blond, skinny, baby-faced young man who lay peering out from his foxhole in case a non-existent enemy attacked.

'How's it going? What's your name?'

'All right, sir. Ranger MacGilloway, sir.'

I could tell from his looks and profuse use of 'sir' that this was a new soldier. I ventured as much.

'Oh, aye, sir. Arrived in battalion six weeks ago,' his Belfast drawl now discernible.

'And how are you finding it, Ranger MacGilloway?'

'Lovin' it, sir, lovin' it. The boys are really friendly and every-one seems on the ball.'

'Where are you from?'

'The Shankill, sir. And yourself?'

I was shocked, but I didn't show it. For a man from the south, the Shankill was the epitome of loyalist Ulster's resistance to us and everything we were. And I was going to have to lead these men, to get them to follow me. It was a tall order. Still, I was immensely proud to have the opportunity.

I didn't falter a second.

'Bray . . . originally. Dublin after that. Right, I'm gonna move on. Keep up the good work.'

'Right enough, sir.'

And almost as soon as it was begun it was over. Introductions aside. Into the meat of it.

The meat of it consisted of training. And training. And training. Some serious drinking thrown in for good measure. And then training the next day. In an undermanned, single-battalion regiment, the last in an illustrious history of Irish regiments of the line, the fear of being cut by a new defence review or drawdown was pervasive. We had to prove ourselves against other battalions; we had to maintain our reputation. And to do this we trained, trained, trained. Booted combat runs that ended in the freezing water of the Firth, log races, stretcher carries, beach runs. There was no guard duty at the palaces and little ceremonial pomp. Instead, life was real and relevant, and it seemed more professional and serious than what some of my contemporaries were experiencing in other regiments. The shine and splendour of Sandhurst seemed a lifetime away, resurrected only occasionally on mess nights. And when the news of Afghan casualties started to beam back to Inverness, I was flung once and for all out of the make-believe never-land of Sandhurst into the reality of shattered limbs and families.

In Sangin a hugely experienced and respected Royal Irish captain was killed in a gun battle. In Musa Qaleh a Royal Irish corporal was just taking over a sangar when a Taliban sniper shot him in the head. The bullet had ricocheted off the helmet of the man next to him and penetrated his. His road to recovery would be long and life changing.

As Somme and Barossa Platoons dug in and faced increasing human wave assaults throughout September 2006, more casualties were taken. A big Fijian was killed instantly when a mortar round hit the bunker he and a lance corporal were fighting from. The lance corporal died from his wounds five days later with his family at his bedside. Paul, my future 2iC, had to go back into that bunker, boots squelching in blood, to pull sentry duty to reassure his men. The next day Luke was hit in Sangin, and Paul, commanding a platoon in a firefight in Musa Qaleh, was seriously injured when a shell hit the roof he was directing fire from and punctured his lung. Only the actions of the doc saved his life.

Days later, as I innocently photocopied a stack of paper, a signal came through on the machine. Jim, my company second in command, had had half his head blown off when he was hit by a grenade when storming compounds outside Sangin. One more life changed for ever. Another Ranger, thought to be dead, comes round kicking and screaming in a black body bag on a chopper. These were only the serious casualties. Far more were wounded.

Such bloody chaos was a million miles away from the library in the fort where we assembled to be given the grim news. As the grandfather clock ticked slowly and we sat in the green chesterfield chairs with sombre faces, our adjutant outlined the serious nature of the casualties to our comrades and friends. The prognosis for either was not good. In the short weeks between Brecon and battalion, war had arrived at my doorstep like a bailiff ready to collect. It wanted me.

But in spite of it all, I still wanted it.

We practise live firing attacks on the barren, rain- and windswept wastes of Cape Wrath. On a Salisbury night, weapons blazing and tanks firing, we tear off planes to seize runways. In an arctic whiteout we stumble through snow three feet deep and watch as our boots and water bottles freeze before our eyes. Throughout it all the sergeant major is on our backs, challenging us, pushing us to do things better, to do things by the book. When, frozen and tired, we fail to post sentries, he stands the whole company to. He introduces the Brecon two-miler as mandatory for C Company soldiers and runs it himself aged forty. He constantly watches the young officers and sergeants alike. He has no tolerance for indiscipline. A tough, hardened Dublin man with an aggressive reputation, he has the strong build and temperament to back it up. His office is full of old Irish regimental history: flags, plaques, awards. His body is adorned with tattoos, many self-inscribed; the Dublin Fusiliers run in his blood. Somewhere I sense there is a compassionate family man, a father, and sometimes when he coaches us on tactics I see glimpses. He oozes confidence, righteousness and, later, I learn to respect him out of sheer deference to experience. Honest and forthright, junior commanders are dismissed as 'shite', platoon commanders often the same. I fear him like I fear failure. And both are intertwined, as failure in his eyes spells failure in general in my eager-to-impress mind. Having the sergeant major nearby is like having a tyrannical Rottweiler snapping at your heels. He is feared by everyone, except Sean, who has returned from war and taken over as second in command.

'That's not how we teach it in Brecon.'

'Well, we're not in Brecon now, sergeant major,' I tactlessly interject, an impressionable one-pip wonder with a big mouth.

The sergeant major fires me a glance that instantly chokes me silent.

'But it's how we did it in Afghanistan, sergeant major,' Sean ventures.

'Well, what use is that, sir? They're not doing it right. That's not what's taught. You've got to let them get the basics right and then let them adapt. This range is shite, sir.'

'Sergeant major, they can't even hear in this . . .'

Sean's reply is lost in the gusting wind and rain blowing in off the North Atlantic. I stand and watch this clash of personalities, experiences and egos unfold. *The clash of the old army versus new, the trainer versus the reality of war? Who is right?* In awe of the combat leader, and drawn to him, I think Sean is. Later I will see just how right the sergeant major was as well.

But for now relations remain fractious.

Another recently returned veteran of the summer 2006 fighting is P.J., the new 7 Platoon sergeant. His reputation precedes him. He has performed brilliantly under fire in Musa Qaleh and is an emerging combat-tested star of the battalion. Steve warns me he can be volatile too. As I bound towards a bunker during a night attack, trying to see what is going on, I am grabbed by a stern hand and flung to the ground like an empty sandbag. I turn to see a towering, helmeted silhouette spitting words through clenched teeth with all the venom of someone who has seen people die from exposing themselves like I just have.

'Sir! Stay the fuck down!' He shoves me away.

P.J.'s shaven head and tall figure make him instantly recognizable, ostrich-like, but he is not the terrorizer I fear him to be. A Southerner, he was a psychiatric nurse before falling into the army. He has a great passion for laughs and a vocabulary of profanities that would make a sailor proud. Tentatively, we begin to build a working relationship based on him keeping me on the right track and me seeking his advice before I do anything. I know this relationship has to work if we are to succeed under the strains of war. Meanwhile, P.J. coaches me through tactics, techniques, procedures, with a patience and goodwill that would put most teachers to shame. When I tend to over-complicate things, P.J. keeps them simple. He looks out for me so I don't mess up, hides it if I do, and protects me from the sergeant major. He makes sure I don't embarrass myself in front of the platoon. And as I begin to develop, the relationship bears fruit. We become more equal, like a parental pair, and the platoon begins to recognize this. After six months we know each other well, share a great sense of trust and humour and run the platoon efficiently. I reckon I've got one of the best sergeants in the army. So does the platoon.

The wind rustles through the long, grassy mound. I stand aloft, looking out towards the English positions and the choppy Firth. I am here to pay my respects, to honour the Irish soldiers who fought with the Bonnie Prince that day. They died in their hundreds, stuck in a bog and mown down by the English guns. But I find more than I had sought. For not only did Irishmen fight on both sides, but a pompous, silk-adorned namesake of mine commanded the victorious English army. I leave, my sense of identity as muddy as that Culloden battlefield.

I trudge down the line of troops kneeling on either side of the dusty road. I am furious.

'Where's Corporal McCord?'

'Down there, boss.'

I move towards him, aware that I am facing a test of leadership. Another officer once told me there comes a time as a junior commander when you must assert your authority. This is it. *Forget liking me. Forget friends.* Somewhere within my depths a peaked-cap, pace-stick-waving Colour Sergeant Collins is silently screaming at me to do something, that this is unacceptable. All the platoon's eyes are on me. Clydey sitting lazily, uninterested as sweat trickles down his forehead. Mac with a 'what are you going to do now, boss?' scowl. No P.J. to back me up.

'Corporal McCord . . .'

'Boss, I'm not going up there. I don't care what you say. We've been walking around here for three hours in this heat and we're wrecked. We need a break . . . I'm not going.'

'Corporal McCord, shut up. We need to get up there now. We can have a break when we're up there. We need to do this now before the shura starts. We have to be in place . . .'

'Sir, don't tell me to shut up. I'm not going. The boys are hooped. I'm not going. Fuck that.'

'Corporal McCord, don't speak to me like that . . .'

'Boss, I AM NOT FUCKING GOING!'

Snap.

'CORPORAL McCORD! YOU ARE A SECTION COM-
MANDER IN THE BRITISH ARMY. I DON'T CARE WHETHER
YOU GIVE A FUCK OR NOT. GET YOUR MEN AND GET UP
THAT HILL NOW OR I'LL GET SOMEONE ELSE TO DO IT.
MOVE OUT IN FIGURES TWO. UNDERSTAND?'

Silence.

I move up the road to the front of the platoon, shaking from
nerves and anger. So is he. I have never screamed so loud in my
life. All eyes follow me, then turn to Corporal McCord.

Showdown. The collective will of the platoon is the prize. The
tension builds.

I sit and wait.

Slowly I see a helmeted, puce face get to its feet. It collects its
rifle. Men start to rise to their feet around him. They fall in. *What
are they going to do?* They move towards me. The tension recedes.

'Boss, this is ridiculous,' he says as he passes.

I let it go, content that we will reach our objective. That I have
won.

And today our objective is critical. As the Paras have been
unable to jump in the high winds, it falls to our C Company to
hold and secure a vital village against DS-led attacks. We do. We
are commended as the best company the DS have seen in years.

And we are picked to join the Paras.

Later, we traipse into a building to rest. There has been silence
between us all day. I take Corporal McCord aside.

'Listen, I'm sorry for telling you to shut up . . .'

'Boss, that was a joke . . .'

'Well, then you need to start acting like a section commander,
not a lance jack. You need to support me when things are tight.
That's what a section commander does. You're on the inside now.
If you bitch I'll tell you to shut up, got it? So don't bitch. I need
your support . . . especially when P.J.'s away. OK?'

He looks at me with a glint of understanding. 'Yeah, boss, sorry. I was tired and hanging . . .'

'Don't worry about it, we all were.'

And, as I sensed at the time, it did come to be a turning point in my relationship with the platoon, with Corporal McCord. It was about me and them. And him. No platoon sergeant, no P.J. 'The day the boss went mad.' And from that stable platform, that setting out of the ground rules, the team began to prosper. Much of what was sowed that day would be reaped on the battlefield in Afghanistan.

KENYA

Nec Aspera Terrent
The harshest trails do not frighten us

Ranger Company Motto

We creep slowly, silently through the tangled mix of thorn bushes and squat, sparse African trees. A full bright moon beams down, silhouetting us and sending our long shadows out against the baked red soil. We lost communications (comms) forty minutes ago, but I have decided to press on. We must find the other platoon's camp and destroy them. I am confident we can.

We slide stealthily over a bare rock face, picking our way, crouching, towards their hideout.

Whisper.

'Boss, d'you hear that?'

'What, Al?'

'Listen . . .'

Above, I hear a deep purring, breathing.

'Boss, that's a lion.'

'You sure?'

As if in answer, a lazy, low growl emanates from the ledge.

'Feck!' I giggle, wide-eyed at Al. 'Let's crack on.'

We can't find their base. Back and forth we cross in the moon-light, searching, scowling. Nothing.

A loud sustained burst of automatic gunfire rolls out across the sky. It is not close. I think of the men I have left at the rear to pro-tect our little recce group. *Compromised.*

We dash back to the group, ignoring lion and thorn bush.

But all is well. Without comms, I reason our base location has been contacted. We trudge back through the bush as the moon dips behind us but are ordered straight back out. We set off into a tar-black world, the moon missing, vanished. Without time to move tactically, we take a bearing for the rock face. The men are feeling it; some are bitching. In the utter blackness the huge blades of savannah grass sweep our faces. We hear lions, sleeping, growling, moving around us. Close.

We lose comms. I move to the front to navigate.

A swallowing blackness. I hit mud and crumple. Davy falls in on top of me.

We've fallen ten feet. Somehow unharmed, we are pulled out by the others.

'Ha! Lovin' it. The boss takes over and snots himself!' Davy laughs.

A growl nearby reminds us of our perilous position. *No comms. Terrain we could break a leg in. Lions. If anything happens to these boys I can't raise help . . .* I weigh this against the mission, a company exercise, which in the grand scheme of things doesn't matter. *It's only two platoons out here, not the whole battalion . . .*

'Hold it, boys. We're turning around.'

We trudge back. I raise comms. The boss and sergeant major are livid. Standby.

A golden-pink morning breaks over the mountaintops and descends to cover the matted undergrowth below. It leaves me in a dilemma. The other platoon has our grid reference. *Forget the platoon harbour; we need to stay small to stay concealed. Stay close.*

It is the wrong decision. Alone, without P.J. to guide me and faced with disgruntled soldiers, I flounder.

The other platoon doesn't find us but as dawn breaks I can hear the Land Rover approach like rolling thunder.

'You! Get over here now!'

I am called away from the platoon.

The new OC is boiling over. Hopping from foot to foot. *He's going to hit me . . .*

'What the hell is going on? What is that cluster fuck? Do you call that a platoon harbour? I am so angry. SO ANGRY!'

'Sir . . . I . . .'

'D'you know where we're going in nine months, d'you? Fucking Afghanistan. People are going to die. Boys are going to die, and that's without incompetent people like you makin' a pig's ear of everything. Where were your sentries? Why were you so bunched up? What were you thinking?'

'Sir . . .'

'Listen to me and listen well. I've seen incompetent commanders in Baghdad kill their men and themselves by taking short cuts. By taking short cuts, not checking things, not doing things right. D'you understand? I'm not having that happen to these boys. D'YOU UNDERSTAND? . . . You can report to the CO when you get back . . . Get out of my sight.'

There is no point in arguing. I have learned that.

Crestfallen, ashamed, I slope back to the platoon.

The new boss took over C Company a few weeks ago. From the north, his good looks make him appear even younger than he is, while a strong, scientific mind underpins a real aptitude for the practicalities of infanteering. 'Resilience and mentorship,' he says. 'Resilience to do the job of the person above you, because you never know when you'll have to. And mentorship. Mentorship to bring on those below you, to develop them.' His watchwords foster a great team ethos in the company. After eleven months with the 101st Airborne in Baghdad, he is full of Americanisms, chewing gum and using military jargon that even we don't understand. His brigade had lost over fifty dead in his time in Baghdad. He has bags of combat experience and has won the Bronze Star for his efforts trying to save two soldiers captured by the militia. Later, he tells me how he had frantically planned air assaults all over the city trying to find them, only for his men to recover their mutilated bodies, having been dragged through the city alive and finally shot. And how he'd watched as a slack commander killed his men by taking short cuts. By then I could tell that I had hit a nerve this day, that he was simply protecting his soldiers from what he judged an incompetent commander. But not now.

I stand shaking outside the new CO's office, a rickety wooden colonial building nestled among some greenery.

What a bad start.

'Mr Bury. This is a big deal. March in and bang your tabs in,' the adjutant whispers.

'Yessir.'

'Sir, Lieutenant Bury.'

'Yes. Come in.'

He is sitting relaxed behind a desk, staring at me. I am trembling.

'Well, Patrick, I'm sorry we have to meet for the first time in these circumstances, but your company commander has raised some very alarming incidents reference your leadership with me. Can you explain yourself?'

He is the first person, bar Steve, to ask me this in the days since I turned the patrol around. The sergeant major has flown off the handle, saying I belong in the reserves. Most of the other senior NCOs avoid me like some highly infectious and ugly disease. The OC has been silent. Paul, my new 2iC, silent with him. I have been shunned. Only P.J. supports me.

'Boss, you did the right thing. You're the one on the ground; you're paid to make the decisions, God's sake. I just wish I was there to stop the cluster that happened after. You need to be careful, boss. They're after your blood.'

I explain my actions to the CO and he listens. At one point I think he even understands.

'Right. Well, this is a training exercise and we're all here to learn, but I'll be watching you very closely from now on. Dismissed.'

It feels worse, shameful, returning to the platoon. I have lost my confidence. And confidence is key. An average, confident leader can command. An average unconfident commander can't lead. Unsure of my abilities, I start to make stupid mistakes. But the boys are supportive.

'Sir, just so you know, I think you did the right thing turning the patrol around.'

'Ah, but *they* don't, Ranger Conboy, and that's what matters . . . Thanks anyway, though.'

Later, as we sit in the scrub wilderness in a baking, broken-down Land Rover, the boss calls me around the back. Calmer now, he lets me explain what happened and listens.

'Right. Well, I still think you made some wrong decisions, but don't worry about it. It's just a blip. A big blip.'

Cheers. I know I messed up afterwards but I'd turn that patrol around again in the same circumstances.

The next day, as the CO looks on, the platoon push themselves to collapse in our attack. Now I need them. They are as aware as I that this could be my last attack. I am touched by their efforts, which see some continuing until they collapse. We hang in there.

We clear dozens of enemy positions in a protracted, exhausting attack, the death rattle of the exercise. And then we are told to clear more. As I lead the platoon up the red silt track, past collapsed soldiers and bushes blazing beside us, I feel their resentment burning more harshly than the sun on the back of my neck.

This is tough.

I look around. What's left of the platoon are red-faced zombies on the brink of exhaustion. Not to mention mutiny. The sergeant major is still hounding us. MacB's boot is flap-flapping, the sole coming apart as he trundles on, Jimpy gripped in his hands. He has walked for twenty kilometres with both. Cupples, our new American-Irish-Lithuanian Ranger, has hobbled all the way. Only later does he reveal his foot was broken throughout. Meanwhile, T, from Kerry and straight out of depot, soldiers on as many fall out.

I am proud of these men.

We return from Kenya as Ranger Company, a specially selected group formed to reinforce the elite Parachute Regiment in Afghanistan. As we head south to Colchester, we leave our regimental family behind, acutely aware that we represent them and wondering how we will compare with the Paras. The pressure is on.

First we must complete an eight-mile forced march with full kit in a Para respectable time, with their CO watching on. Ex-Royal Irish, vastly experienced and towering above everybody, he is a modern-day Spartan. He marches alongside the boys with a stern, vacant stare.

'Y'know,' he thoughtfully says to a junior Ranger, 'it's been ten years since I marched with a Ranger . . . It's a good feeling.'

Motivated, the boys prove themselves.

Throughout the winter we train, train, train. At night. With helicopters. With jets. Clearing mock compounds. Defending Afghan Forward Operating Bases (FOBs) deep in Norfolk forests. The stress of deploying to a war zone adds to the pressure. By now thoughts of our own mortality shadow us, directly corre-lated with the losses in the headlines.

'Sir, your platoon did alroigh' on that exercise. Well done.'

'Cheers, sergeant major.' Things were starting to thaw between us as I began to value his advice and he could see I was developing as a leader.

'Yeah, I'm more worried about the other platoon now . . .'

P.J. confirms as much.

'The boss is happy, the CSM's as happy as a pig in shit. All tick-ety-boo, boss, hey?'

Saying goodbye to family is one of the hardest things I will ever do. I have determined to tell them all I love them in case I do not return. I am as sure as an alive man can be that I won't, so sure I have already picked the songs to be played at my impending funeral. I have seen the tears of regret of the bereaved that haven't said it. On the steps of the officers' mess I fight the tears. My father and brother are the hardest. So many unspokens between men.

Their blue car pulls away, back to green, lush Ireland. I stand and think in my desert combats.

That night, will completed, insurance policy increased, bags on shoulder, myself and Paul walk to the bus in the dark. A huge touchable white moon shines down on the black tarmac road. It starts to snow.

'Any regrets?' Paul asks quietly.

'Yeah . . . A few . . . You?'

'Yeah, a few.' He sighs.

Part 3

TO WAR,
AND ARMS,
I FLY

KANDAHAR

Tell me not, sweet, I am unkind,
That from the nunnery
Of thy chaste breast and quiet mind
To war and arms I fly.

'To Lucasta, On Going to the Wars'
Richard Lovelace

The boys stop joking. The lights go off. In the blackness the thirty-year-old TriStar surges and slows, pitches and groans, like an old tanker in a storm. In our fatigues, helmets and body armour we sit as the plane weaves and ducks its way towards Kandahar airfield.

Please don't shoot us down. Please don't let us be the first. Please.

In the TriStar's cabin we pass the empty stretcher beds for the wounded and disembark into a night world of kerosene fumes and flashing safety sirens that illuminate the dust clouds. We move to a holding area and get our kit. Concrete blast walls surround us as a nervous Air Force rep tells us they were mortared last night. We're not that interested. This is the first step on an escalator that is moving us all inexorably onwards, upwards, towards danger and possibly death. P.J. barks commands, organizing the troops into neat formations for the onward flight.

'Six weeks, boss, six fucken' weeks, that's all. Six weeks and home to Kat. That's all . . .' He repeats it like a mantra.

Matt laughs. 'Got any lucky charms, boss?'

'Yep. I've got a lucky leprechaun. You?'

'Got my wife's knickers in me top pocket. Have done on every tour since Sierra Leone.'

I tell P.J.

'That's nothin', boss. I've got two teddy bears with me. One me ma' gave me when I joined the army.'

We wait some more and fall asleep. Meanwhile, Sangin stirs.

DO AB

Never think that war, no matter how necessary,
nor how justified, is not a crime. Ask the infantry
and ask the dead.

Ernest Hemingway

The Viking armoured vehicle slips out from the District Centre
(DC) under the cover of night. It starts to cross the wide, rapidly
flowing Helmand River at a shallow point, an alien vehicle in an
alien landscape. It is headed for the outskirts of Do Ab, a desert
village of red mud walls and berms built right into the rock face.
Pinprick holes of light puncture the curtain of night. It's a scene
straight out of *Star Wars*.

Inside the Viking are Royal Marines of Bravo Company, 40
Commando. For the last month they have endured increasingly
accurate rocket attacks on the DC. Rockets land inside the DC
itself, just missing accommodation blocks and exploding close to
the command centre. Every day the rockets explode nearer,
every day there are closer calls. Something has to be done before
someone dies. An audacious solution is proposed. These
Commandos are part of that solution.

The amphibious Viking negotiates the torrent and heads for the massive sandy, rocky hills that overlook the DC and the surrounding Green Zone. Even now the Taliban dickers (lookouts) report their movement, but the Marines have a deception plan. Covertly, a Javelin missile team and a gun section are dropped off before the Viking moves off on another, more visible task. The next morning it returns to base after what looks like a routine patrol.

Meanwhile the Commandos begin the arduous trek up the hill face with all their kit. They need to get to the summit before dawn, before they are exposed, and before they are baked by the sun. They do.

They set up a covert OP with panoramic views east. But they are concentrating on one point in particular, Wombat Wood, a thick orchard-like area north of the DC that normally provides excellent cover for the rocket teams to set up in. It is here, almost daily at six o'clock in the evening, Taliban on motorbikes venture in to rocket the Commandos' base. This time the Marines hope to catch them out. They wait.

A radio frequency scanner crackles. Pashto voices.

'Are you ready?'

'Yes.'

'Do you have your friends?'

'Yes.'

'Good. Bring two melons. I will see you there.'

High up in the OP, the Marines are on high alert, scanning the trackways, paths and fields around Wombat Wood. Waiting for them to come. Hoping for them to come.

Hoping they can kill them.

Then, peering through the magnification device on the Javelin, they spot them. Two motorbikes with two fighting-age males on each moving south. They track them until they are joined by others. It looks like half a dozen Taliban in total. They wait. And listen.

Pashto.

'Good. Get it ready there. This time give two to the infidels. Allah Akbar.'

'Allah Akbar.'

The OP commander requests clearance to fire. He waits for what seems an age as they check the situation.

'Roger, you are clear to fire.'

The OP commander checks one last time.

'Have you got lock-on?'

'Yes, boss.'

'Good. Guns standby. Javelin . . . Fire now . . .'

FFFSSHhhhhh.

The missile screeches out of the tube and tips immediately at forty-five degrees, white-hot jets of flame spewing out like a firecracker behind it as small stabilizing fins pop out. The missile levels and fizzes towards its target at a thousand feet a second.

Radio crackle. Pashto. Hurried.

'What was that?'

'What?'

'ALLAH!'

A black tube of dust rises upwards, capped by a wide, sandbrown cloud.

'ALLAH! My leg, my leg! Oh! Allah!'

'Help me! . . . Help me.'

'Gun group, FIRE!'

The Commandos open up with the machine guns, sending redhot pieces of copper flying towards the smokestack. The bullets arc, zip forward, clattering into the group of dead and injured men, immersing them in a red, phosphorus-tipped rain. There is no escape.

Pain is a universal language.

The guns stop. Silence.

Oily smoke wafts out of the barrels. The gunners smile contentedly as they scrape, click, click, make safe their weapons. The missile firer beams.

'Boss, d'you see that? We got 'em! We got the bastards!'

'Hoofing! WHOOOHOOO!'

'YESSSS! HOOOFIN'! DON'T MESS WITH THE BULLDOGS, YOU BASTARDS!'

Seven Taliban lie dead, strewn around their destroyed launcher. Back in the ops room the planners punch the air. The relief, the excitement, these Marines feel is tangible, even a week later when we first meet them. There is nothing sweeter, purer, more self-affirming than knowing you have killed someone who was trying to kill you. You could call it pure murder, but they had triumphed, and they had also escaped. In the battle of wits and method that was Afghanistan, they had managed to pull off a textbook ambush that virtually guaranteed them all survival through the last weeks of their tour. Bravo Company would return home as it went out, not a seat empty, and that was no mean feat.

Plus they had saved our lives, for a while, too.

BASTION

I climb the towers and towers
To watch out the barbarous land:
Desolate castle, the sky, the wide desert.

Lament of the Frontier Guard
Rihaku

We awake in Camp Bastion, the next step on that escalator, to
our first Afghan morning. A bright whiteness engulfs everything
and slowly heats us out of our camp beds. The closer we get, the
more we wonder about dying, and the more we feel alive, more
aware, more sensitive to our surroundings. Outside, the military
equivalent of a fortified Bedouin camp greets us. Sean told me
when he first arrived in 2006 they literally camped under the
stars. Now, thick rubber hangars are sorted in neat rows, their
zip-lock doors billowing in the breeze. Inside, the few working
air-con machines struggle against the sun scorching the outer
skins, sending temperatures within the tents stiflingly hotter by
mid-afternoon.

In the glare I struggle out on to the black plastic walkway and
past the hesco bastion cubes that protect the hangars from rocket

attacks. These are the most common thing in Afghanistan, bar death. Portable, but when filled with sand, excellent defensive fortifications. I cross one of the dirt roads that bisect the huge, sprawling camp. It's a construction site crossed with a quarry, new metalled buildings, rusted trucks and buses delivering wares and people. At the edges of this ever-expanding town, high concrete walls interspersed with lookout towers keep the desert out. Behind me a truck beeps as it sprinkles water to keep the dust down in a desert, and I wonder how much that costs.

Over a breakfast of croissants, fruit and cereal we learn that a Danish soldier has been killed and another wounded in Gereshk. Back out in the sun, as our eyes squint to adjust to the white, we see orange tape running around the phone and internet booths, cordoning them off until their families are notified. The tape will be torn down when they are. I look closer. Around each thin iron stake jutting out of the hard sand are dozens of old pieces of tape flapping in the breeze, a silent, unintended memorial to the fallen.

I collect my rifle that will stay by my side for the next five months and be embedded in my psyche for much longer. It becomes a ten-kilo extension of my right arm, a part of me with a magnified crosshair sight, red-dot pointer, laser beam and infrared/halogen torch.

During the cold night the continuous roar of aircraft and helicopter engines rolls through the desert like a thunderstorm. We sleep fitfully. Morning sees the issue of our body armour, ammunition and pistols. Now is the time for 'allying' your kit, for making it personally comfortable but also looking cool, looking like you are a professional. Dev has explained it to me earlier:

'Boss, you need to get your own pouches, the issue stuff is shit. You need to look ally, not like a dope from the rear.'

'Really?'

'Yeah. Remember, you're working with people out here from different armies who make an instant decision about you on how you look, bust. You don't wanna look a plonker, do you? . . . Plus the boys like an ally boss.'

So there it was. The cool element of war. Feeling cool, tough, powerful. Manly, really. It attracted all of us at some level. Most of us had spent much of our own money buying ally magazine pouches, special blast-reducing wrap-around goggles, torches, fighting knives, backpacks. A mechanic has spanners, a carpenter saws, and so we have knee pads and command pouches. We have been issued most of it anyway, and some of it is very good, but some of it is too bulky or falls apart after a month wading and sweating through muddy ditches. The infantryman takes immense pride and pleasure in his kit; it is his house. We want to look different from the rear troops, to look cool. So we do.

Once, as we patrolled in silent single file over a long dyke, evenly spaced and watching, the still water barely rippling beneath our feet, the bright blue morning sky wide open above us, a jet screamed over our heads so low, so fast and so unheard we all ducked. And then we watched as he pulled up steeply in that white-edged blueness, pulling looping barrel roll after barrel roll, leaving twisting white wisps in his wake. His personal salute to us. Power. And you laughed and you turned to the man next to you and you both grinned. Because sometimes, war too was cool.

I adjust and tinker with my expensive 'ally' pouches, fully aware that having the right thing in the right pouch in the right place could easily mean the difference between life and death. Magazines need to be turned upside down to avoid dust that clogs weapons, easily accessible with the left hand since your now useless empty rifle would be in your right, and not near your chest, otherwise they will expose you when you dive for cover. The med pouch, containing morphine and tourniquet, is carried in the same place by each man, dead men's lessons not forgotten by us. But the real tinkering comes with the spare tourniquet.

Some put it around their upper legs, loose but ready to pull tight in an instant, reasoning that if they were hit there, in the femoral artery, they could bleed out in forty-five seconds. On such decisions limbs were saved or lost, soldiers lived and died. Others went for the right arm, because a hit here, if you were right-handed, meant groping around with a lame hand as you bled to death. At first I kept mine clipped to my body armour, but H, one of my section commanders, warned me off that.

'Boss, see that tourniquet. I wouldn't keep it there. Last time we were here a bunch of guys kept it there and it rotted in the dust and water and sweat. Went to use it and the thing snapped. Bloke almost bled to death 'cause they kept snapping.'

Maybe I should just put it around my neck.

While the machine gunners work out where is best for their oil bottles, cut leather gloves to allow them to handle red-hot barrels and tie bayonets to chest rigs (subsequently reviewed when a bayonet likewise attached took a soldier's eye out in an explosion), I draw my pistol and watch the boys. The mood is sombre. Things are real.

That night we venture into the 40 Commando operations centre for a brief on Sangin. We are there for three hours. The situation is so complicated, there are so many tribal, cultural, political, religious and military dynamics, that I am overwhelmed. *How can we cope with this?* It seems that we soldiers, primarily trained to fight conventional wars, need to be friendly police, social workers, government representatives, aid workers, bomb detectors, engineers, killers, medics . . . the list is as endless as the problems we face. The Marine CO rattles off each consideration, each dilemma, with such rapidity that it leaves my head spinning. It is daunting. *Maybe he's trying to freak us out?* At the end I look around the table. The other platoon commanders are awestruck. Paul looks like I feel. The sergeant major has a stunned expression on his face that scares the hell out of me. *And he's the experienced one.* We are wavering. Even the boss looks a little shaken.

Outside in the darkness he calls us together.

'Look, I know that was some brief. I know what you're thinking; how bloody complicated can you get? But we can get through this together. We've trained hard and we've got a strong team. I'm confident in this team and everyone's ability . . .'

He looks around at us all and continues.

In a short string of sentences the boss simplifies everything, boosts us, protects us, takes the burden on himself and makes us feel like he's sure.

Even though I suspect he's not.

It is a display of pure leadership.

With daybreak comes another brief. A red map, all Taliban held, is projected of the Helmand River valley. Green dots show areas of ISAF control. This is the famous ink-blot strategy, a series of FOBs out of which the West's calm, democratic and peaceful virtues are meant to flow like an expanding green ink sea, searching out other blots, joining up and turning Helmand into one happy, green place. We can see the basis of the plan on the map, but the green blots are only dots in a sea of red. One place is particularly obvious, a thirty-kilometre red swathe between Sangin and where the valley ends in the stunning pink Kajaki mountains with its massive turquoise-blue dam and tiny green dot. In the centre of this red is Sapwan Qala, one of the last Taliban strongholds, we are told. Plans are afoot to put another green dot right there.

The company brass and myself pack our kit and lug it in the

boiling whiteness to the helipad, where we sit and sweat in the midday sun. When we are all assembled and ready to go, a chopper breaks down and we go nowhere. I march off to the desert ranges, salting my new uniform and armour, to watch the platoon attack things. The boys are in a daze, overawed by the heat and the immediacy of what they are about to face. They don't perform as they can. The Marines scream at them, knowing that to not think, to not perform, equals death out here.

As we pack up, Local Nationals (LNs), what we call 'people', try to rush on to the range to collect the brass bullet casings we leave behind. This irritates the Marine sergeant in charge. He screams, shouts, chases, curses and threatens to hit the scavengers, like a maniac who could well be suffering from acute stress disorder. The LNs avoid him gleefully, eyes darting between each other as they bolt on to the empty range after their gold. The sergeant begins to lose himself in an apoplectic, vitriolic rage. I march back wondering what happened to make him so angry, as the platoon wait for transport. They watch, a mute audience as the strange drama unfolds. The sergeant grabs a ragged teenager, shakes him vigorously. He roars.

'I'LL FUCKING KILL YOU, YOU RAGHEAD CUNT!'

The boys don't know whether to step in or not, but the sergeant acts before they can. He screams into the shocked face.

'FUCK OFF! I'LL KILL YOU, I SWEAR!'

He lets go of the teen, who sprints away, shaken.

That evening in the tent the boys tell me what happened. 'Hearts and minds, boss, hearts and minds. That's all I'm saying.'

While we consider reporting the sergeant, I sit wondering if I will end up like him by the end of this.

P.J. and I decide it's time to speak to the platoon, to shove them out from the juggernaut's headlights that they seem caught in. I look at the faces staring back at me in the shafts of light escaping from the tent door. Some have heard hundreds of these pep talks before and show it in their blank uninterested gaze; for others this is their first and they watch me intently.

'Fellas, we know what the mission in Sangin is: to DEFEND the District Centre and the surrounding AO and to provide security so that the government of the Islamic Republic of Afghanistan can create the conditions for further stability and security.'

We've heard it a hundred times. That statement is why we are here. We get the gist of what it means. Keep the Taliban out, show the people that the government can govern inside the blot, let the Afghans run things. Simple.

But it didn't really explain why we were here in the first place.

'Lads, I'm not going to bullshit you with the nonsense we've heard about why we're here and about the schools and women's rights. But I am going to tell you why I think we're here. This is a far better war than Iraq. That was a mess, and thank God we're not being sent there. This one is better. The way I see it, us being here stops Afghanistan being used as a base to attack home. Us being here draws in all the fundamentalists, like a black hole, distracts them and makes them want to take us on. That way they're killing soldiers and not civilians. And that's the difference between us and civvies. We've volunteered, we're paid to do it, and we know what the price is.'

'Plus, there's the drugs thing. If we can stop some of the heroin getting back to Liverpool, Belfast, Dublin, then maybe less people will have their lives and their family's lives screwed up.'

At the time I truly believed it. Afghanistan *was* a better fight than Iraq. It was legitimate, morally cleaner and less sneaky. Less IEDs. Twenty-seven, keen and naive, I really thought we could make a difference, that we could help the Afghan people while protecting British and European streets from that small percentage of disenchanted young men intoxicated on Islamic fundamentalism. I hoped that we could do something about the heroin, but I wasn't as sure. But we had to have something. We had to have something worthwhile that we were risking our limbs and lives for every time we stepped out the gate. It had to be for something, worth something. The military called it the moral component. A purpose, a noble effort. And so I created that, for myself anyway. I wasn't sure about the platoon.

I look around. *Has it resonated?*

'Right, lads, it's time to snap out of the bunny-in-the-headlights mentality. Let's start sparking. We're going to be out on the ground in two days and we need everybody thinking and working at a hundred per cent. Don't be worried; just do what you know. Youse are good enough; just do the basics and we'll build on that. Any dramas, my door is always open. Sergeant B . . .'

P.J. steps forward with his notebook out and glares at them all. 'Cheers, boss . . . Right, ye cock-knockers.' He smiles at his herd.

'Me and the boss have been talkin' and I want to get a few points across from day one. First, this is big boys' rules out here. Ye can fuck the AGAI discipline system right off. Any screw-ups out here will be sorted by me and me only. In my way. Time to snap out of it, lads, right? Got it? Second, morale. This is gonna be a long seven months, boys, and you're gonna need each other to get through it. Me and the boss don't wanna hear any fucken' moanin': "this is shite, that is shite", 'cause it's bad for morale and morale is what keeps us together. If you wanna have a bitch, fuck off and moan with one of your muckers; don't do it in front of everyone. Corporals bitch with corporals, lance jacks with lance jacks, senior Rangers with senior Rangers, and the junior Rangers shouldn't have anything to bitch about.'

We all laugh.

'An' if I catch anyone bitchin' in front of another rank, I'll fucken' knock ye out myself. Got it? Now remember, as the boss said, our doors are always open if there's a drama; just use the chain of command . . . Any questions? . . . Now, detail for tomorrow . . .'

I look around at the platoon, sitting in small, loose rows on benches and the hesco wall. It's a snapshot that often reappears in my mind, them looking at P.J. while I wonder how many will survive. I feel the responsibility.

Matt was taking notes. His shaved head still revealed a tinge of red hair, and his lower lip hung loose as he concentrated on P.J. Since our bust-up we had both learned much, and he had become very supportive of me. We shared a healthy respect for one another, and he had grown into an excellent corporal, whom, most important, I trusted completely. I hoped he trusted me.

Ronnie was looking intently at P.J. and around at the guys. He was built like a long-distance runner, and P.J. quickly resurrected his 'Ronnie the Rib' nickname. A recce platoon corporal, he was hugely experienced and intelligent. He'd just returned from training recruits, eager not to miss the tour his battalion went on and with an inherent distrust of officers. I knew I would have to prove myself to him.

Beside him sat Naf, an immensely popular Fijian with the biggest head P.J. had ever seen and of which he reminded him constantly. Naf was quiet, gentle and fun in that Pacific way. But beneath this quietness there was a determination and bravery that Naf would reaffirm countless times on the tour. With his experience, he had a great understanding of the people we were going out to protect and was guided by a sense of morality, of good, that he refused to surrender no matter how hard survival would become. He was always smiling.

Below him sat Ake, another Fijian, a fiercely proud physical-training instructor with the bulging muscles to prove it. He loved his rugby, and followed Fiji with a passion.

Mac hadn't changed much since our first woodland meeting in Inverness. At twenty, he was soon to be a father. Buoyant and smiling, he was always joking and taking the mick out of anyone he could, including me. He, with others, encapsulated the spirit of the platoon, that spirit, that ethos, that constantly joked and laughed at each other and at the world in such a way that no one and nothing could keep them down. Squeak was another, an always laughing, teasing, machine gunner. He loved mocking me and annoying P.J. In this platoon, if you couldn't laugh at your-self you were finished. Honesty and being down to earth were key. Once, I returned to my dugout to find a donkey Squeak had snuck in standing inside. Another time, while in the shower, P.J. robbed my towel, leaving me with the prospect of walking naked through camp. No high-horse Sandhurst-template officers here.

Ammo had watched me intently while I spoke. He was new and, as with all the new guys, I didn't know much about him. I remembered inspecting the troops on the square before we left, and as I came up to Ammo he had drawn himself up with such pride and self-confidence that I knew, right then, that here was a quality soldier. I would not be proved wrong. Of all the men in the platoon, I always felt he listened to me, watched me the most. Perhaps it was because he was new, I don't know, but he was also deeply, quietly and confidently religious. And later, that made me envious, to have that belief, that strength, out here.

Conboy was the kind of soldier who made me proud to be from the Republic. He had that never-give-up mentality, no matter how long or hard or fast the run was, or how far he was behind. He would finish. And that was that. A solid, dependable Ranger, he was our medic, and there was no one else I would have rather seen coming to treat me if my legs had been blown off and I was bleeding out in a dusty alleyway. He looked slightly comical, monkish, in his oversized combats and thick suncream spread all over his bald head. He had a soft, quiet manner that P.J. always mocked: 'Yessss, sergeant. Nooooo, sergeant. I'm OOO-K, sergeant.'

Lastly I looked at Kav, who was looking a little perplexed. He was a Dubliner, brought up in Birmingham. The boys, as usual, teased him: 'Alwigh', geeze'. I'm from fackin' Dablin, mate.' I remembered his first interview: 'I was beat up in a Dublin school for being a Brummie, and beat up in a Birmingham school for being a Paddy,' he nonchalantly mentioned to me. I'd asked him what were his funeral arrangements, as I had to ask of all the platoon. His answer both shocked and enraged me at the same time: 'I hadn't really thought about it, boss.'

'Well you'd wanna start thinking about it fucking quickly, Ranger Kavanagh. We deploy in two weeks and it's not guaranteed we'll all be coming back.'

And that was the attitude in the platoon. I think, somewhere deep down, we knew we weren't all coming back. I sometimes wonder why that was. Did we create our own reality? Another platoon went out there thinking they were going to have a whale of a time, and some of them did. But not 7 Platoon. Maybe we were a bit more mature. Maybe it was because we had more vets from 2006, young men who had seen it all and knew too well what we would have to endure. Certainly, while I knew the kind of casualties a platoon could take on an Afghan summer tour, P.J. and the others had seen them first-hand. The loss of friends, comrades, Luke; part of the collective memory of the platoon, had an effect. It tempered our attitude. We felt we were here to do a job, a dangerous job, and we were going to do it to the best of our ability so that maybe others didn't have to come out and do it again. The vast majority of the company felt that way. But elements of another platoon I knew had seemed to have set themselves up for a roller-coaster ride in the playground of no consequences. All it took was a few key individuals to create an ethos that could permeate the platoon. Soldiers had set themselves kill targets, and tally lists of weapons fired were discussed like professional advancement, a path to enlightenment, even manhood. A small minority of others who weren't in our company, or even in Sangin, had a real desire to drop bombs or fire missiles, the kind of addiction that after training for so long with these weapons probably made them, in the 'hearts and minds' context, the very people who shouldn't have been allowed near them. Luckily, most of Ranger Company had been brought up on the streets of Northern Ireland and understood acutely the impact that heavily armed soldiers can have on a native population. Even so, soldiers bent on killing for revenge, experience or enjoyment were more common than I had imagined, but less common than you'd think in such a twisted, dangerous world.

But not in 7 Platoon; that was not part of our collective identity. And, luckily, we didn't have any psychopaths either.

I wasn't sure what my role was going to be in this weird and changing war, but I knew it was going to be complex. Sure, I had to move the guys as best I could, given the ground, keep them alive while fulfilling the increasingly dangerous missions and perform a myriad tactical duties that the boys looked on me to do with a hungry concern that fed, nourished, their hopes of survival. But I knew there was more to it than that, even at this early stage. I thought of Colonel Collins's words before Iraq: 'Those that have killed needlessly live with the mark of Cain upon them.' I knew soldiers in Musa Qaleh who were haunted by the machine-gunning of a family in a car, even though they had been ordered to open fire on the suspected suicide bomber. The officer who ordered it felt as bad as the gunner, for he lived with the decision, knowing that his order had killed a family and caused great anguish to one of his own soldiers. But what could you do? It was the situation's fault. Afghanistan's fault. Anyone's but your fault. The whole thing was a swirling, multicoloured sandstorm viewed from a spinning Wurlitzer, which left you sick and never sure of anything and still needed you to make life-and-death decisions in an instant. A second ago.

Or somebody else is dead.

So I felt I had a protective role, not only to protect these young men's lives as best I could, but to protect their psyches, their souls. A responsibility. I didn't want anyone coming back to me years down the line asking: 'Boss, what were you thinking? Why did you tell me to do that?' And I didn't want these young men, free for the first time from all society's rules and regulations, the cans and can'ts, and really little gods in this crazy violent dreamscape, doing things that they, and I suppose I, would later regret. None of these men needed that weight, that mark, and I would do my best to shield them from it. Luckily, others in the platoon shared that sensitivity, that humanity, and an unspoken agreement was formed to get us through this madness in a certain way. Elements of another platoon had other ideas and went about surviving in another way. Maybe theirs was more effective.

But I'm not sure which required more courage.

Afterwards, over a Coke, I speak to one of the part-time Royal Irish officers who commands the protection force for the medevac birds. Another Danish soldier is dead. A kid with a knife stuck in his head. And a badly injured American soldier almost raped by a camel that was confused by his desert combats.

THE DC

The descent to Hades is the same from every place.

Diogenes Läertius
Anaxagoras

From over our shoulders comes the low whocka-whocka of the approaching helicopters. They touch down on the dirt pads, sending a slow, enveloping tidal wave of grit towards us. Swallowed, dust pours down the back of exposed necks, chests and into eyes. Tentatively we await a thumbs up to board. We scuttle back and forth, loading mountains of kit on to the Chinook. The furnace heat blasts us as we move past the down-draught of the engines on to the chopper's seats, back to the relative calm and coolness of the cabin. I make sure I'll be last on so I'll be first off. I don't even know if the boys notice or care, but it's something I feel I should do.

The unstoppable escalator keeps climbing.

We fly high over the barren yellow desert and let our shadow slide over the dry river beds below us. From the rear door I look past the unconcerned gunner to the other Chinook slowly bobbing up and down on an invisible wave. An Apache buzzes like a hornet behind it, guarding. I see my first glimpse of an oasis, no, a green strip, as we fly low now, so low I can see tyre tracks in the pink-red dunes. The gunner sparks to life.

We touch down in a cloud of dust and debris and bail out on to the dirt, hugging our kit against the swirling brown and battering gale. Only hand signals communicate in the roar. We unload our kit in long human chains, pebbles and stones hitting our faces. Quickly the helis load up and soar into the bright blue sky, taking relieved, smiling Marines with them.

The noise dies down. I look around, half deaf, nervous. Handshakes are offered. Welcome to Sangin.

There is one last step. You can only walk this one on your own.

That night the Marines and I creep out of the gate and through the town. Long, comical shadows splay out and grow with every step away from one of the few golden street lamps, bouncing up the ruined walls. I follow Tom, the commander, as he weaves us through ink-black alleyways and quickly over sandy roads. In the shafts of light I see Commandos ahead of me, their night sights jutting out from their helmets as they scan from side to side, seeing all in grainy green and black. We hear music waft through the empty bazaar; Arabic wailing and pipes. I will later learn that at night the bazaar smells different, but tonight all I smell is dryness, dust. The music is closer. We step out of an alley and on to a wide street. Two men, lying on rugs inside a plain concrete open-faced shop lit by a single light bulb, are startled. They look up.

'Salaam aleikum,' a Marine speaks quietly.

'W . . . Waleikum salaam,' comes the nervous reply. We move on.

Tom whispers to me. 'That's a good sign. They're listening to music. The Taliban don't let them do that, so we're probably safe tonight.'

We sit for hours, fighting sleep and asking Tom every question we can as a pilotless drone circles above us. Eventually the road convoy passes and we move back to base, our night tour complete.

The DC reveals itself to me in the morning haze, a ramshackle fortress of ancient Afghan buildings and modern military engineering. Two buildings dominate the skyline, separated by an ever-changing green-blue-brown canal that flows quickly right through our new home. One is fire support tower, a citadel four storeys high, built of concrete and rock that observes for miles around. On the roof is piled sandbag after sandbag. The other is the command centre, an old narco trafficker's palace. I make my way there, past the open concrete courtyard where an empty, forgotten swimming pool now houses the stores of the olive-green canteen tent. I drop down the steps into the dark coolness of the ops room. Fans whip the air. Maps, tables, radios fill the room.

Embedded in the ceiling, small yellow and blue mosaic tiles encircle a large broken mirror. All that's missing is a disco ball. *Looks like that narco had fun.*

'Ah, sir, good to see you. How's it going?'

'All right, sergeant major. And yourself?'

'Not bad, not bad, be better if we get another heli in today. Don't want the boys waiting around in Bastion, y'know?' He laughs and grins conspiratorially. 'I'll show you 'round.'

Upstairs is a TV room with some satphone booths and a malfunctioning refrigerator. Above that, a makeshift gym with panoramic views of the Green Zone proudly displays bullet holes and RPG strike marks in its walls. Above that, a camouflaged lookout tower where soldiers keep watch.

I cross the dirt courtyard behind, passing solar showers and wooden latrines. On a flank I spot the thick mud walls and low ceiling of the accommodation block. Home. Inside is cool, dark and musty. Later I discover this is where the narco kept the dancing women for his shows.

We quickly cross the thin iron footbridge, eyes on the torrent below that will only increase as the mountain snows melt in the summer, to the ANA side of the base, our slick acronym for the Afghan National Army. This is more like outside the wire. Here, smells of spice and shit linger, rubbish lies festering, pots and pans untended. Time does not tick as it does on our side of the canal, but slower, more contemplatively, resigned and interwoven with Allah's will. And it feels like they have more of it than we do.

We leave on our daylight tour of the town, students keen to learn what we can before the Marines hand over and take all their knowledge, all their hard-earned experience and understanding and everything that could keep us alive, with them on that chopper out of here. Kids run up to us dressed in grey and brown cloths, friendly, smiling, their fathers more cautious a few feet away. We move through tight brown mud alleys between thick orange mud walls that reach far over our heads. Through destroyed buildings, landmarks, scenes of past battles with names that are etched on the memories of the second-timers in our platoon. JDAM house, Pizza Hut, Old Governor's House, Pipe Range, the last so named when the Taliban launched midnight human wave attacks up a street near the base, not realizing we had night sights. The defenders literally couldn't miss. Past ragged power cables that hang low, zigzagging across the streets, and wooden or rusting metal power poles with transformer boxes forlornly hanging from them. Perfect for IEDs, the Commandos say. Along empty baked-mud streets with open drains and alleyways for snipers to pick you off. Past rubbish and old white Toyota Corollas whose drivers eye us suspiciously, on to the main drag, the 611, and swiftly, shockingly, into a bustle where things happen quickly, where life is being lived and there is nothing, nothing, you can do to stop it, and what if there's a shooter there or a suicide bomber there and what's in that car and isn't that a man's hand under that black burka and why aren't the kids as friendly why are they staring at me why won't he talk to us who just ducked away there and what's on the scanner 'the British are coming, get ready'. Oh fuck.

We cross the 611 as fast as we can, stopping cars and trying to keep people out of an imaginary bubble we hope will protect us. As we leave the jumbled strip of motorbike shops, DIY stalls, general stores and food suppliers, the noise, the uncertainty and the immediacy dissipates in our wake. We are back on soldiers' ground, where we can recognize and react. We move through a cemetery, hoping the Taliban's sense of respect keeps them from trying to blow us apart here, and head for Red Hotel, which dominates the Sangin skyline. Inside, the red walls reveal a half-finished hotel, five storeys high. Bare concrete corridors, rooms, staircases and empty windows greet us. Shade. And the concrete means less chance of IEDs. We move to the wide, buttressed roof, fanning out to take up defensive positions overlooking the bazaar. Tom calls us forward.

'Right. There, just up from the flyover over the wadi, that's the Northern Travel Agency, known as the NTA. The ANP man that checkpoint when they feel like it, meant to stop and search all traffic coming in from the north. They're meant to be police but they are fucking useless. Out there to the east on the hill is the Wishtan bazaar, dodgy if you ask me, a maze of muddy alleys you get completely channelled in. That compound there with the sandbags is Tangiers, the ANA and OMLT base; some of your Royal Irish boys are there. And south, there . . . on the 611, that's Suffolk, an ANA checkpoint. They actually do search the vehicles. Over there, down that street, that's Haji Nisamedeen . . . back in November we lost a captain there, blown up by a daisy chain. It's full of Taliban. No-go area.'

We return along the 611, futuristic impostors in this ancient town. The smells are medieval, sweet. Sweat, animals and human shit mix with spices, cooking, lambs' blood. Only the fumes of the Toyotas and the motorbikes betray the twenty-first century. We drop into the wadi, under the Soviet-built flyover, while locals watch and the Taliban dick us. That night Matt and Ronnie arrive.

We leave in the early morning, trying to avoid the increasingly menacing heat. The Marines are tense. They have all survived until now. This is their last patrol, and they are taking us new guys to the front line, now called the 'FLET', where they and the Taliban trade bullets and rockets and sometimes blood. I feel for them. We're tempting fate.

We move north. Past a chequered mass of vibrant pink and green poppy fields. Under green, low-hanging trees, their branches catching, clawing at our antennas, faces. Beside mud compounds with thick grainy walls and large rusting iron gates, some bolted hopefully by fleeing refugees. Peering at small mosques, domed and plain outside, well maintained and elaborate within. Around orchards of unknown fruits and quietly tethered goats, through green wheat fields that will soon turn gold. Along and into thin irrigation canals, lined high with mud and channels of water running into the fields. Everywhere there is water, fertility, life bursting up towards the epithermal sun. The river is the saviour in this otherwise arid land, and a thousand years of work has created these watery arteries. We snake towards the FLET in single file, watching, keeping our spacing, bouncing, traipsing through water-filled ditches when a perfect but possibly booby-trapped bridge is just down there. The heat and the wet slowly bake our feet in their boots, a stinging, gnawing pain that won't go until socks are triumphantly pulled off and air and sandals work wonders. 'Better wet feet than no feet,' a Marine jokes as we slide in, and then, on the other bank, turn to pull the next man out.

Scanner. Pashto. Pakistani accents.

'Tell your friends they are coming.'

'Get the PKM.'

'There are about sixty of them.'

There are. Someone we passed was counting us, dicking us. The kid with the prayer beads? The guy just sitting there? The man in the field?

Women in full black burkas clutching small children to their breasts calmly leave their compounds, heading away from us. *They know what's coming.*

We watch a series of compounds across an open sea of poppy fields and spot 'fighting-age' males in browns and blacks and white turbans eyeing us. To cross those fields is to cross no-man's-land. Not today.

We move back through mud rat runs and river paths, smiling and sweating at locals and waiting to see if the enemy will mortar us from Wombat Wood again. The heat soars to a sapping, boiling, infuriating intensity that screams at you to throw off your helmet, rip off your body armour and slump in the shade – you don't give a damn if it's dangerous, this is unbearable. We are dicked again. And finally, finally we traipse back into camp, muddy, pink, burned and blistered, soaked in water, drenched in sweat, dizzy from our loads, but alive.

That night I sit in the halogen-lit ops room. Outside is darkness, quiet, sleep. Intermittently through the night we read or talk quietly as watchkeepers radio in.

'Hades Four Zero. This is Tangiers. Radio check, over.'

'Hades Four Zero, you're OK, over.'

'Tangiers, OK, out.'

Someone fires shots at Suffolk. They fire back. Later, a wounded man comes in, arm bleeding, saying he was shot by the Taliban. The doc treats him.

I like the night in Afghanistan. The sun dips behind the sandy hills to our west, turning them orange, pink and finally a darker brown. The shade spreads out from the RPG-scarred wall we sit beneath as we finish our evening meal. The intensity, the ferociousness of the heat diminishes to an acceptable, almost pleasant level. With night comes a sense of normality, of peace inside the walls, that you like to think extends to the whole of that dusty town outside. Lights go on and then out. Dogs bark. I love walking towards the whir of the ops room and midnight stag, seemingly the only soul awake, alive, in this dead of night. At least you have survived another day, and that feels good. But you are wrong if you think things are normal outside, because somewhere out there men with beards are creeping around readying an ambush, an IED, to try to kill you tomorrow.

Cupples is the kind of man who makes stag go quickly. He collects facts like others collect beautiful butterflies, to be released during a dull moment to be proudly marvelled at. A shy, handsome man, he sits in the olive cloth and wood camping chair in the ops room and sparkles conversations to life. 'Boss, whaddaya think about Putin?' 'What did the Buddhist say to the hot-dog vendor?' 'Did ya ever think about buying a house in Lithuania, boss? I'd recommend Vilnius; it's a great investment. You should go.' 'Here, read this article, it's very interesting.'

He had joined the US navy after dropping out of law school and had been in Naples on 9/11; 'thought it was a movie. Boy, it took them a long time to get us all back on the *Roosevelt*! And then we sailed straight for this place. Well, as close as we could get.' He'd left the navy for Ireland, where he'd met his Lithuanian wife, Vilma. He'd tried to join the Irish army but couldn't get in. 'I missed the craic, y' know, boss, so decided, feck it, why not join the Royal Irish?' He proudly throws Irishisms into his soft Miami accent and he is here to settle a score, a proud American seeking revenge, where, unlike Iraq he pointed out, he felt he'd really find it. Bitterly determined, he is curiously always stumbling and falling on patrol. Interesting is an understatement. After hours of proud discussion, I slip back to my cot, amused and invigorated.

Morning breaks with a wailing call to prayer, a five-minute lament piped from the mosques through speakers we have given them, a pious cry that reminds everyone that Allah reigns here. In the rapidly rescinding blueness, local males get up and make their way across the fields and paths to their nearest mosque, where they remove their sandals and bow and pray, bow and pray on the small ruby-red rugs. As blue gives way to pink, to orange and then to white, you are happy to be in the cool, cool morning.

All ahead is ominous, unavoidable heat, always rising, and hope. Hope this day won't be your last. Prayer punctuates the day, divides it, for us and them, in a way no clock can ever hope to. As the wails cast out at eleven, one, five, seven and finally nine, trickles of men move without thought on paths they have trodden daily for their entire lives and will continue to once we've gone. There are mosques in every hamlet, and fat, important mullahs live beside them. Here, time itself has submitted to religion, moving slowly, ploddingly, sometimes stopping, as Allah's will dictates what happens when; who lives, who dies.

We sit on benches beside our green tent and eat a sickening mix of fried spam, powdered egg and frankfurters. The other option is boiling porridge in the thirty-degree heat. We crave cold, cold milk, cereal, but they won't arrive until headquarters does. The ANA and OMLT have already swept the 611 for IEDs, but that doesn't mean they have found them all. Meanwhile, the distant crumps of the heavy shells remind us that another FOB, five Ks and a world away, is in its usual morning routine of combat. Lunch is an unchanging inedible splodge of curried rice, tinned bony salmon and tinned cheese. We start to lose weight and envy the OMLT troops who can buy and cook fresh food with their ANA comrades. We work rotations, six days of patrols, three days of guard. At first everyone wants to be on patrol, to get some action, but soon stag becomes the preferred choice, with its increased chances of rest and sleep and decreased chance of dying. Throughout the morning the boys on guard are busy as local elders come to the sangars to attend the boss's shura, a sit-down on a rug, have a cup of chai and let's sort it out kind of attempt at building a nation. Because we can sort it out. We want to help you. We know about your culture and we accept it. So let's do this like we did in Northern Ireland. Simple.

The culture quickly impresses on us. We need to understand it, operate with it, in whatever we do. Pashtunwali governs here, an ancient code that regulates society, but not in a way that makes any sense to us. A product of a strategic crossroads swept by invading armies and cultures since time began, this Pashtunwali is a mishmash of cultural ideas and norms, a framework for survival in this hard land. Men wear make-up and rape young boys to show how powerful they are, just like the governor I watch circle the helipad with his entourage billowing behind him. Machismo thinly veils a common, desperate homosexuality in many men, even though Allah forbids it. Hidden women peer through tiny slits when outside the house, yet rule the roost within. If I kill your brother you are honour bound to kill me. If

I seek shelter from you before the rest of your family, or you find me, you are honour bound to protect me from them.

What is this madness?

In those first weeks we learn much of our surroundings and some of it sows seeds of doubt that we try to ignore. We concentrate on the wonderful kids with dirty faces and painted nails and dyed red hair and the smiles and the laughs and not the subversive, strange and, yes, sinister culture or the brown eyes with cold hatred. For now the boys say, 'What's the craic there, boss?' and, 'Aye, that's fucked up,' in their cheerful accepting way. We believe we can change things, make it better, win them over. We're the Irish, after all, the gift of the gab; we'll have the craic and the locals will love us. Simple.

At the nightly brief we sit and listen intently to the situation reports. Most of it comes from what locals report to us: five Taliban crossed the river with a Stinger missile to shoot down a chopper. Two wounded Taliban from last night's attack. Doctors intimidated by Taliban in Wishtan. In Sapwan Qala the Taliban have set up their own courts and are executing those found guilty, two suicide bombers from Quetta are here to get ISAF and are dressed as women, a white Toyota Corolla has a bomb in it, Taliban are extracting taxes in a village in the south, enemy forces plan to attack ANA compound tonight Mullah such and such is giving information to the Taliban there is an IED on the 611 poppy season is coming expect foreign workers the ANP are selling weapons to the Taliban who are now in ANP uniforms kids are being used as dickers twenty fighters moved into the Green Zone they will attack the DC tomorrow . . . We pay attention, take notes and pass it on to the boys and think, think about how we can mitigate the risk, slice those chances.

After the brief, I walk back to the platoon huddled around a campfire outside our accommodation. Laughter drifts out from the camouflage canopy where the Tricolour, Northern Irish and Fijian flags flutter proudly alongside a Ranger flag proclaiming 'Mess with the best, Die like the rest'. Beneath, Naf fries slaughtered chicken and hand-cut chips in a pan. Sandbag and Jihad, our two adopted dogs with noses for danger, lie lazily beside him. Ronnie spots me.

'Boss, you creeping around there with your head torch in your hand for a reason?' he chuckles.

'Yeah. Don't fancy getting my head blown off by a sniper. How far away are those hills, d'you reckon?'

'Bo-ss!' He laughs incredulously with the rest of the platoon.

After that dream I had in Sandhurst I'm not taking any chances.

The nights pass with a flare and an occasional gunshot, maybe an explosion, just enough to wake us and remind us where we are. Sometimes the Taliban try to overrun a checkpoint and chaos reigns, each ANA location radioing in that another base is under attack or overrun only to find out when it quietens, calms, that simply Suffolk has been hit and they're fine. Then the mortars BANG BANG and their illumination shells pop before fizzing down to the quiet, silent fields. Later, lightning splits the blackness. Other nights the boss and I listen to a radio intercept as a Taliban commander issues his orders for the summer, urging his men on to capture and behead Danish 'non-believer' soldiers with their anti-Islamic cartoons, or a local is shot by the ANA for acting suspiciously. It turns out he was handicapped and put up to carrying a grenade towards their outpost by the Taliban.

I awake to a distant explosion that shakes the mud walls of my room. I ponder, roll over and fall back asleep.

I am awake. Commotion.

'TEAM MEDICS TO THE MED CENTRE! TEAM MEDICS TO THE MED CENTRE!'

I squint my way to breakfast and cross a deep crimson pool on the ground. I feel sick. The NTA has been blown up this morning. One ANP bleeds out in the med centre, another loses his leg. Then an OMLT patrol bumps into two Taliban on a motorbike, and a sudden, running firefight ensues as the ANA chase the Taliban and the OMLT chase the ANA through the dusty alleys like a mad-fun-deadly hunt. A shell from an IED is found, while another patrol finds and destroys some opium. Later, another explosion; this time a Royal Irish casualty, blown up when his Land Rover hits an IED and disintegrates. Another day and a man comes in with his throat slit. A baby girl who's been badly scalded is delivered to the gate in a white Corolla by anguished parents. The IRT scrambles to collect them and I think about the pilots risking their lives and their precious airframes to save these people in this violent, harsh land. It gives me heart, conviction, gives us some pride. *Force for Good.*

Just before we leave the gate there's a loud bang. We think nothing of it; they've been test-firing weapons all day. Then word comes through.

'Mass casualties at Sangar 2! ANP have been hit! 7 Platoon stand to! Medics and stretcher-bearers to the med centre!'

We brace ourselves for the violent bloody wave we know is about to crash against us. The lads put on their rubber gloves. Movement. Dashing uniforms. Controlled panic. P.J. lines the platoon up against a wall, controlling them like a team manager launching pairs of substitutes on to a pitch. 'Davy, T, youse are next. Go!'

They race around the corner with the stretcher and into another world. A world they will remember for the rest of their lives.

I watch as they struggle back with a mass of blue rags, blood and bone. The first has both legs missing at his knees, bones splayed open like the white paper covers on a roast chicken's legs, his bearded face white with shock. The next is dead, a bloody pulp, his back empty, missing. One has the top of his head sheared off. More come with lost gory legs or limbs that dangle from long shreds of sinew. Those with the horrific injuries die first. The stretchers are bloody, the concrete crimson, the gloves squelching. Uniforms speckled with blood. Every pair of hands is working to treat, to keep alive in this chaos of field dressings, tourniquets and death. There is utter shock on some of the young Rangers' faces, but others are quietly determined. For many of them, these are their first dead bodies, their first introduction to death, the manifestation of our chosen path and all the tactics and threats we have warned them about.

Afterwards some are particularly bad. McD is shaking and throwing up, a white shell of his former self. Only nineteen, he carried one of the grossly disfigured soldiers. P.J. and I check on him, tell him he did well, and I realize I couldn't have done that at his age. Soon we learn that these deaths were not the result of an IED but of poor RPG handling drills. It reminds us of the unforgivingly violent place we are in, of our own mortality. Not least because the night before I had got the patrol lost in a watery maze of canals and paddy fields and the Taliban threatened to ambush us. The Rangers sloshed and slid noisily while the boss got more irate and the situation got more desperate. We got out, just scared, but freshly aware that survival here balances on a knife edge.

The daily rhythm of violence and rumour continues. A legless soldier bleeds out in Kajaki, screaming into unconsciousness. On an IRT chopper a medic massages a dying heart with his hands. The amputees, the bullet wounded, the shrapnel peppered, the accidentally injured, all evacuated. The phone booths often sealed. We harden a little. A local names the new Taliban commander.

The OMLT search his compound and detain two men. Elation as it's the new commander, then resignation when they're friendly informers. The Taliban wait until our patrol is safely back in the DC, and all our power irrelevant, before they hit Tangiers again. We move in for an arrest op, acting on local intelligence (intel). Nothing. The kids say the Taliban left in the early hours. We sift through empty compounds, desperate for some success, and return red-faced, sweaty, exhausted. Already the constant, unverifiable stream of information worries me. We know nothing, and what can we know in this medieval world of no administration, no records, no fucking nothing but hearsay? *Maybe they're just using us to settle their scores?* Already it feels like we are a hammer being used to tighten a screw. Frustration.

And humour. Tom tells me of some of his Marines, who, when bathing in the canal, are swept naked out of the DC into the Green Zone. Struggling to a bank 500 metres from base, they decide it's safer to run back through the bazaar. They do, two white naked Marines running barefoot down the 611 as the locals stare, smile, laugh and eventually clap. No one knew they were gone.

You finish forcing the last of four litres of warm water down your neck and tie your sandy boots as your stomach churns. You pull on your desert shirt, reluctantly accepting the extra layer in the sun's sweltering heat and roll down the sleeves to protect your arms from thorns and ditches. It is the last thing you want to do, but not as bad as what comes next. You stoop, pick up your exoskeleton of body armour propping itself up like an empty beetle's torso. Twenty kilos, you think. A small bag of coal. You slip this sweat-smelling weight over your head and it tears at your ears. Your shield sits on your shoulders with a dull pain, a forgotten familiarity that, they tell you, lightens with time. You grab the Velcro flap and seal yourself in tight, tight, around your shirt and body so if you step on a bomb it might not blow your armour into your face. Seal is the word, for now your white chest, shaven in case you get a sucking chest wound, is cocooned in this hotness, embalmed. You only feel the first trickles of sweat on your dry shirt, then all feeling is lost in the wet, slimy, salty film that hugs your skin. You check your pouches and finally flap them down, check your pockets and close them. *Everything is so dry.* Your hands lose their precious moisture. Skin peels off them. You oil your weapon one last time, release and pull the bolt, release and pull the bolt. You switch your radio on and listen for the double beep that means it's working this time. You zip and sling your rucksack over your head and let it settle on those shoulders too. You put your head mike on and walk to the gate, watching the guys with the electronic equipment bending under another twenty kilos, the soldiers with the rockets strapped under their daysacks, the guys with the ladders, the medic.

'Hades Four Zero, this is Hades Four One. Radio check, over.'

'Hades Four Zero. OK, over.'

'Four One. OK, out.'

You meet at the gate and vie for space in the shade. You wait. You sit. The terp (interpreter) arrives. You wait. You kneel. The ANA arrive.

'OK, listen in. LOAD.'

A chorus of 'chink scrape click' accompanies your solo as you look at your magazine topped full of red tracer bullets to mark enemy positions, and slide it, check it, into your weapon, pulling the bolt, slipping one of those beautiful red phosphorus streaks into the chamber and checking the safety catch. Lastly, you put on your dreaded helmet. You have been hoping you won't have to do it, that someone or something will cancel the patrol and your head won't feel like it's boiling in a pressure cooker. But not today. You slip on your blast-proof shades.

'OK, order of march three, two, one. Ronnie, take the ANA. Keep your spacing. Keep the bubble. Let's go.'

Your muscles pull hard to get you on to your feet. You watch the electronic-pack-laden Rangers wobble under the strain. You push yourself out of the gate, hurl yourself quietly and personally into the unknown. You hope you will be back.

Behind you, P.J. counts them out.

'Hades Four Zero, Four One leaving on task now.'

'Four Zero. Roger, out.'

You imagine the radio operator scribbling in his logbook. *What else will he have to write?*

'Boss, thirty-eight all in.'

Thirty-eight people to keep alive.

'Cheers, P.J. . . . . Ronnie, slow it down a bit . . .'

I awake to the unusual sight of a flooded door. Outside, a brown world of puddles and mud greets me. This is good; the clouds will keep us cool. We navigate with ease through the Green Zone, wondering as we enter if those fires being lit are an ancient yet effective warning screen. We are absorbing our surroundings, growing in confidence. This stretch of twisted soaking foliage is becoming our neighbourhood. We slip and slide through warm, sticky mud that only hours previously was dust and hard-baked tracks. Skirting around poppy fields, we try to avoid falling into the swamps. It still rains, grey and cold. We come to an overflowing ditch. The ANA and terp cross nimbly on a thin tree trunk. Not us. Too heavy. We wade through chest-high water, weapons above our heads, as the rain splashes the water and our faces. *Vietnam.* We cross, slip, laugh and continue on. The search dog and the metal detectors come out, slowly moving, slithering, falling, coating ourselves in the grey-brown slick. *This is warfare at its most basic.*

Locals peer out from their hanging cloth doors. An old man comes out.

'Salaam aleikum.' I smile.

'Walaikum salaam.' He crookedly smiles back, bewildered at this modern mud man in front of him.

Pashto.

I motion to Arian, our terp. 'What's he saying?'

'Boss, he says he can't believe you are out patrolling in this weather, but he is happy that you are . . .'

'Good. Ask him about the Taliban.'

Pashto.

Arian nods. 'Boss, he says the Taliiibon in this area are foreign fighters, Chechens. He says the IEDs come from Pakiiiston. Men come at midnight on motorbikes, when there are no ISAF, and tell them to stay inside.'

'What about Taliban today?'

Pashto.

'No. Not today. They don't like the rain.' Arian and the old man grin.

I get out my notebook. We ask questions. Do you have electricity? What are your health concerns? Where is the nearest hospital? Is there a midwife available? What about a pharmacy? Is diarrhoea a problem? Where is your water source? Do you have immunizations? I feel like a prying social worker more than a soldier. Other locals tell us the Taliban have threatened to cut off the hands of kids who kick around a football with the ANA. We give the kids chocolate bars and pens and remind them to hide the wrappers. They ask us where we're from and Cupples points to the shamrocks on our helmets; 'Irelandia, Irelandia.' Maybe we can make a difference.

. And always the scanner. Pashto. Panicked.

'The British are here, the British are here! How could you let them get so close without knowing?'

We trudge, like our First World War forebears, back through the quagmire seventy-six boots have created. Above the thick low cloud, call signs like 'Dude' and 'Get Some', with their laser-guided wizardry, swoop and circle in a different, modern universe.

The boys have loved it. Morale is high.

The next day we patrol to a hamlet a few hundred metres south of the DC that we have christened Monkey. Amid the flowing streams, beautiful poppy fields and gently bristling poplar trees sits a maze of compounds, mud walls and a small white mosque. I move to the group of old men sitting beside a well that some NGO has long since forgotten. They are happy to see us, and we go through the water electricity hospital midwife pharmacy diarrhoea has anyone died recently what age questions quickly as they watch me take notes.

One brown-turbaned, white-bearded man speaks to Arian in Pashto.

'What'd he say?'

'He said,' Arian sighs, 'now that it's in your notebook he hopes something will be done about it. He's seen many soldiers with notebooks and not much else.'

I look at him and we share a knowing smile. He opens up. We ask him about the Taliban. 'The governor could round them all up in a day if he wanted to – he knows them all – but they pay him not to.' *And we support this guy?* 'The ANP are drug-addled and corrupt who bully and steal from the people. We respect the ANA; they don't rob us.'

With an undertaking that we'll be back to look at the broken well, we leave.

That night I relay my findings to the boss. Things have healed between us; I have learned much, and we get on well. He's not surprised.

'Y'know, at that first shura I had with the governor and his aides I went in hard, said I was going to hunt down the Taliban if they attacked our efforts to improve Sangin. And y'know what? There's guys in there, s'posed to be on our side, right, bowed their heads, like they're Taliban and I was threatening them! The government shura full of Taliban! The very people who are meant to be on our side! Corrupt bastards! I'm hearing this stuff from everyone. I don't like this governor one bit.'

'It's screwed up, sir.'

And it was.

We patrol down to Waterloo, an isolated OMLT outpost a few Ks south of the DC. Through empty, dusty orange alleys. Over crumbling brown walls. Past a stony hilltop cemetery, where coloured tape billows raggedly in the wind. *Just like those stakes in Bastion.* Through deserted festering compounds, across the 611. The OMLT live a lonely life here while they mentor their ANA comrades in this exposed and unsupplied excuse for a fort. But they are happy; no one but the Taliban bothers them. We learn one of the men on the motorbike during the suicide attack yesterday wants compensation from us for shooting up his bike. It mildly surprises us and our rapidly changing view of Afghanistan. We try to cook parts of our ten-man ration packs, tins of stew and pasta and tomatoes, in small fires that can be seen for miles around. Ake and Naf feed the platoon again while I wonder how I would overrun the base. We try to sleep in the twisted wreckage of an IED-destroyed car, but the wind and cold keep us awake. In the sangars, stoned ANA fire off long streaks of rounds to wake the next sentry for stag.

The next morning we are up and out in the hushed blackness into an area the ANA fear to go alone. We will sweep back up through the Green Zone for five Ks and clear the suspected

Taliban that wait there. If they are here they should come out and fight. But they don't. We are too strong. Instead, all our wary, watchful eyes see are suspicious locals, cold stares, people moving. Everyone is dicking us. Paranoia. The boss prompts us over the radio, experienced, protecting, coaching. We wait as another platoon searches compounds. Something ahead. A sky-blue burka billows over a fat figure storming about in a purple-green poppy field. It sees us and flees. *What's this strangeness? Do I shoot? Is it a woman? I can't, I don't see a weapon.* Maybe the agile, lightly armed ANA can catch it, search it, I hope, but not us heavily loaded, trundling, bumbling foreigners. Later, I wish I had shot. It was likely a Taliban commander escaping in a woman's wedding burka. Later still, I wouldn't give a fuck if it wasn't.

We pass locals and, as intel suggests, foreigners in the fields, harvesting their purple crop. They stand, heads bowed in the sun, cutting razor blade slits into the green pods. Seven slits per pod, they say. Now you can see the hurt and destruction this plant causes, the brown sticky pus collecting on the slits like boiling caramel. The workers watch impassively. ISAF have not been here for a year and won't be again for another. We're just mowing the grass.

We move through the river bed, reeds and shale and stones and tired and cooked, cross that final stream into the welcome safe gates of camp.

SANGIN CENSUS COMPANY

I have made fellowships –
Untold of happy lovers in old song,
For love is not the binding of fair lips . . .
But wound with war's hard wire whose
    stakes are strong.

'Apologia Pro Poemate Meo'
Wilfred Owen

Sometimes we have two or three patrols a day, sometimes we have none. Either way we are tired, always tired. Maybe you wash your kit, read a book, listen to music. Go for a run around the orchard littered with human excrement and stoned ANP to take your mind off things. But you can rarely sleep. It's too hot. And tiredness can get you killed.

There are many ways to die in Sangin. Assassinations, shoot and scoots from men on motorbikes, ambushes of bullets and RPGs, mortars and SPGs, rockets, the usual. But it is the IEDs that frighten us, the hidden traps of old shells and wires that change our soldiers' love for the ground, this ground we've been taught to worship every curve of, every fold, every crevice, this ground that can save us from all the other deaths. But Improvised

Explosive Devices have come between us, so now we don't love. We have been betrayed, but we are still forced to relate, with constant cautious eyeing distrust. Pressure-plate mines to step on, radio-controlled shells to rearrange you, command-wire bombs to trick you, popper mines in electrical boxes, suicide vests on women, suicide bombers in cars, 'chicken switch' radio-controlled suicide bombers in case they back out booby-trapped doors and weapons tilt switch IEDs initiated by your metal detector plastic explosives you can't detect collapsing circuit IEDs to kill your disposal teams IEDs you move to when ambushed. IEDs everywhere.

And nowhere.

And so, while my eye sweeps over my body as I sunbathe, my mind drifts to how I would look without an arm. With a bullet in my chest, my face disfigured, with my leg splayed like that ANP guy. Projecting their injuries on to my body like a disturbing slide show. *Stop it*. I'd never really thought of the detail of it before. And what would I look like afterwards, how would it heal? What about a wheelchair? I wouldn't be able to run any more, but what about swim? *Stop!* Sean called it fate and didn't wear dog tags because he wasn't going to die. I don't wear dog tags but am pretty sure I'm going to die. The sliding scale of rationalizing your own mortality starts. For some, religion is first and last, God's or Allah's will and the comfort in that. But not many. Is it fate? Maybe you think so before you arrive, think there's some interwoven predestined path you're all individually walking, some with buried IEDs, some without. Religion for the unbelieving. Then you put it down to luck. Luck you can influence. You can make your own luck, yet there's still that unknown, that intangible, that makes you lucky or not. Finally, begrudgingly, you accept there's nothing, nothing in this fucked-up place but chance. The unquestionable geometry of chance. A bullet fired from that weapon at that trajectory will move at that speed for that distance while you move at that speed at that angle and it hits your helmet and deflects at that speed and that angle. And hits the man next to you in the face. A bomb made of that explosive at that time placed in that damp earth for that long and you're the point man for that point section at that time so you step on it and are covered in nothing but powder. God? Fate? Luck? No. Chance. There was no God in chance's strange arithmetic, not that I could see anyway. No fate, no luck, nothing but numbers. At least you could influence chance, you could lower the angle, lessen the speed, rotate the point section, really work the numbers, try to survive in these small, life-saving ways. The Para taking cover in a field a few hundred metres from the nearest contact who died with a random single stray bullet through his eye knew it was chance. As does the Marine who watches an RPG burst though his Viking, scream through the legs of the man sitting opposite him, miss an ammo tin, scream through his legs too and out the other side of the Viking. Chance. We all know it and we all respect it. Just submit. The best way to survive is to accept it, accept you're already dead and then you're freed from all the worry, freed from the imagination. For imagination breeds weakness and you need to be tough out here.

Toughness is the hallmark of the other platoon, sometimes at the expense of thought, I feel. There are concerns about some of this platoon. Much of it is down to leadership, that little-understood, catch-all term that supposedly separates those in charge from those who aren't. The other platoon's boss is a competent commander on the ground but infuriatingly stubborn and arrogant at times. I sense he fails to set an example, and out here, where each rule is invariably some sort of safety-induced hardship, that is glaringly obvious. His statements are flung open to interpretation: 'Yeah and if you see any dickers, Bob and Razor, give them the good news.' It all sounds cool and tough, 'ally', but one

man's 'good news' is wildly different from another's and techni-
cally we can't shoot dead someone who is just watching us.
Luckily, his soldiers have enough common sense to understand
this, but a rogue streak begins to form in some elements of this
platoon. When I sit chatting with him in his room, a lance jack
passes.

'Johno, that ammo needs to be sorted. Get a work party to do
it.'

'I'll get someone else to do it later.'

He looks hurt by this rebuke that shows instantly how much he
wants to be liked by his platoon. But he takes it. If he had exploded
in anger or called in his platoon sergeant, the lance corporal would
have been sorting the ammo himself. But he doesn't. I knew I was
no perfect commander, that I'd walked this murky path before, but
leaving his room I thanked my stars I'd had that inkling to stand up
to Corporal McCord when I did. In a way I felt sorry for him
because I knew how easily it could happen.

Slowly, a small but growing rift develops between our platoons,
separating us, like the river that separates our accommodation,
into two ways of doing things, two ways of surviving. At first it is
slight, summed up by P.J. and me in our nightly briefs to the boys,
who question some of the other platoon's actions and motives.
'Don't worry about them. We'll just concentrate on doing things
the way we always have.' Soon, the river that separates us is as wide
as the Rubicon, dividing platoons and men in the dark, twisted
underworld of morality.

Meanwhile, P.J.'s replacement, the legendary, wiry and red-
haired Speedy arrives. A highly competent and highly strung
Military Cross-winner, he throws himself into organizing the platoon with such obsessive-compulsive gusto that we all smile.
Newly promoted and always supportive, now that P.J. has done his
best to bring me on, it is my turn to do likewise with him. With

him is Dev, a laid-back lance jack with an acerbic, deadpan Scouse wit which betrays his intelligence. Of the platoon's questions, his are the ones I fear most. He will save my life twice. Both have brought irreplaceable, indefinable experience to the platoon.

These veterans go straight to the quiet orchard where their friend Luke had died in 2006, to have their photo taken with a plaque they have made for him. 'Luke, we're back' reads their picture. I can feel it is an important experience for them. Speedy is still haunted by his friend's death, determined not to take another casualty.

Another death touches the platoon just as much. 7 Platoon's mascot, Jihad, is shot due to the dog handler's concern it is rabid. We see the hurt on his face, this lover of dogs turned executioner, and we blame it on Afghanistan, on this messed-up place. It disturbs the boys, more so than the suicide bomber or the mutilated ANP, because Jihad was a part of their daily lives, a source of affection in an existence seriously lacking it.

It's 2 a.m., and beneath a bright moon that illuminates the alleyways of the bazaar, the men of Ranger Company are preparing to enter the night. With hushed voices, radios are checked, equipment tested and weapons made ready. We move out at H Hour. Laden with kit and ladders, we clatter and clang and beep and eventually quieten down. Our mission is to clear that hostile village of Haji Nisamedeen, that village Tom called a no-go area and that we've taken his word for ever since. Intel suggests, as always, it's full of Taliban weapons and IEDs.

We scan the 611 as we stride up it in the cool blue-blackness and I leave P.J. with most of the platoon on a roof of some predetermined building. I move around with Matt, and the engineers cut the lock on our target compound's huge solid-iron gate. A darkened world of corridors, open doors and ransacked rooms awaits us. The Rangers clear room by room cautiously, torch beams following rifles into every blackened corner. 'Compound clear,' whispers over the radio. We move up on to the roof just as the sun starts to rise.

As day comes, so does a greater appreciation of our surroundings. By Afghan standards this is a palace. A ten-room, two-storey building with piped water and electrical fittings indicates it was once the residence of a prosperous drug smuggler. We start our search in earnest and soon have a find. Two mobile phone boxes point to the building having been used by enemy dickers. A Pakistani ID card of a fighting-age male. Syringes. Then we find a large bag of a greenish-brown powder. About a kilo of heroin is held aloft in Dev's hand. Most of us haven't seen it before. We wonder how much it's worth as Dev scatters it over the porch and goes back to the roof. Later, the sergeant major reckons fifty thousand.

By now the other platoon is in position as well. With the village sealed off, the ANA arrive, their new OMLT commander skidding his open-top jeep to a halt in a cloud of dust and, with a nod of his cowboy hat, beginning the sweep-through. The villagers comply, and those light, nimble ANA search the entire village in a couple of hours, far quicker than we could.

Suddenly, two white turboprop planes appear over the hills, flying low and fast. They race right over our heads and bank tightly over the Green Zone. *What the hell is this?* Quickly, supplies are bundled out the back, dropping to the fields below.

'Boss, what's going on there?' Matt asks.

'Hold on, I'll check with ops . . .'

'Eh . . . We're just checking with higher, no air planned for today.' *Pakistani Taliban resupplying fighters?*

The aircraft whizz past us as we train our guns on them, tip their wings to whoever is collecting their wares in the field and fly off, low over the hills.

A lot later we learn it was an ally's intelligence service. *Not very subtle.*

The village is checked and cleared and, as usual, we find nothing. As the sun starts to cook our heads in our helmets, the company folds back into base. So much for 'no-go', we wonder.

Weeks later it's no-go again.

That evening we sweep the 611 for IEDs and await another convoy. Somewhere in the darkness someone has fallen asleep, and the convoy turns off the only road in the province and drives along a wadi straight towards the Taliban. P.J. and I laugh as we imagine thirty vehicles stuck in a ravine plodding towards an ambush. *This is meant to be a military operation?* An officer in a Land Rover volunteers to get them. Madness.

'Fucken' hell . . . Always the same,' P.J. sighs as he sits on an old sofa chatting to the ANA.

Finally they pass, a whirr of hydraulics, lights and dust clouds. Nervous rear troops on their monthly venture to the front line pop flares into the night and train their guns on us.

As the poppy harvest continues, the violence dwindles and the rumours persist. With less happening on the patrols and less to keep them busy, the boys' morale starts to drop. Thoughts of R and R become an obsession. 'Boss, when are we gonna get some action?' 'Boss, why are we here if we're just giving out pens and cash?' 'Boss, we've been here for two years. Why are we only doing this hearts and minds stuff now?' And they're right. We are the distributors of hard cash and smiles, not warriors locked in an adversarial struggle with the enemy, but walking targets waiting to get blown to pieces. Such is the nature of modern conflict, of a war for the people amongst the people. The boss had his orders and Paul has his patrol schedule and we are sent out to map the bazaar, store by store, to find old electricity transformers and speak to doctors and question pharmacists. Meanwhile, intel suggests there are two suicide bombers waiting for us near the dilapidated hospital. The doc asks his questions quickly, aware of the threat. We sweat and watch and stop anyone coming near.

'Wadrezha! Gamice porta kra! Ya za de wallum!'

The males stop and cautiously lift their dishdashes and show us their hands. But what about those burka-clad females? What do you do about them? Ranger Williams and Ranger Smith want to know, because they're approaching them fast and they're scared. Do you tell them to go 'round? What about the woman on the back of the motorbike? What about the one with the kids? If we're here to win them over, we can't mess up their lives; we have to take calculated risks. So you ask how many there are and you let the four of them through, because four hopefully means they're not suicide bombers. You feel that tingly, top-of-the-stomach scared, then vindicated, as they pass you and Skills in that dusty alley, their eyes darting from side to side of the slits in their black hoods. They have spotted Skills's exposed muscles as he cradles his machine gun. Chatter. More darting eyes. A burst of girlish giggles. They move on, joyfully oblivious to the parallel universe of threats and counter-threats spinning in your head.

'Are you ready for heaven?' the wraith speaks into his radio.

'Yes, let's blow the infidels to hell.'

'Doc, we need to get the fuck out of here now.'

'No worries, Paddy. I'm done.'

We collapse quickly, and nervously move off, passing the IED-destroyed, sandbag-strewn NTA, an eerie monument to our lack of control. We speak to shop owners and mechanics, fruit sellers and tailors. Always the same questions. Always the notebooks. Hopefully, this time those who make the decisions will actually do something with the information, make some improvements in these daily lives. Because I'm starting to feel like a fraud asking for trust and support from these people and returning nothing.

As I wait in the shade for the information specialists, a kid looks over my rifle. I let him peer through the sight. His face beams at the magnified sights, the laser pointer, the torch. Such modernity.

'Taliban?' I say.

Thumbs down.

'Karzai?'

Thumbs up.

'Bush?' he asks inquisitively.

I give a thumbs down. We laugh.

We return to base, weary. Now we can add surveyors to that long list of duties we perform. 'Ranger Company me arse, boss; more like the Sangin Census Company,' the boys mock.

P.J.'s last patrol sees us up to the FLET and the platoon itching for action to break the monotony of patrols, threats and questions. We scan the now brown and dying poppy fields of no-man's-land and the Taliban try to ambush us. For a while things get tense. 'Jaysus, boss, are you trying to kill me on me last patrol?' P.J. jokes. We avoid the ambush. On the way back, a beautiful little girl is hit by a motorbike driven by a ten-year-old. Her toes are badly mangled and our medic does what he can for her. She will have to go to the hospital in Lashkar Gar, forty miles and a lifetime away. She doesn't even cry.

Afterwards, in the DC, the sergeant major runs up to us.

'That was the closest yet! They were waiting for you! The phone was buzzing off the hook with threat warnings! I was worried, y'know?'

It's unusual and touching to hear such compassion from him. We can see now that he cares deeply about us. Some of the boys are disappointed we have avoided contact. That elusive test of manhood that we all prepare ourselves for as we leave the gate. That I fear and seek, another uneasy paradox in this profession full of them. That we run through in our minds; the little sequence of actions we need to perform and hope we will be able to. So we don't fail ourselves. So we don't fail each other. Anything but that.

P.J. and I tell them it's coming, don't worry, and when it comes they will wish it hadn't. The vets agree. 'Be careful what you wish for' are the watchwords.

To restore morale, P.J. breaks out the platoon quote book and reads aloud at the nightly firelit get-together. 'Ranger Smith said this one yesterday. Jaysus, nearly broke me in two. Me at scoff queue: "Are you the last one?" Ranger Smith: "I am, sergeant . . . but there's a couple more behind me!"' Rapturous laughter. 'What about the boss?' Matt says. 'I didn't say that, Corporal McCord!' 'What? What?' they chorus. 'When the suicide bomber hit us the boss told me to deny the motorbike with a sixty-six rocket!' Rapturous laughter. 'I didn't say that!' I protest. 'You did, boss, you did!' They laugh harder and I smile. The topic turns to P.J.'s imminent departure. The boys love him like a mother, and P.J.'s affection for them is palpable.

'Lads, it's been a pleasure. Just stay safe out here and screw the nut for the boss and Speedy. I'll be thinking of youse every day while I'm sitting on me arse in Brecon! Not you though, Clydey. I'm glad to get away from you! But seriously, look after your-selves . . . I'll be thinking of youse . . . stay safe.'

That night I have a nightmare that I am relieved of command.

In the morning P.J. shakes my hand.

'Thanks for all your support, Sergeant B, it means a lot.'

'It's been a privilege, boss.'

I feel honoured, yet vulnerable. P.J. has had my back through everything, has mentored me closely and now I am naked and exposed. I feel the responsibility of command more than ever.

'Look after the boys . . . And look yourself. I'll see you soon.'

While the wind whistles around base we prepare to leave. The sandstorm is reaching a crescendo as, goggles down, we venture out into the haze. Our mission is simple: to go deep into the Green Zone and establish the platoon in a patrol base for forty-eight hours. Take over an empty compound. See what happens. Keep the Taliban guessing. Collect some intelligence. Reassure the locals. It will be the first time a patrol has stayed this long in the Green Zone, and 7 Platoon's progress will be monitored closely by those in command. We must use this relatively quiet period to get out, learn the ground and develop relationships with the locals.

The dust clouds screen our movement perfectly, and we reach our village without the Taliban knowing we are out of base. As the storm subsides, we look for a suitable empty building from which we can operate. We locate a compound, but it's occupied by a weathered, friendly mullah who begs us not to stay for fear of reprisal. We move on.

No empty compounds. We spot a large concrete building with clear views of the surrounding poppy fields. I send Arian to speak to the occupants. They are squatters, refugees minding the compound for its owners. They refuse to leave, not even for the five dollars a day I offer them. *What do I do?* I can't knock on every gate asking to be allowed in like some desert drab band of trick-or-treaters.

'Arian, tell them I'll give them ten dollars a day. They can stay if they want, but we are staying too.'

They leave.

Our new home has obviously had wealthy previous owners of illicit occupation. The small rooms within the walls are locked

with safe-like doors, and through girdered windows we see tele-
visions and sofas. We get the keys from the family in case the
Taliban try to mortar us. An old Soviet well with a hammer and
sickle proudly embossed on the handle allows us to filter our own
water, while the concrete roof supports the sentries who quickly
fan out to provide over-watch.

We are still sorting ourselves out when a Ranger alerts me to
a build-up of locals outside the gate. I venture out with Arian and
a protection party and am greeted by about thirty concerned-
looking local males. They are dressed in assorted brown, black and
grey dishdashes and turbans, but the village elders stand out with
their white turbans and white beards. It's daunting. I feel like an
explorer greeting an undiscovered tribe. They become friendlier
when they discover we are neither Americans nor infidels, but
they still want us to leave.

'If you are here, the Taliban will come and they will attack you
from our compounds, so we must leave if you do not.'

'Why?' I ask stupidly. This is getting complicated. Like everything.

'Because if we stay, the Taliban will force us inside and attack
you, and you will fire back and we will be caught in the middle.'

'And what if you leave?'

'The Taliban won't come; all will be quiet because they know
the compounds are empty and therefore you can bomb them if
they attack you.'

Catch 22.

We don't want the locals to leave, and I explain that we are here
to provide security for them, to keep the Taliban away and to stop
them intimidating and taxing the village. They say they will leave
tomorrow if we do not. A little girl in a green dress speaks to
Arian. Pashto.

'Why do you work with the infidels?'

'Little one, these guys are not infidels; they are only trying to help us.'

'These British killed my brother last year.'

What can you say? Arian thinks she may come from a Taliban family, sent to spy on the locals. We pass an uneventful night on an Afghan rug.

By next morning the villagers are in the fields, working the wheat harvest. We patrol out around the compound and await the sergeant major, who arrives with his critical, protecting eye and ammo, rations and CWA kit. Consent Winning Activity is our name for giving the locals gifts so they like us. As the elders ask us to leave again, I say this is the first of many small bases in the area. Some are receptive, and they become more so when bags of tomato seed, tea, prayer mats, tools and the ever-popular radios are handed out. We are careful to appease the elders and the mullah. That evening no one leaves.

In the dead of night a cacophony of dog barking alerts us to the presence of someone around the base. A Ranger catches sight of three males just before they bolt off into the blackness. Taliban reconnaissance.

We leave the next evening, and the locals are understandably relieved when we do. The family move back in. We give the village more attention on our patrols, and it begins to feel like we can achieve something. We recognize locals and they do us; smiles are exchanged openly, information covertly.

That night we venture out to catch those Taliban in an ambush. We wind through the black maize fields and creep through darkened alleyways. For all our silence, all our effort, we cannot keep pace with our scent. Dogs telegraph our movement from hamlet to hamlet. We set up on the baked canal path, ready to jump out and apprehend anybody approaching. It's midnight, yet twenty-five degrees. We wait.

Something approaching.

A torchlight briefly streaks down the alley to our right. Dev and Bardsley move to intercept.

Footsteps.

'Wadrezha!'

Two men. They are greeted by locked luminous beams pointing at their heads, cutting the darkness with green precision.

'Wadrezha!' Dev shouts again. They are startled, scared, hesitant. Any wrong move and the boys will end their lives. Adrenalin pumps.

There is an intense, pressurized pause. Lives are in the balance.

I get to the alley with Matt.

'Don't shoot . . . don't shoot, lads.' We calm, soothe, the boys with lock-on in this world of misunderstandings.

After what seems an age, Arian arrives. 'They heard the dogs barking and thought you were thieves, here to steal the copper from the electrical cables.' We apologize for scaring them and give them leaflets proclaiming 'ISAF is watching while you are sleeping'. Compromised, we trudge back to camp, briefly getting lost and irritated in the pure-black maze of canopy-covered alleyways.

I sit in the ops room with the sergeant major and we talk. He's in a perceptive mood.

'Sir, what do you think of what we're doing here . . . really?' He looks at me with a questioning frown.

'I dunno, sergeant major. It's pretty messed up. Seems like it's one step forward, two steps back . . . I'm not sure if we're the right tool for the job . . . It's just wild goose chases in the dark, y'know?' I had kept that to myself until now.

'Yeah, I know what you mean. Damn right. I just don't get it. I thought we were coming out here to help people . . . but half of them don't want our help. You see the way some of them look at you on patrol. What's that about? They hate us.'

'I know . . . Not all of them, though . . .' It's reassuring to hear someone I respect say exactly what I have been thinking. Finally, someone being as honest as the evidence surrounding us.

'. . . And the fuckin' poppies, what's the deal there? We don't get involved 'cause we wanna keep them onside? We don't stop anything under ten kilos of pure opium. Man, there's wheelbarrow loads of poppies in that market nearly every day. How much opium do you think they make? Screw that . . . I thought we could stop that stuff, y'know?'

'Yeah, it doesn't make much sense . . . I s'pose I thought it was about Al Qaeda and all that. That's what I told the boys, anyway. And maybe at a higher level it still is, but there's no Al Qaeda in Sangin . . . No chance. Most of these Taliban are locals. They're part of the same families that run the stalls, man the ANP sangars, sit in the shuras with the boss. How the hell can we fix that? You know the governor? I've heard he rapes kids. He just takes them off families. And he's paid by the Taliban. And we support him? I know I'm not a father . . . but I'd kill him if he did that to my children.'

'Y'know . . . I'm struggling a bit with this. It's just so messed up and hopeless. And we're risking our lives for it, the boys are risking their lives every day. For this place? This place isn't worth the left boot of one of our boys.'

'Yeah, we just gotta try and keep them alive. That's all we can do.'

He looks at me and smiles. 'You're damn right there, sir. Just get them through it, that's all that counts. I've put enough people in body bags already . . .' He smiles but looks away. 'Anyway . . . how's your blokes' morale?'

'Good enough, sergeant major. They're itching for a scrap, but that'll come.'

'You don't have to worry about that.' He smiles again and looks directly at me.

'They're good blokes there, sir, y'know? You're lucky you got good, thoughtful commanders. And your blokes don't complain when I tell them to do stuff either; they just crack on . . . Keep an eye on Speedy, though. He can get wound up easy . . . Yis are doing alroigh'; keep it up.'

'Cheers, sergeant major. I'll do me best.'

'And sir . . .' I look back. He's sitting thoughtfully on the table swinging his legs.

'There's no need to mention any of this to the boys. We still gotta job to do and we need to take pride in doing it well, keep supporting the boss, y'know? . . . They don't need to know if they can't work it out for themselves.'

'Roger . . . I wouldn't've anyway, CSM.'

'Yeah, right, ye little bollix!' He grins.

That night another nightmare. This time a psychic tells me she can feel a terrible pain in my head . . .

Unfortunately, the boys work it out the next day.

We patrol out early into the bazaar and I drop off Ronnie's section in the shadeless, sandy wadi as we move to a busy track. With home-made signs we set up roadblocks to search the locals during the morning rush hour. This is the big one for us, the litmus test of how ISAF and the government are doing in Sangin. A swarm of bikes, Toyotas, trucks, minibuses and pedestrians flows through us, ready, we hope, for paid work on local government development projects. We are wrong. The terps ask the questions, we do the searches, the heat rises. No one knows about Workers' Registration Day. No one cares. And those who do don't want to work for the corrupt local governor, whom they all despise. It is depressing.

For twelve hours we bake in the sun, desperate for some success, some hope. Two people register. From a town of seventeen thousand. It's a blatant indictment of the governor and ISAF's support for him, and the boys can see the fallacy of our task with their own eyes. Still, they professionally man the blocks, cautious, watching, searching, despite local complaints that we are not respecting women and children. Our futures depend on us searching everything. We try to balance protection with respect.

Matt stops a nervous fighting-age male on a motorbike with a mobile and two ID cards in his pockets. They are confiscated. He says he's going to Sapwan Qala for a wedding. Later, we hear a Taliban commander was married in Sapwan Qala. *Bastard*. Two black-robed males watch us and streak away on motorbikes from our checkpoint. Taliban. We can feel it. Under those dishdashes are weapons. We know it. But we can't see them. What can we do? We can't shoot them. Not allowed. No threat. They know that. I eye them through my crosshairs and finger the trigger. They disappear.

Are we weakened by these western rules of engagement in this eastern place? Or strengthened?

Someone reports an IED to another checkpoint. It's confirmed as a well-disguised daisy chain of 105-millimetre shells ready to ruin someone's day. We collapse the cordon and move to that bastioned, familiar roof of Red Hotel. We seek shade as the baking concrete floor forces us to move every few seconds, jolting us from our drowsy, drifting tiredness. I listen as Arian tells me about the Tajiks and the Pashtuns, the Uzbeks, the Pashtun women, Kabul, his hopes.

'You know, boss, Afghanistan is not all like this. These people are uneducated. They are farmers. They need to be educated, boss.'

'But I'm not sure if they want to be, Arian. Isn't that the point?'

'Maybe, boss, but they don't know any better.'

'Well, you would say that!' I smile. '. . . You're an educated Tajik! . . . I mean, they don't look that poor, do they? Those stalls down there are stocked full of stuff . . .'

'A family spends about a hundred dollars a week, boss, on rice and meat mainly . . . But a family can be twenty people, so they aren't rich.'

'S'pose.'

'Kabul is so different, boss. Girls walk around in jeans, there are discos . . . You should go,' he suggests proudly.

'I wouldn't mind . . . Can you get me a flight?' I grin.

'You know, I am saving for a flight myself . . . To Canada. I want to get out of here. My girlfriend is studying in Canada. Afghanistan is too dangerous and too corrupt . . .'

'I know, I know. It seems like all we're doing here is helping these corrupt bastards with their power plays . . .'

My earpiece crackles. 'Hades Four One, you can collapse task. The IED disposal team got on the wrong chopper. It's gonna be a while before they get out here, over.'

'Four One. Roger, out . . . Ronnie, Matt, you get that? Let's get out of here before they change their minds . . . Ake, you're on point, straight through the bazaar. Let's get going . . .'

After fifteen hours we return to base and collapse into sleep. We are lucky. The other platoon are out for eighteen hours until the EOD team arrive and blow the device.

I am sitting on the benches at dinner talking to two newly arrived and keen United States Marine Corps sergeants. I tell them how quiet it is, but not to worry, it'll soon get busy. Cue machine gun firing over our heads from the lookout tower, so close it rattles our brains. The sergeants and I exchange looks and I race to the ops room. Commotion.

'Two Taliban just got into camp! Got in through the disused sangar. The guys in the tower fired at them with the Jimpys. They couldn't see any weapons, but they coulda been suicide bombers. They legged it . . . Think they moved towards JDAM.'

'Fuck's sake,' says the sergeant major, 'they should've shot them anyway. No civvy's gonna jump the bleedin' fence.'

The boss is twitching with anger.

'Go out and clear around JDAM, quick. Catch these fuckers.'

In the turmoil the boys have rushed to reinforce the sangars, and now I need them to get ready quickly in the fast-fading light. It's chaos. The men struggle to find each other, to find their kit. We have just moved into our newly built hesco accommodation and weren't expecting to be on patrol. My fault. We are meant to be ready to deploy in five minutes.

We hurry, panicked, to the gate.

'What about the medic?' I ask Speedy.

'Dunno who it is or where they are . . .'

'Hades Four One, you need to get out of that gate now.'

'Boss, we've got enough team medics; we should be OK.'

Stressed, I acquiesce.

Wrong decision.

We're still waiting on Matt. *Where the hell is he?*

'Hades Four One, have you left yet?'

C'mon, c'mon . . .

'He mustn't have got the message, boss.' We send a runner. Speedy's radio won't work. My aerial breaks. *This is a disaster.*

The pressure builds.

Eventually, I see a torchlight coming towards us.

'Fucking come on!' I shout.

Matt loses it.

'Shut the fuck up! I'm coming!' he pants.

Not again. 'Corporal McCord, don't speak to me like that.'

'Don't speak to me like that in front of the troops.'

He's hassled, I'm hassled.

I go to speak to him.

'Get your hands off me.' He thrashes out.

I am about to boil over but catch myself, acutely aware the boys are watching this scene unfold. Speedy steps in.

We move out after a hasty brief. Nervously, cautiously, through dark rustling treelines and blackened fields. *This could be a trap.* We are on edge; an anxious, dangerous feeling pervades.

Ronnie sees a male carrying something across his body. I send Matt to another treeline to protect us. Ronnie moves in.

It's a startled old man with a stick. He's as scared as us. The whole platoon can feel it. Someone in the blackness is watching us. We know.

We creep south. Slowly, we regain our composure. Our calm returns after the cluster in camp. But Speedy is still frantic.

'Boss, this is a fucking joke. What the fuck are we doing? This is a trap.'

'Sergeant Coult, keep the bitching off the net. Out.'

An artilleryman has been ordered to man the once-empty sangar. Nervously, he approaches. Speedy spots his torch beam. In his agitated state he thinks the Taliban have got around us and are re-infiltrating into camp. He has no comms with me. He brings his rifle to his eye and in the blackness takes aim, despite the advice of Joe Bog nearby.

I hear a single shot.

The red streak races out of Speedy's barrel and smashes into the wooden post inches from the artilleryman's head. He sees where it came from. Scrape, click. He loads his machine gun, as do the others in fire support tower. Things are now completely out of my control.

I'm frantically trying to work out what's happening when hot, red 7.62-millimetre copper crashes over our heads. The boys throw themselves into a black ditch as bullets impact all around, churning the dirt in front of them and biting into the wall behind, raking over them. The weight of fire is incredible, a wave of violence smashing against them. Naf and I are transfixed for a moment and then dive for cover behind a compound wall. Branches break overhead.

'HADES FOUR ZERO! THIS IS HADES FOUR ONE! STOP FIRING! STOP FIRING!' I scream into the radio.

The net is garbled with panicked voices. We fire illumination rockets and flares to show we're friendlies. They fire on us again. Then it stops.

Quiet.

Oh, no. Please, no casualties from that. Please.

'Matt, you got everyone?'

'Yeah, boss, we're OK. What was that about?'

'Boss, 3 Section all OK.'

'Roger, Ronnie.'

'2 Section, Ake . . . you there?'

They are pulling themselves out of the muddy ditch, dumbfounded that they are all somehow alive.

'Yes, boss, we are OK . . .'

Eventually, I raise the ops room, send my locstat and tell them we have no casualties. It's been a close call. The vets say they've never been on the receiving end of such an accurate and heavy weight of fire, which is perversely reassuring.

They tell us to clear JDAM, but Ronnie refuses to do a night search without the mine-detectors we've stupidly left in base. He is right. We watch instead.

We traipse through the gate relieved to be alive but embarrassed about the blue on blue. The military equivalent of paedophilia. It happened on my watch.

I bring the commanders into an empty room and in the darkness we flick on our head torches. We've nearly had half our platoon wiped out by our own side.

I look at Matt.

'Corporal McCord, I'm sorry for shouting at you in front of the . . .'

He interrupts and speaks hurriedly, passionately. 'Sorry for shouting at you, boss. I wasn't angry with you, boss, I was just bulling in general 'cause of the stress . . . I love you, boss. I'd do anything for you . . . I'd take a bullet for you.' He looks at me.

It is not often that a man tells another he loves him. Especially in front of other men. I think of the bust-ups we've had, think of the effort I have made to repair things, to be myself, to respect and protect the boys, to build this team. To earn their trust and respect. And we call it respect because it's easy to say. It's not soft and it's not embarrassing. But Matt has called it by its true name, love. Simple platonic love. This love that motivates men to do the most touching, brave, selfless things for their brothers. A love so deep it burns and tingles in you when it flickers, reminding you there are things greater than you, more important than you, things that last longer than you. Not the lover's love of egos and nurturing and selfishness. It is purer than that, deeper than that. It does not expect anything in return, intense yet dormant, a fiery iron stove that rarely opens. The soul? Yes, that is what it is. And sometimes, out here, you get a glimpse and you understand. You understand why soldiers charge machine guns or hold out to the death while others escape. Love. For love melts fear like butter on a furnace; it transcends it.

Inside, I'm touched. I know that something important yet peculiarly intangible has happened.

Outside, I keep my officer's face.

'Hopefully, there'll be no need,' I reply and look away, embarrassed.

We talk about the team, about man management and stress. I tell the section commanders I need them to support me, that it all breaks down if they don't. They listen and give feedback. Finally, we get points from the patrol so another event like we've just experienced doesn't happen again. We leave a team again.

When I get to the ops room it's a different story. Prepare for bollocking. The boss is livid and rightly so. Paul calms him down a bit.

Out of earshot I am rightly bollocked for the delayed departure and for not bringing the mine-detectors and, less rightly I feel, for the blue on blue.

I keep my mouth shut.

The sergeant major chats to me outside the ops room. That tingly nervous sickening shock still sits in my stomach.

'Lookit, there wasn't much you could've done. You can't control each individual soldier all the time. They make their own decisions out there sometimes.'

'Yeah, but fuck's sakes, CSM, I nearly got half the platoon wiped out.'

He grins conspiratorially. 'Was that your first contact?'

'I s'pose . . . for the platoon on their own . . . yeah,' I realize, embarrassed.

'And a blue on blue . . .' He chuckles. '. . . Don't worry, sir, contact means *with the enemy*; that was just *an incident*. Doesn't really count.'

When we have all calmed down, we realize that blue on blues in this complicated, unsure place are not as avoidable as we'd wish them to be. Heavily armed young men make mistakes sometimes.

Chance.

Violent vomiting and diarrhoea sweep through the FOBs, decimating combat power. I am no exception, making an embarrassment of myself as I whimper on to the doc's stretcher before being cordoned from the rest of the platoon. The rest of the company embrace the tales of my weakness with jesting gusto. The doc catches the other stricken platoon commander breaking the cordon sanitaire even though he knows not to. When I return, the boys ask: 'What does he think, boss? One rule for us and one for him?'

Echo Company, 2nd/7th US Marines, arrive in a cloud of dust, their heavy vehicles filling the helipad with more hardware than a British battalion. They are spearheading the renewed American commitment to Operation Enduring Freedom and their battle honours read like a military historian's shelf; Guadalcanal, Okinawa, Korea, Vietnam, Fallujah. Their hardware is inspiring. As is their attitude. Like Cupples, this is their war. Afghanistan is their Japan; they have a score to settle. Maybe because they are new, maybe because they have that conviction, they are keen, motivated and ready to take risks, more so than us. Their influx breathes new life into Sangin, and they bring with them an asset that will save our lives many times, Gunnery Sergeant Chavez, a moustached, tough, intense man and an Explosive Ordnance Disposal expert. No more waiting for hours on the British EOD team to get on the wrong chopper.

The boys welcome the arrival of the Marines with a flurry of banter and barter. Our sandals for their mosquito nets. Our shamrocks for their shirts. Our rations for their MREs (Meals Ready to Eat). They bring Gatorade and cookies, cheeseburgers and fajitas. They chew tobacco through stag and 'whooyeah' and 'Semper Fi' through the day. Their laid-back, professional manner makes them easy to work with, especially for the boss with his 101st experiences. Their arrival doubles our boots on the ground, and they soon set up another patrol base in the dusty, red Wishtan bazaar. Without them, in the storm of IEDs and violence that awaits us, Ranger Company would be overwhelmed. But we don't know that yet.

Once, in Sandhurst, an American general in charge of Iraq spoke to us captive wannabes. He sweet-talked us, a 'you Brits got all the experience in insurgency, we got all the hardware . . . but we're learning fast' kind of pep talk that just confirmed what the vastly intellectually superior British army thought of itself anyway. Not so now. Over four thousand deaths in Iraq had changed that. The Marines had just co-written the new textbook on counter-insurgency. These guys got it, they understood the environment and they knew how to operate in it. And they had the resources behind them to do it properly.

We begin joint patrolling, showing these Marines the ground just like the Royals showed us.

In the days before R and R I find myself in countdown mode, even though the constant cycle of planning, briefs and orders keeps us busy. I am lucky. I am due R and R after only two months out here. *Should I go? What if I miss their first contact?* But then that old dictum 'be careful what you wish for' kicks in. Most of the wounded and dead out here are the ones who aren't meant to be out on patrol. The long toured, the volunteer, the newly engaged, the one who tempted fate. *No, I'm not messing with the numbers.*

The night before we leave it emerges that our flight out has been postponed. The news is greeted with grins and jokes from those in the platoon who aren't due to go, and silence from those who are.

'Don't worry, we'll still get out,' I tell Cupples, who has volunteered for the unpopular first slot so he can heal his stumble-injured ankle and get back to the platoon and the patrols.

The next morning I sit in the ops room monitoring the net. A Royal Marine Viking convoy has been ambushed in a valley a few kilometres from our base. Their armoured vehicles hurtle towards our location with bullets clanging off their armour and RPGs detonating all around them. We sit tensely, willing them to make it through and listening to their rushed voices call out enemy positions on the net.

'Two o'clock, two o'clock! RPG man!'

'Seen . . .'

'Fu-uck! . . . That was close!'

'Two shooters, four o'clock! FOUR O'CLOCK!'

'Can't see them! CAN'T SEE THEM!'

'Incoming RPG from nine o'clock!'

'Where? WHERE?'

'. . . Fuck this . . . floor it! Drive through! DRIVE THROUGH!'

They do, and we are just starting to relax when I hear a loud explosion outside.

In the silence, a stoic, 'Contact. Mine. Wait out . . .,' drifts solemnly over the net.

The lead vehicle, as it was crossing the Helmand, has been blown up. The noise brings the Rangers out on to vantage points to helplessly watch the drama unfold. Four hundred metres away, a huge plume of black smoke and flame is leaping from the stricken vehicle.

'Hades Four Zero, Mud Two Zero. We can't get to them . . . it's brewing up . . . the ammo is exploding.'

Christ. The poor men.

Everyone is silent, imagining the hell happening just outside.

Bravely, the fire is extinguished and survivors are pulled from the blackened, twisted and smouldering wreckage. But a courageous Marine, whose tour had been extended so he could carry out this final mission, and who was in sight of safety, has died. It hits us all.

The injured are extracted by a medevac chopper as the convoy makes its way into our base. Its members, faces matted with dirt and sweat, are in a state of shock. They sit against the hesco walls and sip water from bottles, staring silently into nothing or bowing their heads. The boss goes up to comfort them, speaking softly with the commander.

The rest of us don't know what to do.

A jet comes in to 'deny' the Viking, to drop a 500-pound bomb on it so it's rendered useless to the Taliban. Disconcertingly, it takes three attempts and three bombs before it explodes again.

It emerges that there will be a flight after all, to collect the fallen Marine. We will also be extracted on it. As we frantically pack our kit, an honour guard forms up on the helicopter landing site (HLS). The chopper lands, and in the swirling dust and debris the honour guard stand to attention with heads bowed, lining the route on to the aircraft. We leave Sangin in solemn mood, watching the desert drop beneath the rear door of the helicopter as the Union Jack covering the body billows in the breeze.

Plucked out of the front line, our arrival in Bastion is surreal but welcome. As I walk to the accommodation with my kit, I catch the clean, rear soldiers staring at me. There is something envious in their self-conscious, curious gazes. I avoid manholes and bridges out of habit, and then catch myself.

It's cooler. There are fresh vegetables, crunchy green apples, succulent steaks, the internet and even cold, cold ice cream. Senses and tastes I haven't used are reawakened.

Safe. Certain.

The 2 Para CO apologizes for extracting us in such circumstances.

I stuff ice cream and cheesecake down my neck. As I scrape my bowl clean, my eye falls on the comments book. I leaf through to the latest remarks. Some fat rear technician wants a Mexican-themed night. A logistician wants an Italian night. In response, a wiry, hardened Para back on R and R has suggested a FOB-themed night. I grin. Ten-man ration-pack splodge for all these complaining bastards. *That'll show them.*

Once we're safe in our air-conditioned rooms, thoughts turn back to Sangin. The Rangers, once so keen to get away, now say they want to return to the platoon, to their friends. Meanwhile, a paternal instinct for the platoon keeps me preoccupied. Every night I glean what information I can from fellow officers about the daily situation reports coming in from Ranger Company. Thankfully, all is quiet.

We all realize, now that we have left Sangin, just how much we are enjoying the soldiering, despite the danger and hardships. We miss the camaraderie of the platoon. Each of us, in our own little way, now somehow feels helpless should anything happen to 7 Platoon while we're at home.

As I whizz through summery, orderly England, colour negatives of Afghanistan flicker before me, overlaid on to offices, houses, towns. Mud walls and alleyways, poppy fields and ditches replace the unfamiliar scenery. *What would that look like bombed? That's an excellent vantage point for a sniper . . . Stop it . . .*

R and R is spent in surreal limbo, half in Ireland, half in Afghanistan. The love of family versus the love of brothers. Safety and selfishness versus danger and selflessness.

You are hooked on Sky News for any information on British casualties. There are. Three dead from a suicide bomb in Sangin. Your breathing stops. Your heart pounds. You realize they are Paras based just north of the DC. You are relieved.

And then you are guilty you are relieved.

Part 4

A STORM IS
THREATENING

WOMBAT WOOD

If one conquers a thousand thousand men in battle,
And if one conquers himself alone,
He is in battle supreme.

Dhammapada
Suttapitaka

The Chinook bobs high above the many golden speckled lights below. In the darkness we could be flying over small fishing boats in the South China Sea for all I know.

My eyes are glued to the round porthole, searching the blue-blackness for those feared surface-to-air missiles they've briefed us about in Bastion. I see it before the pilot, a twirling, spinning, climbing light ahead of and below us.

This is it.

A half-second later, the pilot sees it. Light. Light. Shadows momentarily dance inside the cabin. Streaks of fireworks shoot out of the heli. We continue to close with the swirling light. My heart stops. Everything tenses. *I knew it.*

The missile slows; it's not moving fast enough. We're already over it. It bursts into a halo of gold light.

My heart starts and I breathe again. The damned ANA. *What idiot fires a flare when a chopper is inbound?*

We land in a dust cloud and hold on to sacks of mail as silhouettes dash about us. The heli takes off.

A Fijian voice booms deep in the darkness. 'Welcome back, sir. It's good to have you back.'

I am white with shock. But no one can see. And no one cares.

The boss and Paul are standing outside the stairs leading down to the glowing ops room, sharing a cigar.

'Good to see you, mate. Good R 'n' R?'

'Yeah, brilliant. Glad to be back, though, y'know? Where's 7 Platoon? Have they been contacted yet?' I blurt.

I fear the reply.

'They're out in a compound in Wombat Wood, been there for a few days now and, no, they haven't been contacted . . . yet.' The boss grins at me.

'The other platoon got hit a couple of days ago. They were in that big compound where you guys found the heroin. Taliban didn't like it. RPGs and small-arms attacks. Hit them about five times, trying to drive them out. Set the compound on fire, 'n' all. Guys did well, broke it up and called in 105s and mortar rounds. Mowgs did outstanding . . .'

Mowgs was our attached forward observer, a cheerful, mischievous artilleryman who called in shells if we needed them and were allowed to. He looked like an Afghan, tanned with a droopy moustache and long hair. The boys loved him.

'. . . they were pinned on the roof at one stage, couldn't get a round down range, the Taliban's weight of fire was so heavy. But, yeah, good to get that out of the way. They did well, killed one too. Just your boys now need to get blooded. You know this Sapwan Qala op is coming up soon?'

'I heard. That'll be tasty if it happens.'

'We'll see. You guys could be going . . . though keep it quiet for now.'

'Roger. Will do.'

'You all right? You look sick.'

'Grand. Just had a close one on the heli. Fucking ANA.'

That night I listen to the other platoon commander describe the fire fight, jealous that he has been baptized and I have not, keenly aware of the assured self-confidence he and some of his men now exude.

My first and last trip in a vehicle in Afghanistan takes me out to a new Royal Irish compound at the edge of Wombat Wood, Patrol Base Nabi. On foot you have some control, some say in your destiny. Not so in this thinly armoured hearse. I decide I prefer control to protection and clutch the door handle throughout the short journey, hoping we won't hit an IED. We don't.

The OMLT guys are working hard to shore up the compound before the attacks begin, filling sandbags, cutting tree branches, building roadblocks. Ronnie collects me and H on a quad motorbike and we move to 7 Platoon's compound, deep in the heart of Wombat Wood. I see all the faces I have worried about, but Speedy and Ronnie have easily kept things together in my absence. It seems the lads are glad to see me.

This compound is wrecked compared with our last. No concrete here. A dry dirt floor, thatched wattle roof, mud walls that reveal Hellfire missile-blast scars and thirty-millimetre cannon-strike marks, a badly barricaded gate manned by a dangerously exposed sentry and sandbagged positions on the rickety roof. Not the best.

There are four USMC snipers with us, led by Mad Tim, a master sniper and good-natured killer who quickly impresses on us how much he enjoys his job. The guys swap rations and chat about the merits of the MRE chocolate milkshakes vis-à-vis our chicken tikka. Out here, food is important. More than nourishment; common ground, a distraction, a sanctuary. Morale.

I move into a cool, dark, dirty room and see Speedy sitting by a radio. He is joking with Caylie, 7 Platoon's new medic. A softly spoken northern woman, she has been with us since the blue on blue, one of the very few female medics on front-line duty. Most girls struggle with the weight on long patrols, but the doc tells me she is as strong and determined as any man, and to treat her likewise. I do. She proves herself time and again. But a girl among thirty boys changes things in other ways. She brings a calmness, a softness that all women bring to men, something especially welcome in this hard place. You can feel the platoon's respect for her. The platonic love that builds has another, natural dynamic. They want to protect her. Later, I fear her loss would devastate these young men more than the loss of anyone else.

Un-acclimatized, that night I try to sleep on a cardboard box, sharing my room with a snake, cockroaches, frogs, flies and the unending heat. But deep within, in my stomach, my guts, I feel good. Good to be back.

'Right, lads, close in.'

'Close in, fellas. The boss wants to speak to youse.'

They take a while to settle down, squeezing into the shade of the thick mud portico next to the courtyard. Under the awnings of the rapidly collapsing roof they sit on the dirt floor and look at me.

'Right, does anyone know what day it is today?'

'Yeah, boss, it's Wednesday!'

They laugh. I grin.

'No, the eighteenth of June, I mean. What day is that?'

A hand is cautiously extended upwards, risking the wrath of its peers. 'Is it Waterloo Day, boss?'

'Yeah, it is . . . well done,' I say, growing into my role as history teacher.

'I wanted to let you guys know about what happened on this day 193 years ago and 5,000 miles away, outside Brussels in Belgium . . .'

I look around. Some look interested; Ammo, Bardsley, Naf, Kav. Others look bored; Dev, T. But I have attracted Mowgs and a couple of the snipers, who now lean against the mud arches of the portico and listen, arms folded.

'. . . Fellas, men exactly like you were serving with one of our old regiments, the 27th Inniskillings, and they were on a boat to America when they were ordered back and had to march sixty miles through the rain and the night to get to the Waterloo battlefield for morning. When they arrived, they were ordered to form up in a square in the centre of General Wellington's line and hold it at all costs. Lads, these guys were like youse, from all over Ireland, North and South . . .' I look up at Naf '. . . though I don't think there were too many Fijians, Naf!' Laughs. '. . . They were knackered and soaked but they formed up in a square in case the French cavalry attacked. Inside the square they hoisted the Queen's Colour and the Regimental Colour, emblazoned with that castle we still wear, and these were held by a Colour Sergeant and a buckshee officer like me . . .' I grin, and they do. '. . . and were aiming points for the French cannons. And that's what happened; the French guns saw them and opened up, trying to batter the 'Skins into breaking before they launched their cavalry. And these guys, guys like you, just took it. Stood there and took it, lads. This battle was deciding the fate of Europe for the next hundred years and these guys were right at the centre of it, completely crucial. Each time a cannonball blasted the Colour Sergeant or officer away, another dashed out and picked up the Colours and took his place. They went through something like twelve sergeants and fifteen officers just from holding the Colours, boys.'

I look around. Now most of them are interested.

'The 'Skins had the greatest losses of men and officers of any battalion in the whole battle. At one point the CO of another regiment shouted over to see if the 'Skins needed officers, because there was only one left, and the major in charge said, "no, thanks, the sergeants are more than capable of running things on their own . . ."'

The boys exchange knowing grins.

'. . . anyway, at the end of all this, the 'Skins were literally dead in the square where they had stood, obedient to the end. They lost over 450 men that day, more than we've lost in Iraq and here put together. Makes you think . . . Anyway, Wellington, years later, saw a 'Skins soldier on guard and said, "Ah, the Inniskillings: they saved the centre of my line." But my favourite is the French colonel, who said after the battle, "I have seen French courage, German courage and Russian courage, but I've never seen such courage as the men with the castles." So that, lads, is a bit about Waterloo, 193 years ago today. Hopefully, it gives you a bit of pride. I know it mightn't seem like it, but you guys are continuing that tradition out here today. So be proud . . . Faugh a Ballagh!'

'Faugh a Ballagh,' they chime while I wonder if they care at all.

The generator packs up and that decides things. We will leave this compound today. As we sit in the shade and the sentries cautiously watch, the Taliban radios chatter.

'Boss, the Taliban just said that they will ambush the next patrol that leaves the new compound.'

'Roger.'

We pack all our wares on to the quad, loading it down with

rockets, batteries, water, fuel. I tell the boys it sounds like they're gonna have a go at us and how we're going to try to stop them. Hopefully, it will concentrate their minds.

It is strange listening to your enemy planning to kill you, and even stranger when it happens in real time. We are ready.

Matt slips his section out of the battered gate first, muttering light-heartedly about being a sandbag again. I tell him to stay no more than a hundred metres to our left in the patchwork maze of compounds, fields, treelines and ditches that await us.

I look through my sight. *Right a bit. Right.* The crosshairs drift over the man. They linger. *What is that?* I drop the sight below my eyes and peer over the top. Peer across the deep-green straw-grass field, across the stone-speckled clay ditch and the patches of grey shale, to my target. My cause for concern. He is wearing a grey skullcap and a dirty white dishdash, walking from my right to left, moving from the end of a glistening, rustling, peaceful treeline into an open green field. And he has something strange on his shoulder.

My crosshairs find him again. I see his face. About thirty-five. *Is that an RPG? What is he doing?*

Beside me the terp has already coiled himself up into a ball in a shallow hollow, the only piece of cover in this flat, exposed killing field. He knows what's coming. His scanner crackles.

'Boss, they are going to hit us,' he whispers nervously.

The man still walks nonchalantly, his RPG pointing backwards atop his shoulder. He hasn't seen us. *Even a stoned Taliban wouldn't do that.* He has no idea that I am debating whether to kill him or not.

I decide.

Quickly, the crosshairs find him again, and I drop it low and right, just behind him. My index finger slides the safety catch.

The report pierces the stillness. A grey dust cloud bursts up at his feet. He jolts and stops dead, the RPG on his shoulder tumbling to the ground and revealing itself as a simple green spade. *Right decision.*

Platoon commanders are not meant to fire, but coordinate others' fire. I have just fired my first shot in anger.

It also initiates the Taliban ambush.

Crack.

Matt hears the shot, just as his men are crossing a small ploughed field, long mounds of dried mud baking in the pink evening sun. They run for the closest ditch.

My warning shot has probably saved their lives.

Chance.

A series of whooshes and booms screeches past. Then the sucking zips and clattering crack-cracks . . .

Violence and noise erupt around us, a thundering, roaring, rolling tsunami of greens and blues and browns, of mud and watery ditches and white streaks of rocket trails, of flying copper and sweat and fear. It's rolling over us, crashing around us, sucking us up and in and spinning us like the great wave it is and you twirl and you spin and everything goes calm and clear and you're in the wave spinning and drifting but it's OK, OK, you gaze at the chaos outside as it spins and spins and you roll and roll and who'll get spat out of this, this frothing beast that's firing rockets from its wash and churning bullets as it soars above you and smashes down on you, there is no escape you are all getting soaked when will I get out of this.

Breathe, run, leg grass leg grass leg grass, breathe.

I am standing above a watery ditch. I am safe. A line of olive-green bushes separates immediate death and myself. H's boys are OK; they have moved out of the field, I have watched them, I am sure. Below me, US Marines are firing through gaps in the bushes, red-hot brass casings fizzing sharply as they hit the murky water they crouch waist-deep in.

'Contact! Small arms and RPGs. Wait out!' *At least I remembered the first thing.*

'Get down! Get down!'

The noise is unbearable. Chaos reigns. One ear is desperate shouts and screams, zips, explosions and twangs; the other an amplified tunnel of panic to another world where two radio frequencies scream for my attention like a fraught baby 'Get down, get down! . . . Boss! Bo . . . six o'clock, six o'clock. CRACK-CRACK-CRACK. See him, see him? Fucking th . . . Hello, Hades Four One, this is Hades Four Zero, send your BOSS! BOSS! IT'S MATT. CONTACT! CONTACT! WE'RE TAKIN' RPGs AND MACHINE-GUN FIRE. I'M FUCKEN' PINNED I'M PIN—' DUDUDUDUDU . . . 'Hello, Hades Four One, this is Hades Four Zero, send locs . . . BOSS, GET THE FUCK DOWN GET THE FUCK DOWN THEY'RE OVER THERE OVER THERE! Four One Alpha this is Four One Bravo, I've closed the bac . . .' CRACK-CRACK, 'BOSS BOSS IT'S MATT! ENEMY FOUR HUNDRED METRES NORTH OF . . . Watch the flanks! Watch the flan . . . Hello, Hades Four One, this is Hades . . .'

Overload. I switch off my headset and tell Mac to listen in instead. I need to think.

Matt's section hurl themselves into their ditch, as rocket-propelled grenades skim along the muddy field and explode only feet in front of them, showering them in dust and shrapnel and swallowing them in noise. Overhead, bullets tear into the trees, scattering yellow splinters and green foliage on them and chewing the ground just yards behind.

Ronnie's boys have been escorting the quad motorbike and are caught in the open.

'Move left! Move left!'

'Boss, it's Speedy! It's Speedy, boss! I got the back door, boss, the back door's closed. We're secure, boss.'

With our backs to the uninterested Helmand and Speedy watching them, now the chances of a troubled young man dashing from a compound and exploding himself in our midst have lessened. We are getting a foothold.

An RPG self-detonates mid-air, sending shrapnel screaming around him, and Ronnie finally decides it's time to abandon the juicy target of the quad and rush for cover with his section, who have positioned themselves between it and their attackers, lying on their bellies in the field and firing back at their black-clad enemy. Meanwhile, Matt's section are starting to return fire. I can hear their guns start to chatter excitedly, hurriedly, with a developing intensity that is joined by others, their own wave gathering speed and weight.

'Get fucking 2 Section up here. H! H! He's here, boss. Here. Where? There. H! H! We need to move forward, get closer and get eyes on. Move to that ruin now, Ronnie'll cover you.'

Sweat.

Hands sting, elbows hurt from crawling.

'Roger, boss, moving now.'

What the fuck is going on where are the enemy where is Matt do we have any casualties?

Crackle: 'BOSS! BOSS! IT'S MATT! ENEMY THREE HUN-DRED METRES DUE NORTH, BY THE COMPOUND . . . COMPOUND FIVE . . . COMPOUND FIVE ONE, I THINK . . . AT LEAST FOUR FIRING POIN . . .' CRACK-CRACK-CRACKDUHDUHDUHDUH.

'MATT! MATT! BOSS! DO YOU HAVE ANY CASUALTIES? ANY CASUALTIES, MATT?'

'DUHDUHDUH . . . NO, BOSS, NO CASUALTI . . . THERE! THERE! FUCKING GET HIM!'

'THERE! THREE HUNDRED METRES. LEFT EDGE OF COMPOUND. TWO TIMES TALIBAN.'

'SEEN!'

'SEEN!'

'SEEN!' echo the Rangers.

'RAAAAPID FIRE!'

Bullets start winging towards the enemy. In the hail of copper that clatters and tap-dances around them the Taliban are momentarily suppressed. H's section take advantage and break from their paltry protection behind a mound in the open field and dash for the cover of some ruins, closer to the enemy. I follow with Mac beside me, always watching out for me, protecting me, as I gaze without seeing, distracted by the information, threats and tactics that swirl in my head.

There is a fleeting lull as the insurgents duck away.

Radio. Pashto.

'We have them. Sustain the attack, sustain the attack.'

They fight back with renewed vigour.

Whooosh BOOM. ZipzipZIPZIPCrack-crack-CRACK-CRACK . . . whoOOSH BOOM.

'THERE! FIVE O'CLOCK! RPG MAN!'

In an instant Mad Tim has whipped his sniper rifle from his pack and, standing waist-deep in the soaking ditch, is searching for targets. The insurgents are firing from different mud-walled alleyways, popping out in small groups, letting off accurate bursts and disappearing again. Just as a masked and black-robed fighter pops out with a primed RPG pointing our way, Tim's magnified sights find him.

'SEEN!'

The shot sends the fighter sprawling backwards.

'I GOT HIM, I GOT HIM IN THE CHEST, MAN!'

The tsunami has crashed over us. We are soaked, bedraggled,

gasping for air, but we are intact. We are slowly regaining control through the muscle memory of training.

Matt pulls his men back, out of the killing area, and forms a baseline.

'BASELINE!' the Rangers repeat.

Another rapid fire. By now H's men are firing as well. Matt has shown me the enemy positions. The Taliban cannot match our heavy weight of fire. Forty times that of a platoon in the Second World War.

The incoming stops.

'WATCH AND SHOOT! WATCH AND SHOOT!' comes the order to stop firing and look for the enemy popping out of cover.

'WATCH THE FLANKS! WATCH THE FLANKS! DON'T LET THEM TURN US!' Eyeballs sweep quickly and nervously over shoulders, scan and scan, waiting. The civilians have vanished. Anyone near us now will die.

The mortar controller radios his barrels and lays them on to the compounds should we need them. Overhead, jets are hurtling towards us at a thousand miles an hour.

The terp's ear is glued to his scanner: 'Boss, boss! They have broken off the attack and taken a casualty.'

Then, panicked: 'Boss, they are preparing to mortar us.'

Oh God, we are so exposed. Please no.

'GET INTO HARD COVER! INCOMMMMINNG!'

There is no hard cover. We press ourselves into the mosque ruins, into the broken walls and shell craters, cradling, hugging, fucking the ground. Please save me. Please save me. Please don't fall on me. Not me, somewhere else somewhere else anywhere else.

Tension. All is quiet. We are all locked in our own selfish thoughts and bracing for the worst. The infantryman fears the mortar almost as much as he does the IED. Just the distant, puny pop and then you are alone with that shell somewhere above you and pure randomness, you think, chance. But there is an art, a world of trajectories and numbers and angles that is trying to unite you with that deadly spinning bomb that drops silently like a raindrop in a muddy field and sends shrapnel and dirt and black and grey smoke spewing out to find you, kiss you, grab you, and fling you back to the ground you so love.

We await the explosions and hail of shrapnel, already damaged by the psychological impact.

But the real impacts never come.

The ANA rush out of their base to our aid and begin pursuit of the Taliban as they flee to their safe houses to hide their weapons. As the lull lengthens, Speedy and Ronnie move back to the abandoned quad and get it away to safety.

'Hades Four One, this is Four Zero. We need you to exploit those firing points. See what intelligence you can get.'

We move carefully, scanning, scanning, nervous, as the locals start to return to the fields.

'Boss, he's one,' says Dev.

'He's wearing the same dishdash as the guys on the firing point.'

I am staring into the face of an indignant seventeen-year-old. His eyes gleam menacingly with his hate for me. *Is this our enemy?*

Matt and Dev search him. Nothing. They smell his hands for cordite.

'Boss, he fuckin' stinks of gunpowder.'

'No. I can't smell it.'

I'm not sure. Maybe I don't want to believe he is our enemy. That this is really the face of what we are fighting.

'Fuck it, let him go. I can't smell anything.'

'Boss, I reckon that guy was firing at us.'

'Me too.'

'Well . . . let's watch which compound he goes to and record it.'

Reluctantly, Matt and Dev release him. He moves to his compound, where his father emerges and shouts and beats and kicks him into the compound.

Wrong decision.

We look for blood spatters, for signs of success. For signs that this little skirmish took place. Nothing. We need something, some proof, for in days our little battle, our little test of manhood, will be forgotten to all bar its participants. But for us it will become a hidden part of us for ever.

The locals say they were waiting an hour for us. Six of them. That they heard one of them screaming and he was dragged away clutching his belly in agony, dying.

Good.

We trudge back to camp under the pink-orange sky, and as we near base we slip into private contemplation. How did I do? How did my friends do? How did I react? Did I use the right tactics? Did I let my buddies down? Did I let the men down?

Luckily not. The Taliban ambush had been foiled at a cost to them, not us, and we were now baptized in that muddy water that soaked our heads, trickled down our pink cheeks and sucked our uniforms away from our bodies. It was different from the suicide bomber because it was just us and it was sustained. It was a proper contact, *our contact*. We felt good that we hadn't let ourselves or each other down. That we had each other's backs, that we performed our individual tasks that, when combined, formed a cohesive whole that kept us alive. That we hadn't been frozen by fear.

I did OK. I can do this.

As we traipse into camp, the adrenalin gone, we realize how exhausted we are. The rear troops look at us in wonder. They've heard the whole thing from the safety of camp. Probably tried to watch.

One REMF looks at McD, a mess of dirt, sweat and water. He turns to another voyeur, smiling.

'Fuuu-uck that.'

When I find out later, I want to bayonet the man in the face.

I am hardening.

BAZAAR

The road to Hades is easily travelled.

Diogenes Läertius
Bion

In the dry wadi the market is bustling, a maze of poles, plastic sheeting, wooden tables, goats and people. Two stoned ANP lazily patrol through the crowds. A motorbike skids to a halt on the edge of the throng. A man jumps off and walks quickly through the mass of beards and brown and grey cloths. He closes on the ANP swiftly. Behind them, he draws a small pistol.

Pop-pop.

We are in the bazaar, only metres yet a world away, among the browns and oranges and walls and alleys, the shit and the cooking, the oil and dust.

I hear the toy gun pops. *Ake firing flares?*

The ANP slump to the ground, one dead, the other dying, bleeding from crimson, skull-smashed head wounds. The assassin runs through the crowd as it parts. He reaches the motorbike, the engine guns and they tear off. It is over in seconds.

We move to the wadi, helpless heavily armed pebbles in the

tide of locals that are silently but quickly flowing out of the market. *What has happened?*

A man in a brown waistcoat and white dishdash shouts at me as he walks briskly past.

'What's he saying?'

'Boss, he's saying what is the point of you being here if you can't even keep security a few hundred metres from your base. He is angry, boss.'

I feel embarrassed. Useless.

The ANP slide the limp corpses on to a pickup. The sergeant major puts them in body bags beside the ops room. An IED goes off against the US Marines a few hundred metres from the DC, but they are only blasted by dust and stones. A suicide bomber detonates at another FOB, killing two Marines, leaving two others and twelve women and children horrendously injured. Intel suggests they'll try to do the same to us. Sixty Taliban are preparing to overrun Nabi. Four hundred broke out of Kandahar prison. Two suicide bombers on motorbikes in the bazaar. Get ready for Sapwan Qala: you're going.

SAR PUZEH

We few, we happy few, we band of brothers;
For he today that sheds his blood with me
Shall be my brother.

Henry V
William Shakespeare

The intelligence officer reads from his papers: 'Enemy forces: reports suggest up to 250 fighters in this area, a mixture of hard-line and ten-dollar Taliban. They are armed with an array of weapons, from small arms and RPGs, through to RPKs, SPG-9s, three times 82-millimetre mortars, 107-millimetre rockets, Dushka and ZPU .50 cal anti-aircraft machine guns, possibly even AGS 17 automatic grenade launchers. Enemy intentions: it is assessed that these fighters will strongly oppose any ISAF presence in this area, which is deemed their vital ground.'

Je-sus.

'Thank you . . . Adam, did you get that? Please outline your plan. We are all listening intently up here.'

The small radio speaker crackles.

'Well, sir, my intent is to launch a large company air assault into the town of Sar Puzeh, south of Sapwan Qala, in order to recce the bridge on the 611 and to gauge local attitudes toward ISAF troops . . .'

I stare at the speaker and scribble notes furiously. Around the large square table adorned with maps, notebooks and senior officers I sit self-consciously, a student in my first exam. The atmosphere is professional, serious, as it always is in the newly arrived headquarters. Officers, clean and quiet, come and go, adding murmurings to the whirr of the cool air-conditioning machines and the rustle of papers. The Spartan CO listens intently.

'. . . Sir, I will take four platoons, 7 and 9 Platoons, a large Fire Support Group [FSG], plus my HQ from FOB Gibraltar, 7 Platoon Ranger Company, and a Royal Irish-mentored ANA platoon from Sangin . . .'

'. . . And I'll be bringing my tactical HQ along too, Adam.'

'Yessir. My scheme of manoeuvre is to air assault in two lifts of three Chinooks into a desert heli landing site east of the 611 and Sar Puzeh town. I will then send a platoon to recce the bridge before moving the company in bounds, with the Fire Support Group and the Ranger Company platoon over-watching us, through the Green Zone, hopefully conducting shuras, gauging local support and giving out medical aid. If it all goes to plan, we will consolidate overnight in the Green Zone and extract ourselves by heli the next day . . .'

'Yes . . . Understood . . . thank you . . . I'm not sure it will go to plan. What intelligence is suggesting is that we'll have to fight our way in and fight our way out. I don't think we'll spend a quiet night in the Green Zone.'

Neither do I. From my junior position it looks like we are picking one of the most heavily defended, fanatical Taliban towns, just down the 611 from their capital of Sapwan Qala, and thinking we may be able to go in and just talk to them. We are going into a scrap. That is plain to see.

I stand up to leave. The boss brings me over to the CO. He towers above me, eyes half closed like he is taking aim, sizing me up.

He shakes my hand powerfully and stares at me, a testing, manly stare.

'Well, are you ready?'

'I am, sir.'

You never really are.

I give orders to the platoon and finish by predicting how I think it will go. We are excited we have been chosen to go by the boss; to represent Ranger Company. We are going to fight with the same Paras we trained hard with for all those wet months on barren Yorkshire hills. I feel the pressure to perform, knowing success means other Ranger Company platoons will be picked for other air assaults, the pinnacle of all we espouse to do.

I don't sleep before we depart, but lie and think. Over and over the plan repeats itself in my head, over and over the tactical solutions to this going wrong, to that happening. We don't know what we're going into, but there is a feeling it's going to be big. *Thank God we're in the second wave.*

In the stillness of the Sangin night we move to the HLS, padded and armoured exoskeletons on the outside, tingly nervous yet determined inside. In the darkness, the ANA platoon arrives, led by Tony, a Royal Irish colour sergeant from the Republic. The sergeant major and the boss come to bid us well as the signaller frantically tries to get our radios working.

'You gonna speak to the platoon, sir?' the sergeant major hints in the blackness.

I nod.

'Right, 7 Platoon listen in: we know the plan and we know our part in it. Let's get switched on. Let's get focused. Let's fucking get out there and do this and get everybody back. Hit the ground running. Watch each other's backs. Let's show the Paras we're as good as them. Remember the big three. What're they?'

'Communication, boss,' says T.

'Target indication and fire control, boss,' says Chips.

'Changing positions, boss,' says Ammo.

Good. They are focused. We hear the choppers approaching. As the boss wishes the platoon good luck and happy hunting, the sergeant major takes me to one side.

His eyes are watching mine.

'Sir, this could be fuckin' serious, y'know? But youse can do this, youse are a good platoon . . . Look after them, sir, bring them all back.'

I wholly revere this man of experience and knowledge and am glad of these reassuring words of support. Command can be lonely, and it's heartening and unusual to be told you are doing all right. The emotion in his voice reveals the rarely seen deep compassion he has for us. I can see how worried he is, like it's his child's first day at school, setting us off into the unknown.

I look at him.

'I'll do my best, sergeant major.'

And I will. I will do everything I can to keep these men alive.

We sit in the green-black hue of the cylindrical Chinook cabin, together in noise but alone in thought. I can barely see the faces of the platoon, sitting in two long lines along the fuselage, facing each other through night-vision goggles and yellow blast-reducing shades. There is time to think. Time to think about your own death, time to think that you don't want to let anyone down. Time to worry if the HLS is hot. I look around, at the knee pads and weapons balanced on their barrels, bullets wrapped tightly around them and held by leather fingerless gloves. Everybody is silent. Everybody is thinking. *Timeless. The same kind of thoughts as they prepared to jump in on D-Day.*

As we fly through the inky night, the sergeant major and the boss walk back to the ops room to listen to the situation bulletins coming in from HQ on the aircraft radio net. It crackles into life as Apache pilots relay targets to each other.

'Sir, it's a hot LZ. I knew it, sir, they're goin' into a hot LZ. I fuckin' knew it.'

And we were.

Red tracer silently streaks past the portholes. *Opposed landing. Hot LZ.* The heli banks and pitches. Hand signal. Thirty seconds.

'STAND UP. RADIOS ON. CHECK OTHER MAN.'

Silently, men click switches and tap their buddies on their shoulders. Thumbs up. Mac hands me my aerial to hold under the rotor blades. *Keep it low . . . snipers.* The chopper twists sharply in the darkness and flares hard, tipping the rear ramp downwards and sending the light blue desert soaring towards us. The ramp goes down. I let go of the overhead straps.

This is it.

'LET'S GO! LET'S GO!'

I tear down the ramp, a black snake of men on either side of me, light blue dust in front and terrific noise above, clutching at my rifle, scrape click-cocking it as I run, trying not to slip down the ramp, making it on to the ground, running through the billowing blueness and jumping on my belly. I peer through flying dust at the snakes of men arching around on either side of me, their tips moving closer until they stop, a black-dotted circle of protection on the blue gravel ground.

The noise heightens, the dust blows harder. I can't hear any firing, but you couldn't anyway. I can't see any, but I can barely see anything. The heli is up, climbing out of there as fast as possible, chased by the now noisy red lines. The noise begins to recede like a tide, the dust drops out of the air. Quickly, it is silent. I stand up and let go of my aerial.

'Hades Two Zero, this is Hades Four One. Radio check, over.'

Silence.

I try again. Nothing.

The CO is trying too. The radios are down.

Disaster.

Leaving the platoon in all-round defence, I move to a blackened huddle of men, seeking the Para company commander in charge.

'OC C, OC C?' I whisper at the men kneeling together.

'Up there, mate. D'you guys get in all right? Looked cheeky from here.'

'Saw some tracer, alright.'

'You're lucky, mate. First wave had to get an Apache to take out a bloody Dushka. Fucking madness. He's up there.'

Whispers.

'Sir, I'm Paddy, OC Ranger Platoon. We're here and we're ready to go, but our radios are down.'

'Paddy, good stuff. It's not just your radios, mate; it's everybody's.'

'What?'

'Yeah, it's gonna take a while before we can sort it. We've had some resistance from the Green Zone already. Plan's still the same: you guys move up with the FSG and stick with 'em. Send one of your sections to guard CO's Tac and we'll get moving as soon as these radios are done.'

I move back to the platoon and detach Ronnie's men to protect the CO's group of antennas and satphones. The rest of us creep across the shale floor towards the black tufts of men lined up on a rise at the edge of the HLS. The clumps are large, heavily laden with Javelin rocket launchers and machine guns. Their backpacks droop from their shoulders, filled with golden reels of ammunition.

We join them and extend their line along the ridge.

Whispers.

'How's it going? I'm Lieutenant Bury, OC Ranger Platoon.'

'All right, sir . . . Your radio broken?'

'Banjaxed.'

'Right. Mine's working. I'll keep you informed on our personal radios; switch to Charlie Three so we can all talk.'

'Roger. Happy with the plan?'

In the darkness I think I am talking to a corporal, not an ex-infantry instructor and veteran.

'Yes. You?'

'Yeah.'

'Good . . . I'll keep you in the loop, sir.'

I creep back to the platoon and sit and explore my surroundings through the green haze of my night goggles.

We sit atop a ridge, really a gentle, rounded rise that runs from the black jagged mountains to the left of us to the 611 to the right. Over our ridge, where we need to go, I see more ridges and dips, a time-frozen sequence of mellow, rounded swells whose stones and sand shine light green in my scope. These cylinders of shale end abruptly in steep bluffs and cliffs at the 611. I pan right, looking into the deep-green blackness of the Green Zone punctuated by green-white sparkles of illumination from compound lights. The malevolent jungle stretches for two Ks across, channelling the never-ending Helmand, and ends on the other side of the valley in the same looming black line of sandy hills that overlook Sangin. I pan up the deserted 611, towards a cluster of lights, flat roofs and mud walls that betray the centre of Sar Puzeh.

Something large and white screeches over us and we instinctively huddle into ourselves. A short, unnatural, imposed silence. A mighty echoing explosion and a flash of white light: 107-millimetre rockets. *Thank Christ that missed.* We wait for the radios.

We are losing momentum.

Finally, I see sticks of men moving off. Overhead, the drone of two Apaches thumps the air like dragonflies. The Para platoons close on the bridge and the town. Tracer is exchanged, harmless and beautiful from our vantage point, deadly and noisy down there.

Our personal radios relay information, an out-of-sync commentary on the fighting below.

'Dickers popping out all over the place. 9 Platoon have seen armed men. They've already killed one and are firing at others.'

RPGs whoosh and boom.

I clip down my goggles in time to see a thin green laser beam illuminate some intended target, unbeknown to it. An Apache sparks into life, swooping down in a louder THUMPTHUMPTHUMP and then releasing a ripping low brrrrrrrbrrrrrrr noise. I watch the tracer hit and splay out from whatever its explosive bullets have just destroyed.

Commentary: 'RPG man dead. 9 Platoon clearing compounds. Bridge has been recced. It is only a culvert and will take a convoy. The OC says get ready to move out as per plan.'

'Roger.'

We climb to our feet as the sporadic firing starts to ease off. Blackness is losing to blueness, and the white tip of dawn crests the hills over the Green Zone, now slowly melting into green.

We move off, spaced and wary lines of men, scanning the peaks and troughs in front of us, as below the Para platoons clear through the last compounds before straddling the 611 down to our right. Behind, Tony's OMLT troops and their ANA follow us. There is no noise but the wind catching my mouth mike and amplifying into my earpiece. Occasionally, steers from Matt and H permeate the silence.

'Bardsley, left a bit, left a bit, stay off the ridge line.'

'Ammo, keep eyes on that compound coming up: that's where we need to get to. Could be enemy in there.'

We are now the forward troops in the advance down the 611, creeping on our sandy sea high above the matted maze of fields and foliage below which the Paras have begun to sweep through.

We crest a rounded wave, and in the next trough are revealed the blue-black walls of compounds just off the 611. A shallow V-shaped dip runs down to it, some ancient tributary long baked dry. The right side of the V finishes in a ridge before dropping sharply to the 611 below. In the blueness I kneel, shielding my torch as I check map and GPS.

I close Matt in. Whispers.

'That's compound 41. That's the one the OC wants us to get eyes on.'

'Roger, boss.'

'H is in the next dip to our left and he's got eyes on the other compounds over there. We can observe these compounds from here.'

The FSG commander walks over to me. He is so heavily laden, the dawn shades of blue and black so striking, that the scene resembles an astronaut's moonwalk. He is concerned.

He gestures to the top of the ridge line.

Whispers.

'Sir, I need to get up there with my guns. I can't see anything in this dip. I need eyes on the Green Zone for the blokes moving down.'

I look at the ridge. Here we are shielded from the menacing black-greenness by that ridge. Up there we mightn't be. None of us knows for sure what is on the other side. All is quiet.

He's the FSG commander. He has his mission. I am here to protect him.

'OK . . . Matt, we're going up there, see what we can see. Turn your guys in line as they are and take it slow.'

We move off, a wide-spaced dotted line of soldiers scaling this small ridge. I am in the middle, Matt's men to my left, the FSG commander just in front of me, his FSG team behind to my right, our formation a loose V like a flock of seagulls. We creep up the rise. It starts to expose itself as flatter than anticipated. I crouch and look to my left. *Good.* Matt's boys are doing the same, advancing slowly, doubled over, peering towards the crest. The FSG commander strides forward, trying to see the ground below. *His antenna's fully up.* We have almost crested the flat-topped mound. Our horizon reveals itself further with every stride. The dark Green Zone deepens below us. *This is dodgy.* The FSG commander surveys the scene. I am just behind him. The rest are behind me. White dawn sits on the hills.

Red streaks of light. Straight for me.

Captivatingly slow.

So fast.

I tense. There is no time for anything else. No thought. No feeling.

Flashes pass me, low left, near my hand. More flashes, streaks all over me. Straight at my head. Somehow flashing past my right ear. A double kiss of air ripples my ear. CRACK-CRACK-CRACK-CRACK.

I am alive.

'GET DOWN!'

'INCOMING!'

I hit the dirt, heart racing, adrenalin pumping, every nerve in my body working in overdrive, sensing, feeling, responding. Out of the corner of my wide, quivering, hyper-alert eyes I see the commander drop to his knee.

'THAT COULD BE FRIENDLY!' someone shouts behind me.

They are right. It could be. I have heard those beautiful red sticks before and they sound like ours.

I turn to the FSG gunners to my right, anxious to stop them engaging if it is.

'DON'T FIRE! DON'T FIRE!'

They can't see over the ridge anyway.

More incoming. CRACK-CRACK-CRACK.

I hear a faint cry.

I turn my head.

The man to my front is now slumped on the crest, his back towards me, collapsed.

'MAN DOWN! MAN DOWN!' I shout.

'Man down!' echoes over the ridge line.

I look to my right. The three young gunners are staring at me, a mixture of shock and bewilderment. A look that asks: what are you going to do now, boss?

Shit. Shitshitshitshit.

Time is beginning to warp, slowed by the intensity of what is happening to us.

I look at him again. His hand slightly raised, lying on his side. He's alive. But he's completely exposed. I am the closest to him.

I sense the gunners are scared. I don't know if I speak or shout to them.

'Stay here. I'll get him. Don't shoot, it could be friendly.' *No friendly would shoot at us twice . . .*

Those young faces look at me and nod.

What are you doing?

I drop my rifle. I won't need it.

Go.

I don't know if I run or crawl.

I close on the slumped, helmetless figure lying above me. His hand is down. I can't see his face as his back is towards me. *Please be OK, please don't be shot in the head, please don't be a mess. I couldn't take that . . .*

I think someone is shooting at me. I can't remember.

There is nothing but me and him and fear.

The dash to the commander is only fifteen feet. I run marathons. Yet this is the shortest longest most intense run I have ever made. I relived it almost every day until I wrote this. As I did this whole sequence.

I get to him and hit the ground. He is faintly murmuring, turning white.

Fuck. Rushed: 'You're OK! You're OK, buddy! You're OK.'

His hand moves slightly in recognition. *Hold his hand, he's dying. No one should die alone.* I grab it and squeeze.

A faint receding pressure.

'You're OK. You're OK.' I desperately try to reassure us both.

Straining, I turn him over, dreading what I will see. Nothing. He is perfect. Still breathing.

I try to drag him down the slope while I lie on the ground but I can't. His kit is too heavy. *He must have a thousand rounds in that daysack.*

Bullets clip the ridge.

Stand up. No, don't. Stand up. I stagger to my feet and grab him by the daysack. *This is dangerous.* Slowly, heaving, I pull him down the slope. But it is too slow. I will get shot out here. I have never felt so alone in all my life. I am flagging.

Suddenly, a blur of desert camouflage: somebody is by my side. The loneliness melts. Energy. Strength. An arm grabs the man's shoulders and we pull hard, determinedly. He is released, sliding quickly down the slope behind us.

Then Dev is by our side, throwing smoke grenades and dragging him too.

We are in the bottom of the dip.

'MEDIC! MEDIC!' I scream.

I am frantically trying to get the only working radio off the back of the limp commander.

The Para lance jack and Dev are cutting his clothes off furiously. We expect to see some horrible wound, but there is none.

Panic. 'Where is it? Where is it?'

Someone else arrives – Bardsley, I know now – and he quickly sees the small cigarette burn on his chest. He expertly applies a seal. He is a nineteen-year-old.

'Hold his hand. Hold his hand,' I plead as I tear the radio out of his daysack.

Suddenly, it is day.

Bullets splatter around us.

'CONTACT FRONT!'

Oh Christ. This is getting serious. Bullets smash straight up our little dip from the south, peppering the ground around us, sending mushrooms of dust erupting into the air. Things are getting desperate; there is no cover. We are now in an L-shaped ambush, an infantryman's worst nightmare.

'MATT! MATT! Deal with that! I've gotta get comms.'

Matt is already turning his men towards the compounds again, peeling them around into a baseline to suppress the shooters to our south. Our weight of fire drives the insurgents momentarily back into their compounds, but their firing has stopped Speedy and Caylie the medic getting to the casualty.

I get his radio working while the others treat him.

I call the OC: 'This is Hades Four One Alpha, Man Down!

Man Down! Possible friendly fire. We're in contact from the south too!'

'Hades Two Zero Alpha. Roger. It was not friendly fire. We know where you are and haven't engaged.'

Speedy and Caylie get to him. As the rounds zip around her, she calmly checks the man for vital signs, as our little clump of desert camouflage sits vulnerable and exposed.

She looks at the Para.

'I'm sorry . . . There's nothing I can do. He's gone.'

Even amid all that chaos, there is a silence as we all look down.

'Well, then . . .' Speedy sighs, looking at me. '. . . It's a T4 [Triage 4 – dead] then, boss.'

I nod and hand him the radio to send the bad news to the Paras. It is a body blow to his FSG, who loved him dearly. They have just lost their sergeant major. The backbone of the company, the sinew of a battalion.

Lee, a Para corporal, takes command of the FSG. We are all only one bullet away from death or promotion out here.

I move to control the fight to the south, where harassing fire impedes our efforts to extract him. Still under fire, Speedy eventually gets him out of the dip back to the safety of a quad. But the heli extraction is called off.

Our Jimpys finally convince the insurgents to the south to move away, and we watch as they attempt to hide their weapons under their flowing white dishdashes and brazenly walk out into the fields under us. These are not civilians.

I see one. He is an older man. I can see a rifle stock protruding under his gown.

'Smith! Five hundred metres, two o'clock, ditch in field.'

'Roger, boss.'

Jets of flame leap out of the Jimpy, lazily arcing towards the

Playing soldiers, Ireland 1990. I am in the centre

One Pip Wonder. Commissioning at midnight, Sandhurst, April 2006.

Paddy's Day in the best regiment in the British Army.

7 Platoon survivors, Kenya 2007.

Above: A chubby and white 7 Platoon at the start of the tour, Sangin DC.

Left: In contact after the suicide bomber. P.J. and 7 Platoon echelon through.

Green Zone patrol. Cupples is forward left, wearing shades to protect his eyes from blast fragments.

Corporal McCord Nav checks in the ever growing Green Zone.

2 Section 7 Platoon.

Harvesting the poppy.

Myself and Ranger Cupples in another dusty, dangerous alley waiting for it to be swept for IEDs. He was always right behind me.

Ranger Company provide honour guard for a marine killed out side the DC when his Viking hit an IED. I sit on the chopper next to the flag-draped body.

On patrol near the bazaar.

Above: US Marines cross Green 78. Like Green 12, it is a constantly dangerous and fought-over bridge.

Left: 9 Platoon in the bazaar.

Searching locals in the bazaar; a tense experience for all.

Above: US Marines in contact in the Green Zone. Note our shamrock worn for luck. We developed close bonds with the Americans.

Right: Things get tense in the Green Zone near Monkey.

The Soviet-era anti section mine which an inquisitive Dev found in a telegraph box, thus saving our lives.

Digging out the Vector, 10 hours in. Soon after this picture was taken we were contacted.

Left: The boss on the walls of PB Armagh.

Below left: Tricolour with Amhran Na Bhfian and Northern Irish Flag, PB Armagh.

Below right: 82mm mortar shells wired as a daisy chain and buried by Green 12. Ronnie somehow found them with his eyeball.

man. He starts to run as explosions of mud and water trail out behind him, closing rapidly. They are just about to catch him when he makes it to the safety of a compound.

'Fuck's sake.'

Below, the reports from rifles and machine guns tell us the Para platoons are engaging small groups of Taliban all around them. They pop out of doors with RPGs, run from treeline to treeline with rifles and AKs, shoot from roofs with machine guns.

As the sun rises on a millionth morning in Sar Puzeh and maybe its first or fifth or tenth of war – *who knows?* – it becomes increasingly obvious that this is getting big. No chance of a shura today.

We wait and fire at the flood of Taliban coming into the area, through ditches and alleyways, paths and compounds. With the dead sergeant major's radio I relay information to the OC and the other platoons, letting them know where they're going and where I think we're being shot from. They are in their own world, pushing south, clearing compounds amid the green foliage, trying to get level with us and killing the Taliban in the process.

The ominous sun begins to burn. Bullets are still clipping the ledge and zinging over our heads. Occasionally, often enough to worry us, RPGs scream over our heads in white plumes and explode harmlessly near the mountains behind us. Apaches are circling, destroying. The battle has begun.

I receive word that the Paras below are level with us, that the ANA behind are ready to go. The OC tells me over the radio what he wants to happen. I move the platoon and the FSG down towards the compounds. Matt and Dev kick in the wooden door, fingers on triggers, safeties off. An old woman and a child come out, crying in the chaos. The terp sends them to a darkened room. We move in and fan out, defending the ragged walls as bits of metal slice the blue sky above us at a thousand miles an hour.

Sweat. Heat. Thirst. Adrenalin still pumping. Eyes wide, taking in every minute detail. Alive. Every muscle, every sinew, every nerve every sense every blood cell every corpuscle every brain cell working in overdrive a maximum like a drug a high thinking faster acting faster one hundred and twenty per cent concentration hit top gear total clarity in control. I can do this.

'Speedy, H, Matt, Lee, close in for a brief.'

They walk up to me as I sit on a muddy ledge, dribbling sweat on to my open map.

'All OK?'

'Yep, boss,' they answer, looking straight at me. Looking for direction in this madness.

'Good. Right. 7 Platoon are here, compound two-four. Seen?'

'Seen.'

'9 Platoon are there, compound two-eight, just ahead of us. Seen?'

'Seen.'

'We are here, four-five. The OC wants us to move down to two-four and then up and over that high ground there to the south . . .' I point to another frozen shale swell that overlooks us threateningly, now turning orange in the sun.

'When we go up there we'll get shot at, so keep it fast. Matt, you're first, then me, then you, Lee, then H, then Speedy. Move out in five.'

It is over quickly. We are all operating at maximum capability, with a clarity and concentration that is rarely equalled. I eyeball them all. They look at me. They understand. No questions.

As I watch them walk away to brief their men, I sit on that ledge gazing at a dirty yellow oil bottle and have an epiphany. I have just dragged a dying man to safety. In all this bedlam I have given a brief which these men whom I respect know was as good as on any training exercise. In the middle of this battle they trust me and my judgement. I think Colour Collins would be proud if he saw me now.

I can do this.

And that was it.

A second later I realized this man and the army were finished. I had proved myself to myself. I had done what I wanted to do.

Consumed the experience.

Whatever.

We move off, around the back of our compounds, trying to find a way to compound two-four that will shield us from the screaming violence in the air. We walk tentatively beside a high mud wall as bullets chip and bite the other side. It ends abruptly above a small plateau that descends in a scree slope to the 611.

Matt goes for it. He runs out with his section. He gets to the ledge before bullets impact the ground around him, wisps of dust twanging chillingly close.

I peer round. He's made it. I look at Mac. He looks at me.

'Let's go.'

'Right behind you, boss.'

Breathe, *go*, boot shale boot shale zipzip boot shale boot crack-crackcrack *thatwasclose, zigzag zigzag, just like training*, boot shale boot CRACKCRACKCRACK *tooclosedown!*

We dive into a slight depression. *This is madness.* Bullets skim the top, washing over us like drops from a gigantic watering can. *We stay here, we're dead.*

'Go!'

Up, boot shale boot shale, *nearlythere* CRACKCRACKCRACK *jump . . . phew*. I skid and roll down the scree and slide into Matt's men hunkering behind a small mud wall. Bullets whizz down the 611 beside us. Across the road I can see some of the Paras. Others are further down the road fending off the Taliban.

'Boss, it's H. Did you make it through?'

'Yeah, H, but be careful. They have it covered. Keep moving.'

There's no other choice.

We watch in relative safety as twenty feet above us H's men break from the wall. The enemy fire increases immediately, bursting all around them as they move along the exposed bluff. Some of the young Rangers dive to the ground, their love of the ground overcoming their tactical awareness. H, a twenty-two-year-old from Rochdale, stands up, completely exposed, bullets bouncing all around him. He screams and kicks at them to keep moving, to keep them alive.

They scramble forward and slide down to us.

H looks at me.

'Fuckin' hell!' He grins knowingly and looks at his men.

'I fuckin' told you to keep moving, didn't I? And what d'you do? Tryna get me killed, are ya?' He smiles.

We cross the 611 and briefly enter the compounds the Paras have just cleared, passing the nonchalant CO's group, who listen intently as the OC briefs me. It's like stepping into a different, calm, unconcerned world. Like HQ. In a way it's inspiring. In another way it's disconcerting. *Surely they don't understand the threat they're facing or they wouldn't be sitting around like that?*

Ronnie winks, draws hard on a cigarette and tells me that as they moved out in the darkness with the CO Naf spotted something suspicious. They just had time to form a defensive baseline and fan out before they were hit, bullets almost nailing them to a wall. They repelled their attackers, killing two Taliban with a grenade round that blew their heads apart.

We move off.

Matt first, straight up another bluff, and the crash of rounds starts again, this time accompanied by the tear and boom of RPGs. The furious, short sprints up these bluffs leave us gasping, sucking for air, our body armour expanding and contracting rapidly on our heaving chests as hands steady us to the wall that protects us. We all make it.

Below, the Paras identify where the insurgents are firing at us from. Clatters of bullets and the chatter of radio traffic indicate targets. We sit behind our orange wall, helpless, as RPGs are lobbed at us, the Taliban trying to get them to self-detonate over our heads to impale us with shrapnel. An Apache thumps overhead, low and mean. A burst of flame and a fizzing screech send a Hellfire missile into one of the compounds with another rumble that rolls over us. I sit listening as something drops on top of the engineer next to me. We jump out of our skin, too slow for anything else, as an empty plastic missile tube crashes to the ground. Then the casings from the cannons start to rain down, red-hot cylinders of brass that fall in sheets like a heavy rain cloud releasing its load.

'Arrrghh! . . . Jesus!' Soldiers swipe skin-melting shells from their necks.

Below, on the covered, camouflaged edge of the Green Zone, the Paras are having a good time. They spot Taliban reinforcements moving round, trying to flank them. They kill them. A sniper pair are killing individuals hundreds of metres away. As the Paras force their way south, insurgents jump out only metres in front of them; the soldiers react quicker and kill them. They leave their bodies where they fall, crumpled in wet ditches or cut into pieces on the road. High above in the barren desert, it is not so good. We are being constantly shot at and rocketed and can't tell where from. We sit and take it.

We have been fighting for over four hours. A pattern emerges as we bound forward over these open rolling swells, getting shot at all the time. We are drawing their fire, moving targets for the Taliban. When they open up, they expose themselves to the Paras below and another round of combat takes place. A compound full of insurgents holds out against everything the Paras can throw at them, the thick mud walls even resistant to the Hellfires that smash into them. Artillery is called in. The heavy shells whistle and spin through the air on their trajectories over our heads. The noise instantly lifts us on the ridge. We know what awaits those trying to kill us. Those that sap our morale with their constant screaming RPGs. Noise is power in this battle, and we're about to exercise ours. And they don't know it yet. We look up at the whistling.

'Haha. Get some of that, you bastards.' And we smile at their impending doom.

Massive CRU-UMMPBAAANGS echo simultaneously across the morning valley and dusty geysers of black-grey-brown shoot up from the compounds. Shrapnel scatters everywhere, carving through leaves, trees, fizzing into wet ditches. Silence. The dust drifts. Crackcrackcrack. It starts again.

We bound forward over another orange-brown hill, the ANA right behind us, bullets whizzing, sun baking. Past ruined, crumbling mud walls that leave us exposed. Matt's section runs for the next compound, across a cruel, seventy-metre bare patch. We run in rushes of two, sprinting, dodging, hoping. Myself and Dev cross last as bullets whip up around us. *Last is always worst. They know you are coming.* We get across, but it's close, and tumble down a stony cliff into cover. Mac should be next. We wait.

He's not. I try the radio. Nothing.

'Shit . . . Dev . . . Where are they?'

We cautiously peer over the ledge. Nothing. No firing.

'I can't see them. Something must've happened . . . We're going to have to go back and get them.'

We bolt back up the bluff. The firing starts again. This time running into it, I can see we are in the sights of a different firer. Red tracer is streaking towards us. It is accurate and it is conserved, not like the usual sprayed shots we face. A sharpshooter. The same firer who killed the sergeant major. Immediately, bullets kick at our feet and over our heads.

I hear Dev cry out behind, turn and see him fall into a shallow hole. I keep running for another depression.

Dive. CRACKCRACKCRACK. Breathe . . . breathe . . . think . . .

'Dev! Dev!'

The firing has stopped already. *He can't see us.*

'Dev! You OK?'

'Ahhh . . . Boss, my knee! I've wrecked my knee.'

'Can you run? We can't stay here.'

'Yeah, I think so,' he echoes back.

'Right, let's go.'

He's waiting for us. We rip out of cover and sprint for the wall. Again the red tracer starts immediately, this time just over our heads. *He must have a scope . . .*

We get to the wall.

'Mac, Mac!'

'Yes, boss.' His head appears around a chink in the wall.

'Where the hell were you? You split the callsign,' I demand, heaving for air.

'Boss . . . H got hit back there too; had to suppress to get the FSG boys out. You were gone before I could tell you.'

This is getting crazy. The Indians are circling the wagons.

Another exposed bluff. Another shell of a compound. Another wall crumbling to reveal us to the sniper. One side is safe, the other death. Speedy is stuck in another shallow hole. Another string of bullets clip the ledge in front of his helmet.

The ANA watch from behind the wall, safe. There is nothing we can do.

'Boss, it's Speedy,' he says calmly into the radio. 'I'm with some of the FSG in that dip in the ruined compound. We're safe, but we're pinned. There's a sniper out there, and he knows we're here.'

'Roger, Speedy. Our snipers know. They're looking for him; give us a steer if you can.'

Speedy slowly winces over the edge. Bullets thump the dirt inches in front of him. He tumbles back down.

'Fu-ck that, boss,' he says, laughing. '. . . Somewhere out there!'

We cross a small track that is covered by fire from the sharp-shooter. Red bullets tear up it and impact past us in the indifferent mountains.

He is close, he can see us and he is behind the Paras.

We are in a hamlet of compounds. Protection. He can't see us in here. Another Corolla is nervously checked for traps, then its tyres shot out. The platoon fan out, kicking doors in, clearing buildings. Occasionally a mud-dulled report echoes back followed by 'compound clear' on the radio.

H: 'Boss, you better come to the next compound – think it's five-one – there's loads of women and kids and they're scared. We need the terp.'

I turn the corner and run down the road to the door. Bullets fly past, but their zip tells me they are not close.

Inside are a small courtyard and a garden shaded by a thankfully high wall that keeps the Taliban from seeing into it. There's a gaggle of women and children, the women dressed in black burkas and green velvet dresses, the dirty kids in deep blue and green cloths. The terp goes to work for the first time since we landed.

'Boss, they want to leave.'

'I wouldn't recommend it. It's hardly safe out there. They can stay with us; it's safer here.'

'No, they want to leave. They don't want to be around ISAF and the fighting.'

I look at the noisy crowd. I am indifferent in all this madness. 'They can leave if they want. Tell them to wait for a lull and go north up the 611. I'll tell our troops, but I can't tell the Taliban. They must understand that.'

'Yes, boss, they do.'

They leave, and we investigate our new surroundings. Built into the beginnings of the bluff is a small room, covered in heavy ruby velvet rugs that adorn the floor and hang on the walls. It is cool. We enter and search well-stocked dressers, full of women's hair dye, make-up and tights.

'Boss, what is this?'

We collapse into the room, exhausted, sweating, guzzling on our hot and dwindling water supplies. *Six hours.* Outside, bullets skim overhead and RPGs continue to explode as the Taliban try to coax them into our compound. Jets swoop in to strafe ditches, their cannon disintegrating whomever they hit. The gunships are out of ammunition. A bomb is dropped on someone somewhere.

We are tired. The adrenalin slips away. We begin to think, to process what just happened. A mental slide show is playing in my head. Different scenes roll before my eyes. *How did those bullets miss my head?* Caylie bandages Dev's knee. We eat. I speak to the FSG, tell them I'm sorry about their sergeant major, the same sergeant major who I later learn helped me into that ambulance in Brecon. I thank the lance corporal for helping me drag him out, *for saving my life.*

Quiet inside, sporadically noisy outside. Someone peels back a velvet curtain.

'Boss, there's loads of beds in here.'

'What?'

I gaze in. There are. A mass of deep red velvet-cushioned beds, a large sea, a continuous pleasure palace.

'No fucking way! This is a fucking whorehouse! A whorehouse in the middle of this place. In the middle of a battle, in the middle of a Taliban stronghold! I thought these fellas are meant to be strict Muslims.' I can barely comprehend our discovery.

'Dirty bastards. No wonder there were so many kids around.'

The terp interjects: 'You know, boss, when a Taliban fighter dies in action, his wife is very poor afterwards. Often his friends support her only if she sleeps with them, if she becomes a prostitute.'

Madness.

9 Platoon are in other compounds close to us, and they have made a discovery too. Kilos and kilos of brown sludge stocked in rusting 200-litre drums, distilling equipment, sacks of opium, chemicals, lumps of heroin. A heroin production plant. Millions of pounds' worth of drugs. *Who are we fighting here? Muslim fundamentalists? Or drug lords?*

Maybe that's why they're fighting so hard.

They blow it up. The cloud of brown dissipates slowly in the air, drifting as it shades out the sun over our compound.

Over the track, Tony's ANA trade RPGs with the Taliban like for like, standing up and loosing them off in their general direction, the Afghan way of war.

We are glad for their noise.

The OC radios me. I can hear the contacts reverberating in his mouth mike.

'Hades Four One, this is Two Zero Alpha . . .' crackcrackcrack . . . 'We need to get ammo and water in and we need to get the body out. I need you to secure an HLS. It'll have to be up

near you guys; we won't get a heli in anywhere near us. Recce it
and let me know where.'

'Roger. Most of the approaches here are covered by that sharp-
shooter; we'll do our best.'

H has the perimeter, so I close Matt in and tell him the plan.

'We'll try and work our way up and round the back. You know
the space we need, so you let me know if we can get it in . . .'

'Yeah, boss, we'll need about half a football field.'

We move off, hugging the walls, towards the orange-grey
mountains looming over us. The shale starts to rise in little cliffs
as the track peters out. We move on but suddenly those red-
tipped streaks crack around us, dancing, zigzagging, fizzing in the
sand like atoms bouncing off each other.

Matt jogs back to me, sweating, his face puce and dirty.

'Boss, I can't get through there, they've got it covered.'

He's right. We can't. I look around. Back down the track, 9
Platoon are in contact. H's section are getting shot at whenever
they put a head over the wall. And this sharpshooter with the red
bullets has covered the only way I thought we could get through.
We are stuck.

'Hades Four One. Heli inbound in figures ten.'

I look up. *It's too risky.* To our right, a small, steep precipice
rises sharply above us. On it is perched the walls of another mud
compound. Higher than us, it is obviously covered by the sharp-
shooter. Decision time.

'Right, Matt, the chopper's inbound in ten. We can't go down
the 611 'cause 9 Platoon are being hit. We can't go over H's wall
'cause they are being hit. We know we can't go that way. The
only way—' I point to the cliff face '—is up there.'

We both know it is a big request. It is not an order. It is something more profound. We both know what the consequences may
be. There is a pause.

Matt looks at me. I stare back. There is a deep, unspoken understanding.

Now I am the bailiff, come to collect. Cashing in my chips. All those arguments, all those jokes, all the respect, everything boils down to this. Trust. Brotherhood. Love.

He looks up at the cliff.

'Yeah . . . no worries, boss.' He looks back at me and then he turns to his men.

'One Section, saddle up, we're going up there.'

He points and they stare.

'We've got to secure this HLS, get that body back, get the heli in or we'll run out of ammo and water. All the other ways are covered and this one will be too. Heli is inbound. Clarkey, you're first. Full belt and don't stop, not even if one of us goes down. Keep going. Then me, then Bardsley, then Cardwell, then Smith. Dev and the boss'll follow on. Get ready.'

They line up, laden with kit and ammunition, ready to sprint up the slippery scree slope. I can only watch events unfold from the safety below.

'Go, Clarkey!'

He runs.

'Follow me!' Matt goes.

Clarkey tears up the slope. He is halfway up, then bullets start to kick around him. Matt is moving straight into them. Straight through. They are committed.

Bullets kick all over in an intensity I have never seen. Smashing into the wall behind them, the ground in front of them, millimetres over their heads. They duck and flinch and keep running. Clarkey gets around the corner. Matt gets around. Bardsley gets around. But Cardwell is struggling, twenty extra kilos of electronic equipment pulling his long legs back. In slow motion I watch a dust cloud appear an inch from his nose, at his heel, as his knee punches high, under his rifle. Everywhere. *He can't get through this.*

He does.

Smith and Dev are readying themselves. I grab Smith's shoulder.

'STOP! STOP! IT'S SUICIDE! STOP!'

They agree.

The firing stops as suddenly as it started.

I am stunned. It is the bravest thing I have ever seen.

'Matt, you guys OK?'

'Yeah, boss, all OK . . .' he says, laughing nervously. '. . . That was close . . .'

'Too close . . . The rest aren't gonna make it up to you; it's suicidal. You'll have to crack on with what you have.'

'Roger, boss, will do.'

'Hades Four Two Alpha, this is Four One . . . They got through . . . four of them. I can't get anyone else over that cliff.'

'Roger. Well done. That'll have to do.'

Four men secured the bullet-raked HLS. Ideally, you need a platoon.

The downdraught of the Chinook flings pebbles and dust in our faces, its underbelly swinging towards us as it pitches tightly in a turn, a hollow magnet for all the Taliban bullets in this valley. I can hear the cracks get fainter as the Chinook slams the air over-head and the engines drown out all noise.

At the HLS the chopper touches down in a square of walls only fifty feet wide, its rotors slicing the air just over their tops. Matt's men and a Para colour sergeant, who has just torn up the 611 with the dead body, work furiously to unload ammo and massive sacks full of water, and then load the body. In the roar, bullets continue to silently hit the dirt, the ramp, and ping into the Chinook.

It takes off quickly, banking hard, away over the mountains. The cracks grow louder until a crescendo of gunfire is crashing against it. They get away.

The heat rises but the battle subsides. Matt's men come back panting, pink and drenched in sweat with warm bottles of water for us. We guzzle them and fill our Camelbaks as we sit in the harem. The bullets and RPGs have stopped screaming over our heads. All is quiet. In a darkened corner of our velvet-ordained whorehouse, Joe Bog, a huge, quiet Fijian, is squatting on a cushion, slowly tilting backwards and forwards, gently humming. On his head is a bandanna, tied tight. He rhythmically twirls a green velvet flag, keeping the swarms of flies away. *Apocalypse Here.*

Both sides are resupplying, recharging. More fighters are coming to take us on.

Nine hours.

It kicks off again. The same pattern, though we are safe now. The Paras pound the same compounds. Another strafe blasts chunks out of something. Another artillery salvo destroys the same compound. It doesn't seem to be stopping. But finally, as the intense heat fades and the sun dips behind the mountains behind us and everything turns beautiful and orange-pink, the battle ebbs to a sporadic burst and then nothing.

Have they melted away?

We rest as the OC and CO plan our next step, not fancying the alternative plan of a long march into the desert. After thirteen hours of getting shot at, we are exhausted, dizzy from dehydration, drained.

Mac, Dev and myself make our way down the now quiet, safe, dusty track towards the 611. Locals appear and we train our red dots on them, shouting, 'Wadrezha!' Jumpy, scared of suicide bombers, we point them back into their houses. Forget hearts and minds. I want to survive today. We make it to the 611, where a small stall has opened selling orange sodas to the bedraggled and sweating Paras. Dev buys some for the platoon as we walk cautiously along the shale sand of the 611 towards the OC. He is sitting in the shade of an unopened stall. I sit beside him.

Soon, two more antennaed, sweating desert figures arrive. I recognize the Para Platoon commanders. Nick has lost a stone and Murray displays a large droop moustache. Last time I saw them we were in an Afghan culture lesson in Salisbury, being taught by a beautiful, bright female corporal. Now she is dead, blown up days ago, and we are fighting hard.

'Everyone OK?'

'Tickety-boo, sir.'

Murray and Nick send a wink and grin my way. The OC speaks assuredly.

'Good stuff so far, lads. Well done . . . We're gonna try and break out of here under the cover of darkness, out towards the mountains behind us, then back to our insertion HLS in the desert. Paddy and Murray; your guys lead the way . . . have the quad up with you. Then the ANA, then Nick; you watch our backs. I'll be in the middle with the CO's group. Move out 22:00. Any questions?'

We stroll back to the harem and, relieved that we won't be tabbing for miles, I brief the platoon. Darkness falls, another blue-black cloak over the mountains and Green Zone, another million twinkles shining through the holes. Some sleep. I can't.

We move out, creeping out of our door, down the track, along the 611, past black silhouettes of Paras lining either side. We turn back up the slope towards the ink peaks of the mountains, past uninhabited, ruined compounds, blue walls, dark alleyways. Our goggles flicker green and anthropoid-like, white glowing circles of light omitting from the eyes of those we pass. We trudge up the shale face, climbing, clawing forward, higher, until the blackness of the Green Zone pans out below us. The only noise now is the quad bike gunning itself up the scree and then sliding forlornly back down. Our hearts pound. We are exposed.

I raise the OC. 'The quad can't make it up the slope. It's a no-go.'

'Roger. Wait out.'

Below in the ruins, the CO and OC consider our predicament. A crackle.

'Hades Four One, change of plan. Close back down to my location. We'll extract up the 611. It's the only way we can get the quad out. Ranger and 7 Platoons lead the way. Keep it fast and quiet.'

We all thought it.

You are kidding me? Back the way we came? This is too risky. They're still out there. We'll get ambushed from the Green Zone.

We traipse back down to the 611, legs aching, heads spinning. Our platoon lines stretch a hundred metres, spaced out and alert. We move off: 7 Platoon, C Company, 2 Para on one side of the track, 7 Platoon, Ranger Company, 1 Royal Irish on the other. If we are hit now, in this close terrain, we'll be wiped out. Nervously, we all scan the blackness, tensing at each bark, each rustle of leaves, everything. *This* . . . I search for the word as I scan . . . *is audacious.* We are doing exactly what we shouldn't be, retracing our steps, yet doing exactly that might fool those wraiths out there, somewhere. Fingers hover over safety catches.

We get through and turn off the 611 into the light blues of the desert. Murray is leading the way. I am hallucinating, strange black shapes morphing in front of me as my mind wanders from tiredness, dehydration.

The pace is relentless. We need to get those behind us off the 611 fast, away from danger.

A call comes over the radio from Nick at the back. 'This is

Hades Two Three. We're all clear of the 611, all clear of 611.'

I can hear the relief in the OC's reply.

We march on, into a sandscape bowl with towering black peaks. I can see Smith and Cardwell struggling ahead. I shuffle up to them.

'What's wrong?'

'Boss, I'm seeing stars and I'm about to shit myself,' Smith says desperately.

'Me too, boss. I need to stop.'

Feck. Not in front of the Paras.

But I know these men are exhausted. I radio the OC.

'Sir, we need to stop. I've got guys who are going to go down up here.'

'Roger. OK, halt there. Maintain security.'

We collapse in a bundle in the sand. I feel ashamed to have called a stop. But soon there are hushed groans, whimpers, all around us. Soldiers, both us and the Paras, crawl off to black clumps of bushes to disgorge watery diarrhoea. Others vomit over themselves uncontrollably. Soon medics are busy dispensing saline solution and Dioralyte to the stricken soldiers, whose bodies, now we are out of danger, succumb to heat exhaustion and dehydration.

We sit and recover for half an hour. Then we move off to the HLS.

As we wait in the blueness for the Chinooks to arrive, men sleep, utterly shattered, but I don't feel safe yet. I watch the CO stand aloft and speak into a satphone.

'Roger . . . Roger . . . understood . . . Roger . . . I understand . . . Roger.'

He hands the satphone back and briefs the OC. C Company's FOB has been attacked, civilians have been accidentally killed and the ANA have mutinied. Not a good day.

The welcome sound of the Chinooks rolls around the hills,

stirring the men from their crouched slumbers. We're out first. A run to the black chopper, a crouch in the fuselage, the engines tear through the sky. We're away.

Please don't get shot down now.

Twenty-three hours after we last stood on the DC's wide helipad, we emerge from our parallel world as if by time machine, jogging wearily off the ramp into the blackness.

'Speedy, all in?'

'All in, boss.'

The men slowly line up facing the hesco walls.

'Listen in. Remember your drills. Unload.'

Scrape, chink, click, click.

The boss and the sergeant major are there to greet us, to welcome us back, but we are in shock, wide-eyed, silent, just like those Marines we'd seen after the Viking exploded.

No one says anything as we slump back to the DC. The boss and the sergeant major give out ice-cold Pepsis that restore morale like a warm hug. It is reassuring that they are here, that they care, that they want to understand.

I sit on a bench watching the men. They are too tired to joke. My mental slide show starts again, preoccupying my eyes in a blank stare. *Click*. Red streaks past my head. *Click*. Sergeant major lying in front of me. *Click*. The gunners looking at me. *Click*. Matt leading his men through the red hail of fire. *Click. Click. Click.*

The sergeant major spots me and walks over. He rests on my table. I gaze at nothing. He says nothing.

'I brought them all back, sergeant major.'

The words hang in the Sangin night.

'You did, sir. You did well. I thought we'd lost one when that casualty came in. I knew it was up where you were. I was worried the whole day, seriously worried. The boss and myself were glued to that radio net; sounded crazy.'

'It was, sergeant major . . . It was.'

Speedy and the boss join us, guzzling on cold Pepsis.

'You know something, boss? That was the heaviest fight I've ever seen . . . I can't believe we got through that . . .' The 2006 veteran's voice trails off.

'You did well, did very well. We're proud of you, and you should be proud of yourselves,' the boss says quietly.

And in a way we were. We had all been tested in battle. We had learned more about ourselves and each other in those intense hours than in all the time that had gone before. Most of us were proud of the way we had acted, relieved that we hadn't let anyone down, and honoured. Honoured that we had fought with the Paras, that we had held our own with them. Honoured and proud to have fought with each other, to have dug deep into ourselves for each other, to have endured for each other. That there was something greater than our own individual suffering. The warrior ethos. Those cold stakes of war were binding us tighter. We were becoming brothers.

I wish I could say we achieved something, but I don't know. We fought for thirteen hours. We killed many Taliban, or whatever they were. We destroyed millions of pounds' worth of heroin, or whatever it was. We proved that the culvert was crossable. We showed them we could strike when and where we chose. We won. Or did we? What was the legacy of this, apart from the experiences etched on to the consciousness of those who fought there and the terminal experiences of those who died? It had to be for something, surely? Some greater good. Maybe it was sweet revenge. Maybe we had been part of the biggest battle to date and that, in a Boy Scout pride kind of way, was cool. But the fact was the Taliban still held Sar Puzeh that night. We didn't.

And if we went back, there'd be the same fight again.

I wish I could say that as 7 Platoon, 2 Para and 7 Platoon, 1

Royal Irish marched side by side out of Sar Puzeh, each man glad they had experienced and survived a real battle, glad for the test that had proved most of them men, that that was it. Our war was over. We had done what we came to do.

But war is not like that. It is violent. And it is constant.

Six days later I'm sitting on a bomb.

HAZARAGON

Ooh a storm is threatening
My very life today . . .

'Gimme Shelter'
Rolling Stones

Thirty hours later we are back out, exhausted beyond all com-
prehension. As we sit by the hesco, waiting for the ANA to
decide whether they are going to launch their convoy or not,
we slowly roast inside our kit. The heat is incredible, the hottest
day yet, and we know the hot days like a baker knows his oven.
The doc's thermometer reads fifty-three Celsius. *Fifty-three
Celsius. They can't send us out in this.* But they do. They have no
choice.

I am seeing stars before I exit the gate. We only have to make
it the 600 metres to the bazaar, to the shade, but I am slurring my
words after 100, the red-orange glow in my head expanding,
consuming me. Our water packs are as hot as tea. *If we get hit now
we're dead; we wouldn't last five minutes in contact.* Anger burns inside
me for risking our lives like this.

In twenty minutes we make it to a half-built concrete mall and collapse in the shade. Commanders are vomiting everywhere, soldiers the same, red-faced, dizzy, weak. I have lost sixty per cent of the platoon in twenty minutes. Dev runs across the road to a stall and thrusts dollars into a child's hand, scooping a frozen crate of orange pop into his arm and scurrying back to the vomit-covered mall floor. The icy cans lower our temperature and give us sugars as Caylie tends to the worst cases.

'Boss, these two need to be extracted.'

I send a request and soon a vehicle is sent to pick them up, risking the crew's life too in this IED-infested town.

We trudge back to camp, seething in anger, wilting under the sun. The doc checks everyone over. We intensely respect the doc, the only man out here who tries to save life rather than take it. The same doc who saved Paul's life in Musa Qaleh. There is some good expectation management. We are back out that night. We have to. Another convoy coming through. There are simply not enough of us to rest a platoon.

At Red Hotel a skeleton guard watches our surrounds as the rest of us collapse on the roof. We try to sleep, too tired to care any more. But we can't, the latent heat from the cement scorching legs, backs and hands through our uniforms.

Exasperated, desperate, painfully tired, we join the guard rotation on return to camp.

We leave at three in the morning and slip into the Green Zone unnoticed, winding our way along the shale banks of the Helmand in the deep black night. Our progress stalls and flows as metal detectors beep and flash, picking up possible IEDs that need to be investigated. We push on. In the half-light US Marines move to our left, through the fields and ditches, past the canal, into the target area; a supposedly Taliban village called Hazaragon. Word comes that the Marines are in position, an outer cordon ready to protect us as we slip through. As dawn arrives, we wait for our watches to hit H Hour. They do.

7 Platoon stagger to their feet and charge forward, slowly building momentum. We cross open mud fields at the sprint, ladders clanging off knee pads, weapons jingling, feet crunching. Unopposed. We reach the compounds and spread out, through the alleyways, into the orchards, over the streams, past the mosque, past the NGO's handpump well. *Near the mosque with the well there is a brown gate; this is our target compound.* So intel has informed me.

In the darkness I find the gate. We fan out, ready to defend ourselves and wait for other troops and the NDS, the Afghani CIA, to arrive to show us exactly what they want searched. They stroll into our cordon. It emerges they have less of a clue than us about the compound and they were providing the intel on this operation. *If they don't know, how the hell are we meant to?* Hearts sink.

We spend the next eight hours searching compounds and finding nothing but one of our spent illumination shells and some documents. The Taliban spend the eight hours watching our forces and preparing their ambush.

The boss tells us to collapse task, and we leave first, exhausted again from the heat and lack of sleep. We move up through the edge of the Green Zone, through the green cornfields that are starting to sprout quickly upward towards the ever-present sun, along the same ditches with the same trees and past the same compounds as the same people watch us with the same stares.

Radio: 'Boss, see over there on the right, 200 metres. They're dicking us, something is gonna happen . . . I don't like this.'

'Yeah . . . Roger that, Ronnie . . . If anything does, make it to that bank to your left. We'll move in bounds . . . Fellas, keep your eyes peeled. I think this is gonna kick off.'

We dip out of the exposed field into the more protected shale bank, still cautious but now relieved. The dickers have gone.

Back on the cordon the boss and the FSG are resting in the shade of a treeline as the Marines begin to move off. The boss sees a worker sprint from a field to a compound.

He knows what's coming.

'STAND TO! STAND TO! MAN THE GUNS!'

Soldiers struggle to their feet and scramble on to the jeeps to man their machine guns.

RPGs scream through the small gap between the vehicles and explode over the Helmand behind them. Bullets ting-tang off the jeeps, somehow missing their occupants, and rivet into the ditch, where the Marines are scrambling for cover. The gunners swing their fifty-cals and Jimpys in the direction of the firers. The Marines unleash with everything they've got. A huge blast of violence surges towards the ambushers, smashing compound walls and flinging one fighter back down an alleyway in pieces. A Marine is firing his mortar in frenzied, rapid succession, desperate to get rid of his heavy bombs.

We hear a wave crash behind us and then another, huge swell build to a towering blasting crescendo and roll back.

The mortars land.

I turn to Naf, looking back in their direction. 'Jesus, I hope that's outgoing.'

It is. And soon it is over. No casualties.

'Those dickers just made sure we were too far away to get involved and then they hit the cordon.'

'Damn right, Naf.'

We are starting to feel like a blindfolded heavyweight boxer fighting against an agile bantamweight who keeps landing blows.

They don't need us down there with them. We're glad. As we turn for base we're glad of another thing.

That we weren't anywhere near it.

We are changing. The draw, dream, gleam of combat is losing its allure.

We move out in the afternoon heat, out of the back gate and over the shale and stones of the Helmand's bank, feet already soaked in its refreshingly cool tributaries. In the deep green cornfields locals in brown and grey cloths stack the dried poppy stalks, firewood for winter, or watch us as they lean against a spade. Dirty barefoot kids with blue and red eyeliner run back and forth, giggling, screaming, pointing. We move on, cautiously, as an informer has told us a sixteen-year-old and a fourteen-year-old are planting IEDs here. The metal detectors sweep the ground, beep-beeping, while those holding them make life-or-death decisions: either to halt the patrol in this searing heat and investigate or to leave it, reasoning it's just a piece of old metal in the earth, so common in this war zone.

We follow the same muddy ditches, the same green treelines that hundreds of patrols have followed before. There is only so much land to walk on, only so many routes to take, that we struggle to avoid setting patterns. Patterns equal IEDs. Our only option is to walk right through the farmers' fields, avoiding the ditches that give us cover from small-arms ambushes.

It also annoys the farmers.

'What's he saying?'

'He says why do you walk across his crops, boss.'

'Tell him we walk across his crops because the Taliban put IEDs in the ditches. Tell him if he tells us where the IEDs are we won't have to walk across his fields, we'll go round.'

'He says he doesn't know where the IEDs are.'

'I bet he doesn't.'

Ake is out in front, zigzagging his line of men from field to treeline to ditch to field. The wind is cool when it blows, revealing in unison the pale green underside of the trees' leaves, like nature's own revolving billboard. I watch Ake's progress, squint out across the fields and in my head pick ground to fight from. We move for a thick treeline that will give us good cover.

As we approach, the last man, Bish, a Para sniper, notices a white plastic bag tied to a tree billowing in the wind. Ake is practically on top of it. We stop, pull back. Check around it for wires, antennas, ground sign. Nothing. Bardsley goes forward with the metal detector. There is a reading but it is weak. Whatever is buried is either small or deep. Too deep for an IED. We go firm along the treeline and investigate further, carefully searching the undergrowth by hand as a sniper watches out across the fields. Nothing. Bardsley lies down on his belly in the dirt, hands outstretched in front of him, and slowly, tentatively, scrapes away dirt with his bayonet. I wait beside him for ten minutes as he scratches the earth away. *It wouldn't be that deep . . .*

Six inches down. Nothing.

He looks at me. I'm still not sure.

'Check with the detector again.'

He sweeps over it.

Surprise. 'Boss, there's something there. It's six inches wide.'

I radio Ronnie, the search team commander, the expert.

'Boss, check and isolate again, check everything.'

We all sweep our surroundings, using boot, gloved hand and eyeball. Nothing.

We have been sitting for twenty minutes. The Taliban know where we are.

Bish decides to have a better look. He moves to the hole and starts digging deeper, hand outstretched, head as far away from the hole as possible, as his bayonet tears out small chunks of earth. Nine inches. A foot.

Something.

Something hard. Something hard and wrapped in blue plastic.

We pull back immediately, unsure but not taking any risks. Not for the first time, Gunny Chavez and his US EOD team are called for. Meanwhile, Bish and Mowgs bolt after a suspicious child and catch him. He tells us eight Taliban are planting IEDs, that there are two suicide bombers further south. The EOD arrive minutes later with their Humvees and laid-back attitude. I meet them.

'How y'guys doin'?'

'Good. You?'

'Good. So whattcha got here?'

'Not sure. We saw a plastic bag on a tree. Got a reading and isolated . . . twice. Found nothing. Dug down a foot and found something wrapped in blue plastic. It's metallic . . . We've got the cordon, here's the grid reference, no civvies about . . .'

'Roger that. How's about we go and take a look at this thing then . . .? Ramirez, get me my box.'

And that is it. In goes Gunny.

We wait, crouching in a dried stream bed, watching the fields and reporting suspicious movement around us. And all movement around you is suspicious when you have a bomb in your midst.

'FIRE IN THE HOLE!'

'GET DOW . . .' BOOOOOOM.

A haze of dust drifts across the fields. The ops room crackles in my ear, berating me for not warning them of the explosion. I didn't know either.

'HEY! WHAT'S GOING ON OVER THERE?'

Across the field a Marine cups his hand to his mouth.

'CONTROLLED CLEARANCE EXPLOSION. IED CON-FIRMED. GUNNY'S GONNA BLOW IT. STANDBY FOR MAIN DETONATION . . . AND GET INTO PROPER COVER . . .'

These guys weren't like the British EOD. They didn't mess around.

We wait again. I watch the Marines lay explosives and scuttle away.

'GET DOWN!'

A huge boom rolls over us, shaking the ground and sending large, heavy clumps of soil spiralling down on us sixty metres away. When the cloud of dust dissipates, I stroll over to Gunny, who's slowly chomping on chewing tobacco, looking uninterested.

'You guys were really lucky, man.' His fist holds aloft a web of wires. 'Hundred-and-fifty-five-millimetre shell, battery pack, radio device, command wire and antenna.'

'But we checked twice . . . Where?'

'Command wire buried a foot in the ground, ran to the tree with the bag on it. Battery pack and remote device buried at the trunk, under some grass, antenna ran up the tree like a mast to catch the signal from the firer. They're trying to get round your electronic equipment. It would've blown you guys to pieces.'

'So it was radio-controlled *and* command wire?'

'That's what I said.'

Gunny didn't suffer fools.

I thank him and, turning white with shock, walk back to the platoon. There was no way we could tell. No chance. I was sitting on it for half an hour, the rest of Ake's men nearby.

The hundred-and-fifty-five-millimetre shell is lethal out to forty metres. It would have been carnage.

We turn for camp. I am shocked by how close to death we were again. Sobered and scared. *I thought it couldn't get any closer than Sar Puzeh. Now this.*

When I return to camp, my face is a green-tinged white. I am quiet and stare blankly as another slide show preoccupies me. The sergeant major grins.

'You alroigh', sir?'

'No . . . That was too close. We were sitting on that bomb for fucking half an hour.'

I walk off.

Maybe our patrol skills had saved us, frightened off the firer. Maybe our equipment had saved us. Maybe the firer wasn't even there. Who knows? What if Bish hadn't seen the bag? What if it had blown up Bardsley? *What if . . .?*

Chance.

GREEN 12

If I don't get some shelter,
Yeah, I'm gonna fade away . . .

'Gimme Shelter'
Rolling Stones

We are sitting on the wooden benches in the white kitchen tent when an eruption of noise tells us the other platoon have been ambushed.

'Where are they?' I say, sliding my body armour over my head as it claws at my ears.

'South of the bridge at Green 12. Get ready,' Paul replies.

We are slicker now. Within minutes, everyone reports to our accommodation. We have Caylie. We have our artillery observer. We have our terp. I brief the commanders, they brief their sections and we are loaded and out of the gate in ten minutes. Experienced.

The contact still rages as we move down the sandy canal path. We cautiously sweep our way south, soberly eyeing the holes dug into the path, ready for IEDs. It is eerie voluntarily moving towards violence, danger, when you are not involved in it. *What's happening down there? Where are they?*

The contact dies down and then peters out, to my relief.

We reach them soon after. A matted bunch of soaked uniforms, hyper-alert eyes, adrenalin.

'7 Platoon coming in!'

I wait for it to echo down the line, then move to the platoon sergeant, who grins wildly.

'What's going on?'

'Good to see you, boss. We were just crossing that field back there and they opened up on us. Eight firing points, they got behind us, had us surrounded for a bit. Couldn't call in the 105s, too many civvies about, so we had to fix bayonets and charge them . . . Think we got six of the bastards, though. That'll teach them . . . The fuckers had locked the civvies into their compounds and fired from them.' He smiles and shakes his sweaty head.

This is the platoon I have concerns with, but they definitely have their strengths too.

'Sounds tight. Where do you want us?'

'We're hooped and running out of battery power . . . our sniper shot an RPG firer just down there. Can you exploit it for us?'

'No worries, will do. You guys OK?'

'Couple of heat casualties. Sergeant Major will be down to extract them.'

We move south and find the evidence. A primed RPG, a belt of brass bullets, casings and a bloody dishdash, the only proof that this ground has recently been contested, the only proof that those we fight are actually mortal.

The trophy comes back with us and is passed to the ANA.

SOUTHERN
TRAVEL AGENCY

Ooh, the flood is threatening
My very life today . . .

'Gimme Shelter'
Rolling Stones

A deep tiredness has set in to Ranger Company. Meanwhile, the violence is gushing over us like a storm tide, seeping everywhere, every alleyway, every village, every ditch. Changing us. It seems like everything we do is reactionary. We just respond. And always too late. We're not sleeping, it's too hot, and we're on patrol every day, trying to stem the flow. Legs continually ache, exhaustion clouds our thoughts, blurs our decision-making ability, crushes our morale. 7 Platoon have not had a day off in a month.

In this atmosphere of stress and exhaustion, men become fractious; frictions begin to flare. Platoons argue over when they take over guard, their best chance of sleep, and about whose turn it is to go on patrol, their best chance of death. The difference in approach between us and the other platoon widens to a deep chasm. We hear rumours of strained relations between commanders. At least our team is holding together. Faced with the poor chances of our own survival, with death permeating everything, with the cheapness of life and the Afghan disregard for it, our morality, our compassion, diminishes within us. We try to keep our empathy. Our humanity. But it is getting harder.

We patrol out to the edge of the bazaar, to an area we call Foxtrot. Foxtrot is a maze of brown mud stalls blasted to oblivion by our bombs and rockets. It is destroyed and deserted, a ghost town of warped metal shutters, collapsed roofs and a bombed-out clinic with the occasional junkie wallowing in a shady corner.

Golgotha.

'I hate this place, boss.' He pulls himself slowly to his feet now, the point where men have slowly swept forward another few yards with their detectors.

'I know what you mean, Naf. It's a shithole.'

'Y'know, boss, when we were first here in 2006 it wasn't like this, it was bustling, there was a Chinese restaurant just over there . . . People lived here.' He stresses the words with a smile to contradict the scene in front of us.

'What happened?'

'I don't know. We left after a few weeks, and when we came back the place was like this . . .' He trails off in thought, scanning around him.

Our search of Foxtrot reveals some mortar shells, a rocket, fuses. EOD collect them.

That night the platoon sits around the fire after our brief. A new photo of the bazaar has been released, showing it as a bustling, prosperous hub of activity. Alongside it is a photo taken in 2007, with fewer people but still busy. Alongside that is one from 2006; just a solitary soldier in a deserted, boarded-up bazaar. The caption reads 'Improving Sangin'. I tell the platoon about it.

Naf flashes his wide conspiratorial grin.

'But, boss, before we arrived in 2006 it was busier than any of this.'

The ANA and USMC follow up our search the next day, sealing the bazaar and sweeping through Foxtrot again. They find the .22 pistols used to assassinate the ANP, a pistol, two grenades, RPG rounds, ammunition and magazines.

In Sangin, this is success.

Meanwhile, the southern checkpoint is attacked. Dishdashed fighters break from the crowds and pull AK47s from under their robes, firing as they run forward. The ANP rattle rounds back at them as locals run for cover in the stalls, bullets bouncing every-where as the Afghans blat rounds at each other from the hip.

Like everything, it is over quickly. A dead Talib lies trickling his warm blood on to the 611. Another is dragged away scream-ing by his comrade, shot in the guts and dribbling blood down alleyways and tracks that the Marines quickly follow but find nothing. The shrapnel-peppered ANP come in for treatment; one lucky man with a bleeding scorch streak in his armpit where a bullet passed straight through.

A chopper takes some of 7 Platoon away on R and R and gives us new recruits. Speedy and I are worried. We are wary of the extra responsibility of looking out for soldiers straight out of training. The platoon is experienced now. We operate like a well-oiled engine, each cog crucial in keeping us running. These arrivals will be weak cogs. They'll fuck with the numbers. So we watch them, mentor them as best we can. Until they are up to our standard, have our experience, we can't guarantee their sur-vival. Even then we still can't.

They learn fast.

WISHTAN

Gimme, gimme shelter,
Or I'm gonna fade away . . .

'Gimme Shelter'
Rolling Stones

The storm rages.

The Marines cautiously patrol the maze of deserted alleys and walls of Wishtan, their night scopes scanning the blackness. But no one sees the hand over the wall. No one hears the grenade as it gently rolls in the sand. No one knows what is about to hit them.

A flash instantaneously lights the Marines. From down an alley a cloaked figure fires a long burst of 7.62 which jingles and clatters its way off the walls towards the wounded soldiers. An RPG impacts near them, covering them in dust. The uninjured fire back. It is over.

Six mangled Marines are extracted to the DC. Fibulas and tibias gleam white out of the bloody mess of twisted limbs, groaning voices, whitening faces. The doc does his best. Two lose legs.

It lasted twenty seconds.

GUMBATTY

War! Children! It's just a shot away,
It's just a shot away.

'Gimme Shelter'
Rolling Stones

And rages.

The other platoons are in two compounds in the Green Zone. Intel suggests the hamlet of Gumbatty is a Taliban resupply route.

It is.

The Taliban contest our excursion into their territory. They simultaneously attack a compound and a foot patrol. They get to within fifty metres. They are repelled.

Near FOB Gib, a blue on blue from an Apache's cannon wipes out a platoon command group and a section, devastating the C Company we fought with.

The OMLT find a radio-controlled IED in a compound. They detain two locals.

An ANA pickup hits an IED en route to Nabi. It explodes.

Small-arms fire erupts.

ARMAGH

No beast so fierce
but knows some touch of pity . . .
But I know none,
And therefore am no beast.

Richard III
William Shakespeare

And then stops.

Patrol Base (PB) Armagh is established, a large, defendable compound in the most affluent and beautiful part of Sangin. A shallow stream glistens as it runs beside the dirt track; overhead, glades of oaks scatter green shade and cause the sun to twinkle above us. Apple and pomegranate orchards, well-kept fields of vegetables and tomatoes are sectioned off by ancient mud walls. Huge cement compounds of pale pinks and blues and whites, some with their own mosques, interlock to form this hamlet of Gumbatty. This enemy nerve centre.

Armagh is well placed to intercept the Taliban, who are crossing the Helmand from the west and infiltrating into Sangin along the bridges, canal paths and tracks south of the DC. Intelligence, it seems, has got it right. As soon as the other platoons set up in

Armagh, Sangin goes eerily quiet. No attacks on the ANA. No ambushes on the Marines. No IEDs. Nothing. Only the rumours of war persist, like a steady stream springing from our new well of intelligence in the Green Zone.

Maybe . . . Maybe we've got it right . . .

For the ten days the other platoons man Armagh, 7 Platoon happily remain on guard and recharge. The hectic pace slackens, but the war does not.

An explosion drowns out the morning birdsong. A brown-grey mushroom cloud appears in the middle distance. We watch, mildly interested.

'Where d'you reckon that is?'

'Somewhere near PB Viking. No one out, is there?'

'No. We're just making sure . . . Hopefully, it's an own goal.'

'That'd be good . . .'

It is. A young man in his twenties has tried to lay an IED on the 611. It went off as he was doing so. His arms are sheared off, his face blown away to reveal a mat of bloody flesh, pebbles, white eyeballs with pupils gone, his scalp torn off. I watch as the mutilated body is dumped outside the ops room by the ANA, another body for the sergeant major to deal with.

And I was glad he was dead. It was funny. He had tried to blow us up, and the stupid fucker had blown himself up. That was gratifying, warming, pleasant. But later I see photos of his body and I feel sick. Somewhere within me, under the hardening crust, compassion still pervades my thoughts. *What about his mother, his family? What a waste of a life.*

My compassion lasts less than twenty-four hours. As we debate whether to return his body to a mosque before sundown, like the soft, moral, Geneva-bound men we are, the Taliban prepare to ambush us at the mosque. Luckily, we don't have the manpower.

The family can collect him later. Then we find out about the ambush. Rage.

Fuck them, the dirty despicable bastards. Is nothing sacred? Ambush your enemy as he returns your dead? Honour? You bastards. YOU FUCK-ING BASTARDS. I WILL KILL EVERY LAST ONE OF YOU.

Since Sar Puzeh I am struggling with this war. I am struggling with the random geometry of chance that permeates everything we do, that makes us second-guess everything. Struggling with accepting I am dead and the inevitable loss of compassion that goes with it. Struggling with our enemy. An enemy that says it is strictly Islamic yet runs harems and makes and takes drugs, an enemy that uses handicapped kids as mules for suicide bombs, that executes children for going to school. I start to hate them. Hate them for what they are doing to me. Hate them and their terrifying suicide bombs that separate us from the locals. Hate them for eroding me.

Do they hate us the same way?

Yes.

And I hate the locals for not standing up to them. For har-bouring them, sheltering them. For not returning our smiles. For not being human. For hating us. For watching us walk over IEDs.

Not all of them . . . Not all of them.

I sit in the halogen whiteness of the ops room with Cupples and a US Marine. We talk about 9/11, about the new GI bill, about MREs. About the war and our little part in it. Now the Marines are as resigned as us to their fate in this ruined place. But the two Americans have something I don't. A belief. A personal interest in the mission. They still have some conviction in the cause. Whatever I have is draining away, seeping, bleeding out of me into the gutter of corrupt child-abusing hopelessness I see every day.

After stag I return to the accommodation, where Squeak and McD are wearing pink fluffy turkeys emblazoned with WKD logos on their heads, giggling and jumping about. It's the twelfth of July and the 'I love Ulster' T-shirts appear out of nowhere.

'Here, boss, you can have one!' Squeak teases.

'Get lost.' I grin.

'Jaysus, round about now back home the party'd just be starting . . .'

'Bring on the Buckfast!' shouts Mac.

'Oh aye, and d'you know what? I'd still be pissed from last night . . .' says Davy.

'Dead on.' They laugh.

We sit outside the accommodation and talk about the Glorious Twelfth, a day alien to me yet one that raises the spirits of many of these boys, who are as proud of their heritage as I am of mine. We talk about sectarianism and the hardliners on both sides. 'I'd have nothing to do with those fellas, not me.' It can be a touchy subject, but Davy, I find, reflects the views of the platoon. They seem glad, proud even, of the Southerners in the platoon, of their 'rebel' boss and their fellow comrades as we sit and mock each other's colloquialisms. Even Naf and Ake join the celebrations, swirling a Northern Irish flag overhead while trying to sing 'The Sash' in broad Fijian accents.

I ask Speedy about his experiences of soldiering in Northern Ireland.

'Didn't really like it, boss, too close to the bone, y'know? . . . Once I was on patrol and some young fella shouted at me, "Fuck off home, you British bastard." So I turned to him and said, "I am home. I'm from Park Road . . ." That shut him up!'

Such character and cheerfulness are great remedies to the ills outside the wire. Ten minutes with these men restores my lagging faith in human nature.

It is an honour to serve with these men.

There are others it is not an honour to serve with. The chubby, useless uniforms that share our accommodation block and sometimes fly the flimsy, toy-plane excuse for a drone. While our bodies are white, whittled and spotted with rashes and nicks, theirs are bronzed and plump. While we patrol and fight almost every day, they sit in camp doing nothing. When we return, soaked, puce and tired, they are sunbathing. At night, as we try to sleep in our cots, they stay up watching Ross fucking Kemp documentaries of Afghanistan on their laptops, un-tired, keeping us awake with the gunfire and explosions that we seek to escape from in sleep. The differences between us are right in our faces. We are out fighting the war. And they are in watching it, a world removed from all the thoughts, feeling and stresses we endure. And they don't even know it most of the time. They don't want to. 'Fu-uck that,' they said. I hate them. Hate them for always being first in the queue for food, hate them for sitting around listening to music while my men guard them in sweaty sangars, hate them for everything they are and everything we're not. I hate them for their ignorance. Hate them because they will survive. When I see these men, I say it, think it, feel it, with deep venom. We all do. Rear. Echelon. Mother. Fuckers.

To calm my anger I have to remind myself I volunteered for the infantry for the very reasons they didn't.

Luckily, the sergeant major is looking out for us and has targeted the slackers. Amid the surge of reports of a Taliban attempt to overrun the base, another sangar is manned. Despite their pleas, he insists the rear troops man it. Soon they want to sleep too.

Meanwhile, Mac asks me about the patrols rotation, an unusual question from a Ranger.

I tell him, but I'm curious. 'Why's that, Mac?'

'Well, boss . . .' he says thoughtfully. 'The way I figure . . .

Each patrol day is a day you can die . . . So I've got nine days I can die before R 'n' R.'

The REMFs didn't have to deal with that.

Another night patrol of US Marines steps on an IED. Another alleyway of chaos. Another rush to extract him. Another bloody stretcher. Another radioed 9-Liner calling for a medevac chopper. Another fight to stabilize him. Another dust-off in the helipad. Another leg lost. Another life changed.

Sangin barely stirred. Everyone slept. The ops room whirred. I didn't even bother waking Paul; he was exhausted, and what could he do? A note was made in the logbook. A report went to headquarters. The war went on.

Tomorrow we are down to Armagh.

I have an ominous feeling. So does the platoon.

Something is going to happen.

We reach Armagh, having lost a new recruit to heat exhaustion on the way. Hands are shaken, smiles exchanged, briefs given. The area, it appears, is riddled with Taliban.

We patrol the immediate vicinity with our sections led by H, Ronnie or Matt. I accompany them purely to lend support, to set the example. I feel it's important to share risk with those I lead. We quietly stalk through the green twinkle of the orchards, sharp branches seeking our eyes, flecks of light on the ground, brilliant sun above us. *Our secret garden.* Visibility in this green undergrowth is fifteen feet. Our best weapon is our ears. There is a thrill to this, an excitement. This is real infanteering. What we joined for. Creeping about in the jungle. Us against them. Fingers on safety catches, eyes on stalks, controlled breathing, hand signals. *Vietnam.*

Today a farmer has diverted an irrigation ditch to flood and feed his orchard. We slosh and slide through it, wet yet thankful for the cold water in our boots. I slip into a ditch, stumble and fall backwards with a small splash, emerging a second later soaked from helmet to boot. Skills offers a leather-gloved hand and a smile as he silently pulls me up. We are enjoying it. Twenty feet from the walls of Armagh and a different universe. *Space is subjective.*

We pass a wall on which kids have painted black drawings in charcoal. Jeeps, Chinooks, jets, guns and explosions jump out from the dried mud, prehistoric murals of our contemporary conflict. The childish wonderment and excitement in the sketches of military hardware remind me of the herds of bison and elephants that jump from Neolithic caves. Brilliant, timeless, sad.

The locals are glad we're here and come to let us know. But in each shura where we listen to their problems there are prying Taliban eyes.

Sometimes we startle an old farmer sleeping in the shade of his orchard in the afternoon heat. Sometimes a kid turns a dusty corner in a tight alleyway and looks at us in wide-eyed disbelief as the point man puts a finger to his mouth, whispers 'Ssssssh' and smiles. Sometimes we talk to locals to tap a new vein of intelligence, their eyes darting nervously across the small green rows of vegetables. Once, when I am up front, we silently bump into a fat, black-bearded, evil-looking man in a brown dishdash. He is surprised but cool. I am surprised but cool. He looks at me, his brown eyes deep with a hatred that asks, 'What are you going to do now, infidel?' 'I'll blow you away . . .' my eyes reply. '. . . We both know you are Taliban.' 'And we both know I have no weapon,' his glare retorts. He breaks my stare and strolls away, leaving me, my stare and my regret in the orchard.

We are in Armagh a day before we understand the quiet: the eye of the storm.

A resupply of rations and radio batteries is needed. We move out to clear the track of IEDs. Hyper-alert, we leave and emerge into another dusty alleyway, another line of dusty walls. Progress is painful in the heat. The point men sweep overlapping arcs in front of them on the track, in the gutters, up the walls. We try to read the secret language etched on the landscape, warning locals of the lurking lethal traps; notches carved into walls, discarded petrol cans, twigs arranged like arrows, piles of pebbles. Ever cautious, beeps halt us as the point men lie down and dig with their bare hands while we kneel and watch.

Eyes scan the track. Every stone. Every dip. Every shade of dirt. What's that? And that? Is it natural? Is that a wire? Don't walk there. Step there, there and there. We've stopped. What's that? Don't kneel there, kneel here. Careful, careful. Patience. Patience. Christ it's hot. Patience. Watch. Watch. Is that a dicker? That kid? They are just walking by. Maybe there are no IEDs. Maybe it's safe. Maybe we're paranoid. Maybe they know where the IEDs are. Bastards. Smile. Hearts and minds. We're moving. Up. That's it. Step there, there. Did they sweep that? Careful. Watch.

In these alleyways full of detritus we average a hundred metres an hour. Five feet a minute. And still we miss it.

We turn a corner. The shallow stream runs beside us in the glade, pebbles glistening in the sun and rolling slowly downstream. Another place to hide IEDs. Dev is annoyed. Our progress is too slow. He closes behind the point men with the detectors and draws his bayonet to help them investigate the dozens of readings they're getting. They sweep up to a small bridge that could easily hide a bomb underneath. They pass an electrical box on a telegraph pole. Dev carefully pokes it open with his bayonet, showing his experience, as the point men have missed it.

'Boss, there's something here.'

'OK. Drop equipment and come back.'

They do.

'Right. Let's isolate. Get into the compounds, check all the walls. Get on the roofs. Everything.'

I move forward with Dev. Fifteen feet. Ten feet. Five feet. There.

We creak open the rusty box. A blue plastic bag with taped-up things inside. Wires everywhere.

'It's probably RC [radio controlled],' says Dev.

He moves on to a roof. Behind the glade someone on an opposite roof bolts off.

The firer.

I take a picture for EOD and call it in. We cordon it off.

Gunny arrives, all shades, moustache and intensity. I show him the picture, give him the info. He moves off. No suit. Just him and the bomb.

All goes quiet. Just the tinkle of the stream. Beautiful. We wait. I get impatient.

'What's happening?'

'I don't know. Gunny doesn't like to be disturbed when he's working,' the Marine replies as he leans against another pole.

'Can you find out?'

He looks at me slowly and reluctantly moves his mouth to his radio.

'Hey, Gunny. What's going on down there?'

Anger. Stress. 'I told you guys not to fuckin' annoy me when I'm working. Jesus Christ Sponanza.'

'He don't like it when we ask him.'

'I gather. Sorry, didn't mean to get you in the doghouse.'

Later, Gunny returns trailing wires and holding the plastic bag.

'Don't annoy me when I'm working.' He glares at us.

'My fault.'

He chews his wad. Calm. 'RC device. Soviet anti-section mine, designed to pop into the air and take off your heads. Pretty lethal.'

He's already walking away. 'Jesus . . . Thanks, Gunny.'

'Yeah . . . y'all look after yourselves down here, y'hear?'

And he's gone.

Back in Armagh the platoon is happy, despite the close call. Chance. Maybe that was what we had the bad feeling about. Maybe not.

The next day another platoon finds something at the back gate. Gunny arrives. We show him a picture. He goes to it. Hundred-and-five-millimetre shell RC device, well hidden and dug in. We have been lucky again.

Morale slumps. It is plain for all to see that we are 'fixed', that military term for 'stuck'. The Rangers ask difficult questions: 'Boss, what are we achieving here?'

'What is the boss at, risking our lives down here?' 'Does he actually care about us? We could lose four blokes down here in an instant; it's too dodgy . . .'

I tell them why we are down here, that we've really made a difference to the locals, that we've opened a new intelligence source, that the attacks have stopped. But they are unconvinced. So am I. I have a bad feeling that only those on the ground can have. Superstition.

That night, a resupply turns to disaster. Tired and walking a vehicle along the track in the blackness, Naf misses a turn. The armoured Vector continues on a rapidly thinning track. It gives way and the Vector slides into the stream, stuck. It's not getting out. Paul comes out to survey the scene and agrees. We'll have to deny it. We set up a cordon in the alleyways around it.

Our vehicle mechanic (VM) arrives with extraction equipment.

He agrees with Paul. We tip the hearse into the stream and start ripping the equipment out of it.

Not good, but it's only a vehicle, and a useless one at that. This happens in war, this is friction.

But it will not be denied. The word is someone in HQ thinks that it would look bad. We must get it out. We must man the cordon through the night and dig it out. In the middle of a war zone. Madness.

A Vector costs four hundred and fifty thousand new. What does a dead soldier cost? Sixty thousand tops. We'll pay for this with our lives. Seven lives and thirty grand left over.

The other platoon arrives, as exhausted as us, and takes over the cordon. With the mechanic we begin our work, chainsawing trees, pickaxing the track, knocking down walls, shovelling dirt. It is exhausting, brutal hard labour, yet the men work hard. The VM and his team work heroically, as do Naf's section, and it's inspiring to see them rally around their commander as their limbs and eyes ache with tiredness. Nearby in the darkness the Taliban chill us all as they signal each other with hyena catcalls.

Dawn breaks and we still work, snatching sleep in twenty-minute rotations. The heat rises and we remove our helmets and body armour to work. Inch by inch we get closer. There is a contact on the cordon as a lone gunman sprays bullets into the orchard, sending us unprotected workers scurrying for cover. The Taliban use the chaos to arm their IED. After sixteen hours of graft by all of us, VM, engineers, rear troops, everyone, the Vector is freed. It's obvious to us that all rear troops aren't like those we live beside. Tired and silent, we move back to Armagh, angry and hallucinating, but proud of our effort.

We collapse into sleep and later make one of those decisions that have repercussions for many people: the other platoon will sweep the track to allow the vehicles to return to camp. Our luck, no, our numbers, are about to run out.

A Land Rover's rear tyre rolls over the earth, pushing down on a wooden bar buried four feet under ground, towards twenty kilos of packed home-made explosives. The metal on the under-side of the bar touches the metal of the battery charge. A spark completes the circuit.

Flashsilhouettes.

Noise.

The three-tonne vehicle, bristling with weapons and crew, is hurled by an invisible wave, up, into and through a three-foot-thick wall, rolling and spinning as it goes. Its occupants are blown ten feet clear of the vehicle and are strewn in the orchard.

Inside Armagh, I run to the radio. I know what that was.

Ears ring. Silence. Then there's shouting: 'Contact! IED. Casualties. Wait out!'

In the shattered night there is chaos. Rangers are regaining consciousness, coming round under trees, slowly realizing what's happened to them, timidly checking their legs. They're still there.

Others can't feel anything.

The stream of information starts to flow amid the shouting and bedlam outside. Speedy jumps on to the quad and tears out of the gate without a metal detector to collect the casualties.

'Hades Four Zero! Hades Four Zero! . . . Contact! IED! Get that tourniquet. Four casualties. Where is h . . . four casualties! We need immediate medevac . . . Where? Where? We need immediate medevac with neck stretcher, one of them is para-lysed . . . Maintain security! Hades Four Zero, you there? Standby for Zap numbers and injury reports . . .'

Gunfire smashes the silence.

What are they firing at?

'We're clearing compounds red.'

Revenge. On empty compounds. I can understand their desire to hit back, but this seems unprofessional. But I am not the commander on the ground.

In the makeshift ops room I relay the information back to the DC where the Quick Reaction Force are mounting their vehicles and preparing to tear down the 611 to collect the casualties. There is no time to sweep it. They run the gauntlet. And get through.

Outside in the blackness, a Ranger has been bitten by a scorpion and is lapsing into nervous shock. In the confusion the quad tips Speedy into the stream, knocking him unconscious and nearly paralysing and drowning McD. The medics work furiously on seven casualties. Meanwhile, I send the increasingly bleak details back to the DC.

Disaster.

The casualties get evacuated, and we wait for the damage reports to trickle in from Bastion. Good news. Speedy and McD will be back to us. The other wounded are miraculously lightly injured. Even the paralysed driver may make a full recovery. But the Land Rover is an unrecognizable mangled mess. A million numbers, calculations, angles have computed to save their lives. Pure chance.

The other platoon is as enraged as us. We knew this was going to happen. We knew we'd lose people if we stayed down here. And we have.

The following day the boss comes down to speak to us. He has an open forum, explains why we're here, explains the progress we're making, the good we're doing. He raises morale. We man new sentry positions, which mean less sleep, and start cutting down trees so we can see out to the 611, to stop these wraiths planting IEDs on our track. Engineers arrive with explosives and chainsaws. We are staying.

That night the Taliban howl outside our walls again. H crashes out and fires two warning shots in the blackness. They stop. He returns. They start again.

I think about the other platoon's response to the IED. Aggressive, safe, yes. And if they thought there was a threat, allowed by our rules of engagement. But it worries us.

Two explosions rock Armagh's walls and for a second, as the silence recedes in the gunfire, we look at one another and wonder what is happening. Then I scramble to the radio to send another contact report. Up on the ramparts, RPGs are detonating below the sentry positions, bullets biting into sandbags as sentries take cover from the fusillade. Men don body armour and helmets and rush to the walls in shorts and flip-flops. Others rush to cover the gates, protecting against a possible suicide bomber ramming through in a Corolla.

A huge weight of fire erupts and peels across the carpet of green below. Soldiers are now ducking under the lip of the walls, reloading as another shoots, and then slickly taking their place as they drop to reload. *Just like in that FOB in wooded Norwich.* Our rate of fire is staggering but inaccurate. In the jungle below us we can't see our enemy, can't even see the distinctive wisps of smoke when he fires. So we fire where we think he is, grenade rounds popping and arching through the air playfully before exploding with a dull thud. On the compound floor, Brecon's beloved fifty-one-millimetre mortar barks into life, raining bomblets seconds later on to a treeline. Meanwhile, a mortar fire controller sends his message: 'Amber 22, Fire Mission. Over.'

'Amber 22, Fire Mission: Send, over.'

We know the OMLT are running to their mortar to lend us support. This is a team effort.

'Roger. Grid . . . Nine Four Three . . . Eight . . . One One.

Target: enemy in the Green Zone. One round, fire for effect. Read back, over . . .'

Two kilometres away, the barrel kicks in to the hard mud floor of Nabi. The mortar round sails silently up through the air, levels out, then plunges down to the Green Zone. CRUUMPH.

It feels good. We are powerful.

'Right, fifty. Three rounds' fire for effect.'

CRUUMPCRUMPCRUMPHHH.

He's calling them in fifty metres from our wall as we try to box the Taliban in, to stop them escaping. Jimpys rattle the undergrowth, rifle reports staccato under their bursts. Slowly, the noise dies down to an occasional shot.

Then it starts again. After all we've thrown at them, their courage is admirable.

More explosions, more RPGs, more bullets. We have the upper hand and are not scared. Safe behind the walls, it is enjoyable, exhilarating even, like an archer repelling a medieval siege from behind his battlements. It starts to quieten. Somebody in the other platoon blows a Claymore mine on the perimeter when it is obvious there is no need to.

Why did they do that?

I monitor the radio from the safety of a darkened room.

All goes quiet.

In another room is Mark, an eighteen-year-old Ranger who is sobbing uncontrollably. He is incoherent, inconsolable. Tears run down his cheeks, his eyes are stained red. Battle stress. I watch as Mac tenderly reassures him.

'I . . . I . . . I thought . . .' he sobs. '. . . I thought they were mortaring us . . . It just got to me . . . Remember . . . Remember Wombat Wood when they said they were going to mortar us and we were stuck in the open . . . I was so scared . . . I just froze . . . I'm sorry . . . I'm sorry . . . I don't wanna let the boys down . . . oh no . . .' He moans agonizingly. 'What'll the boys think of me . . . what'll they think?' He lets out a pained, guttural, animalistic groan, emanating from deep within him.

'Well,' says Mac, his arm around his shoulder in fatherly reassurance, 'they already think you're an eejit, so you've nothing to worry about there!' Mac grins and Mark struggles to turn his lips up to a faint smile.

Such tenderness in this hard place. A shout draws me away.

'Paddy, we're firing an LASM,' the other platoon commander yells down from the ramparts.

'OK . . . At what?'

'A dicker . . .' Screech, boom.

A Light Anti-Structure Munition is designed to blow apart small buildings. It is a new weapon. We have not fired it yet. Perhaps that's why they fired it at a man standing on the roof of a building 400 metres away.

I am starting to lose patience with elements of this platoon. Some of them moan and shy from fatigues. Some of them want to blast off every type of ammunition, every rocket, anything that bangs, just for bragging rights. For a few, this is a free-for-all, their own private playground where they can ride anything they want without the consequences. Because what rules exist out here? Only the easily malleable rules of war. Which our enemy, our invisible enemy, ignore. Nothing else.

Our rules of engagement? Of course. But they are open to interpretation and cannot cover all circumstances. The Geneva Convention? We hope so, but we wouldn't bet our lives on it, though sometimes we have to. For the first time in our lives the rules that govern us are enforced by us. And when we go out that gate, us only. Power. We can make up a story if we like. Who would know? The boss or the sergeant major stuck in the ops room dealing with a million and one issues? No chance. We could shoot whoever we want out here and say they were Taliban, say they were a threat to our lives. But we don't. Because we have professional pride and because we don't want to. We don't want to kill needlessly. Even sometimes when we want to, we don't. Because somewhere within us something tells us it's wrong.

My mind drifts back to those old Sandhurst lessons on morality, to the basics. *Don't lose your compassion, your humanity. Don't lose yourself. Don't allow the men to lose themselves.* Morality. And that is the only rule we have left. The one last sinew that binds us to your society.

But what if you did want to kill without reason? What if you didn't care? What if you didn't want to, but now you don't care because this place and all its random violence is terrifying you, threatening you, hardening you – what then?

I can't trust some of that platoon to make the right decisions. Some of them are fully aware that down here they are indeed deities of their own little universes. But we have to inhabit these worlds with them, and because we share the same uniform, they are creating our reality too. So we become wary of them and their destructive adventures.

Most of it is down to leadership. The platoon sergeant is on R and R, so a few core personalities, men I don't trust out of contact with the enemy, let alone in, have come to dominate the other men in their platoon. It feels like the platoon commander lost the respect of his platoon months ago. It was the little things that added up, the little things he didn't do. God knows, I felt that way sometimes. I was no great commander, but once you let those things slip, as a leader, you had no right to command. You had lost your moral authority. All you had was those pips on your shoulder, and if you had to resort to those you were definitely not leading. Let the small things go and soon you couldn't enforce the big things. It didn't really matter that he could command in a fire-fight. That was becoming the easy bit. It was black and white. Now the real decisions were murky, grey, and getting greyer. The real decisions were in the spaces in between the rules of engagement. It was the moral calls that mattered now. The moral decisions that the soldiers looked to us for. Shoot now? Or now? Kill then? Not then? Maybe he thought he was different. Special. But his men didn't. And neither did mine.

Attached personnel roll their eyes and dread going on patrol with an unpredictable platoon. We hear a man has been shot during a contact. It is unclear if he was Taliban or not. But rumours are whispered of others pleased with themselves for doing it. Heads are shaken. Curses uttered.

Later, I wonder about their attitude. They go in hard and aggressive, they protect themselves first. They take no nonsense and are first rate, hardened combat troops. Fixing bayonets and charging down an ambush had proved this beyond all doubt. But I don't think that is how we are going to win this war in the long run. Yes, we have to be ruthless and violent at times, but almost instantly afterwards we have to be soft and smiling again. For every civilian we kill, accident or not, uncles, brothers and sons are pushed towards the Taliban. So we have to tread lightly on those who are not our adversaries, like Colonel Collins said. Especially in this morphing, hazy conflict where we fight both an enemy who won't play fair and the constant, enduring feeling of being under threat. Here the locals, even if they are untrust-worthy and indifferent, are still our best form of force protection. Sometimes they even tell us where the IEDs are. If we lose them, we lose everything. We have to maintain our softer approach at first. We have to smile and we have to joke and we have to be friendly, even if it is the last thing we feel like doing. We have to respect them. We have to avoid shooting them if we can. We have to treat captured Taliban correctly. Otherwise we might as well not bother coming out here.

And otherwise we just might lose ourselves.

I know there is a balance to be struck between morality and operational effectiveness, between softness and hardness. I know it's a fine line to walk, but one we have to walk nonetheless. I think back to our nightly briefs. As the fire's flames licked our feet and sent dancing shadows over our faces, P.J. always strove to keep the soldiers sharp, aggressive and ready to fight their way out of any situation. 'I would rather be judged by twelve than carried by six' were his watchwords for the platoon. And he is right. The robustness he bred into 7 Platoon, especially at the psychological level, stands us in great stead as Sangin descends first into violence and then survival. We balance protecting ourselves with trying to win over locals as best we can. Elements of the other platoon do not.

Those that don't come to embody everything we are trying not to be.

They are corroding us. Just like our diminishing chances of survival are corroding our compassion. With those hidden IEDs seemingly everywhere, how can we all survive? And yet all our thoughts turn to survival. Somewhere deep, unconscious, amongst us, we assimilate our own deaths into our beings, constantly preparing ourselves, weighing up the chances, hoping. When we are alone we hope we will live. Hope we will see our families again, our friends. Hope we will be able to live our lives, that they won't end out here now before we have done what we desperately, oh so desperately, want to do. And you hope it won't be you. That it's someone else. Anyone but you. You can't escape from the survival instinct. That selfishness we all harbour.

Until you walk out the gate. Then it goes.

Meanwhile, the other commander infuriatingly contradicts my

orders, confusing the men, causing unneeded friction. Speedy is about to explode because of him. Only a senior corporal's tight bonds from 2006 with him and H hold the team together.

The sergeant major arrives in Armagh after R and R, his eyes expertly sizing up our defences in seconds and delegating work to improve them. He is angry.

'I just want you to know, sir, that resupply wouldn't have taken place if I had been here . . . You were setting patterns, and that's what got youse blown up. I'll do things differently from now on . . .'

Mark is extracted back to the DC, and we move into a work phase, demolishing mud walls, building sentry positions, hacking holes in concrete walls, removing junk from the compound, clearing an HLS. The platoon is weary but they work hard. It will take days but we're up for it. Elements of the other platoon moan, their complaints eating us like rust. When they go out on their section patrols, their platoon commander does not. Instead, free from company HQ, he runs his own little adventures. Things get tense. I too am about to explode.

A wall needs a hole smashed in it to allow us covert passage out of the orchard. I tell the other commander, when he takes his patrol out the next morning, to use explosives as a last resort, for it will give away the location. After stag, I roll over on the floor and fall asleep.

I am awake. It is day. The walls are shaking. An explosion rolls along the valley floor. I move to the ops room. The other commander is sitting there. I can barely conceal my wrath. It's like he's testing me. *Don't argue in front of the men.*

'What was that?'

'Oh, they just blew a hole . . .'

'Why aren't you out there?'

'I thought I should stay . . .'

'And why the fuck are they blowing holes? I said knock it down, use explosives as a last resort, they've only been out there fifteen minutes . . .'

He is uninterested and obstinate. I am furious. The men see us arguing, see us tearing apart the very threads that hold our team together. This is hell. I am ashamed of myself for falling into it. Ashamed for the damage I have done.

When the patrol returns I collar an engineer.

'What did he say to you?'

'He said to blow a hole in the wall, so we did.'

I knew it.

Later, I check the sentry positions. In one sangar I find un-helmeted, un-armoured, bare-chested members of the other platoon with pistols drawn on two locals who have come to give us information. Because they are nervous. Because they are scared. Because they don't care about anything but their own sur-vival. *This is getting out of control.*

That night we sit in another black alleyway waiting for another road convoy to roll and creak past us. I hear the hydraulics hiss, then the engine roar to a crescendo as the driver stamps on his throttle.

'H, what's he doing?'

'I dunno, boss. I'm going to check it out.'

Too late. The driver releases the clutch and lurches towards the tight hesco chicane that blocks the 611. There is a screech, a tearing sound, a clunk. I pull myself up off the warm dust and go to investigate.

'Boss, the first one's just got through. He just rammed it, boss, and nearly got stuck. I don't know what he's at . . . nearly ripped the trailer off on the chicane.'

'What the hell, H? He's meant to use the tractor. What was he thinking?'

The reality is he isn't thinking. And neither is the next driver. The whole mission rests on them getting their heavy loads to roll over the Sangin flyover so we can judge its load-bearing capacity. This is the last chicane before the flyover. He is a REMF. He is scared. He also has orders. His orders have told him, and us, that on reaching an obstacle he is to demount the heavy tractor on his trailer, move the obstacle with it, drive through and remount the tractor. Simple. But the orders haven't counted on his fear.

I watch as the second truck drives up to the chicane. It stops, golden headlights beaming through the night dust clouds before it. It reverses.

Good. At least he is not as stupid as the first one.

And then the engine guns and it charges forward. Another screech, another tear, another hiss. Then a furious, panicked revving of the engine. No use. He is impaled on the chicane. Fixed. Stuck.

I cannot believe the stupidity I have just seen. This driver has just jeopardized the whole mission. For tonight this convoy is special. The Kajaki dam is due a new turbine to boost power output for the locals and to deliver some sign of progress. This is meant to be the trial run.

We wait while my rage rises inside, morphing me into a terrible, frenzied animal. *I'm going to shoot that idiot bastard.* Rage. It swirls in my head as we wait. That driver becomes the focus for all my anger, all my negativity, all my hopelessness in this shithole that is Sangin.

'Fuck this.'

I walk to the stalled truck where the driver is shining at his mess with a torch and a curious, foolish look on his face.

'What's your name?' I demand.

'Sergeant Smith, sir.'

'You are a fucking idiot, Sergeant Smith, and I'm going to remember your na . . .'

'Paddy, calm down.'

It's the boss. He takes me aside, out of the glare of headlights and orange flashing lamps.

'What happened here?'

'Sir, that fucking idiot just rammed the chicane with his truck! Now he's ruined the mission, totalled the truck and put our men's lives in danger waiting here protecting him . . . All because he disobeyed a direct order . . . I can't believe it; he should be bust, sir.'

'All right, we'll deal with that later. I'll wait here until the mechanic comes. Your boys man the cordon and stay alert – it'll be a long one.'

It is. We return to the DC just before sunrise.

Fucking REMFs. I hate them.

MONKEY

I know indeed what evil I intend to do,
But stronger than all afterthoughts is my fury,
Fury that brings upon mortals the greatest of evils.

Medea
Euripides

The next morning the boss, sergeant major and I sit outside the ops room in the pleasant sunshine joking about the convoy and the moronic sergeant. Talk turns to Armagh, and I outline my concerns. They both share them, and the other officer will be watched very closely from now on. We hear of more deaths. Doug Beattie's guys have lost a sergeant outside Lashkar Gar, and C Company in FOB Gib have had a point man blown up. The tally we keep in our heads flicks up two. We think of the men, of their pain before they died. Of their families getting the news. And of our own deaths. Our own families.

The ANCOP drive into the DC in a flurry of skidding Ford pickups and shouting. They are from 'up north' and are toughened fighters, non-Pashtuns whose reputation for hardness precedes them. Within hours they are fighting against the governor's personal militia whom they found privately taxing the bazaar shopkeepers. The ANA take their lead from the ANCOP and start fighting the NDS, who have been taxing locals outside their base. As a result, an NDS agent, who had been sitting in on the boss's security shuras, defects to the Taliban along with his knowledge of our intelligence and network of informants. Later, a child with his arms blown off is brought to the DC by his father for treatment. He had his son making IEDs. Meanwhile, a radio intercept tells us the ANA are trying to sell their weapons to the Taliban. I think about the REMF sergeant, the other platoon, the crazy Afghan infighting, the corrupt governor, the indifferent locals, the survivalist tribalism. It is incredible, the madness of it all. *With friends like these . . .* Clausewitz called it friction, but out here in Sangin it feels like more than that. It feels like fallacy. It feels like folly. Like a waste of time. And lives.

At night we sleep outside on our cots, avoiding our oven-hot accommodation blocks, hoping we don't get mortared. Earlier, Naf and T had been burning some rubbish when a mortar bomb landed feet from them but failed to explode. Chance. The nervous sentries hear rustles, see shadows, and so rocket flares fizz into the sky, arching above us in their golden magnesium beauty, sending jumping, flickering shadows over our cots in long, dimming tongues of black. I try to forget the weak spots on our perimeter. I try to forget how I know they can get in, slit our sleeping throats and get out. Fear. I twist and turn and try to sleep in the clinging heat. Try not to sweat. But I can't. So I stagger to the canal. The slow, low strip that flushes with cool, sometimes ice-cold meltwater from the mountains. I wade in and chat to another who can't sleep. The water soaks my shorts, and my T-shirt clings to my chest. My wet sandals clip-clop me back to my cot. Dripping wet yet cool, I fall asleep.

But sleep is no escape. Miscued air strikes bomb us. Naf vanishes in an explosion. Our compound is overrun, a grenade machine gun jamming as they climb up our walls.

'Boss, you were screaming in your sleep last night.'

'Really? What was I saying?'

'You were shouting, "Load the GMG! Load the GMG!" Freaked me out, boss . . .'

In the daylight, all you can do is laugh.

A hack has arrived and sits self-consciously on a bench in the food tent, desperate for some tales of ardent glory. He wants the guys' from 2006 stories. No chance with 7 Platoon's vets. They are livid.

'I'm not talking to him, boss. He wrote us out of history in his last book.'

'Oh, he wants to talk to us now, does he? Maybe he should have thought about that when he wrote his book. Fucking parasite.'

Now I suppose I am.

A defence minister's visit equally annoys the boys. They obediently put on what they dub 'the greatest show on earth' for him. Thus, I am glad when he walks up the FSG tower in his sweat-soaked summer shirt to survey the scene and a contact erupts in Wishtan. *They can't put a positive spin on that.*

Another visitor is one of Britain's armed forces commanders, a greying cold war pilot. A flabby, limp handshake and a silly question confirm our disdain for the RAF.

But they are not all like that. Our brigade commander visits the DC to plan the turbine operation. He is hugely intelligent and a very experienced commander, the kind of man who gives us the impression he excels at everything. Which is heartening, as rumours swirl that the only reason the turbine is going in, against military advice, is for Bush's legacy or, worse still, for profit.

We all admire the head of the army, a hard-working, straight-talking general who has fought single-handedly for our morale-boosting packages to be mailed without charge and boosted the public's appreciation of us. We feel like he is in our corner, has our backs.

Later, we leave the DC and painstakingly clear along Pipe Range. Up front, as always, are Davy and T. Davy is a twenty-nine-year-old from Belfast, a shaven-headed big-mouthed character who finds something to laugh at in everything around him. His humour consistently buoys the platoon, on patrol, in camp, everywhere. A senior Ranger, he has become a rock in the platoon. As is T, in his early twenties, from the other end of Ireland. Quiet, chain-smoking and professional, T is yin to Davy's yan. They complement each other perfectly. They have to. Both are point men of the search team, the most dangerous job in Sangin. They rely on each other like only point men can. With every step, every sweep of their metal detectors, every suspect reading, they surrender themselves to their counterpart. Trust. Total trust in the other's ability. Total trust in his judgement. Their lives in each other's hands. And the pressure of knowing that if they get it wrong not only they but their friends will die too. Side by side, they cautiously sweep the sandy track, only thirty metres from base, because they don't trust the sentries over-watching it as they trust each other. They are fully aware of the large game of dice they play every day with their lives and limbs. But they do it for each other. They do it for us. They take the risk for us. They endure for us.

I learn much about courage watching them chat, joke, sweep another suspect pile of rubble and move on.

I ponder the reality of hidden traps these young men from north and south share and the bravery and trust with which they continue. Despite all the madness, all the negatives, their relationship embodies something heartening. Something hopeful.

Pride. *These men are a credit to our island of Ireland.*

The sand of Pipe Range changes to mud as we enter the Green Zone. We carefully cross the canal and check for IEDs on the rickety dirt bridge known to us as Green 12. We patrol into Monkey. Smiles, laughs and inquisitive glances greet my return to this quiet, happy hamlet. This time we have fresh American dollars to spend on Quick Impact Projects for the locals. On buying hearts and minds. We drop off Speedy and H's men in a treeline outside the village as locals flock around my small group and invite me to sit with them. The atmospherics are good. The elders greet us warmly, children run and play about. Only the fat mullah, with his hazy eye, I do not trust. We are discussing the painting and carpeting of his mosque when an explosion shatters this tranquil scene.

A blast of hot air, then dust washes over Squeak and McD. Then the roar rips at their ears. Speedy, Caylie and Joe Bog are enshrouded in cordite as red-hot chunks of shrapnel slice through the air searching for flesh. Ears ring in high-pitched monotone. Blackness. Dust. Smoke. Earth. Flashes of daylight. Quiet.

Confusion.

IED. Speedy's position.

We run for the shelter of a compound wall. Strangely, somewhere within me I feel everyone is all right.

Silence.

Speedy's voice bursts on to the net. Maddened and deafened, he shouts again and again.

'HADES FOUR ZERO, THIS IS FOUR ONE BRAVO! CONTACT! IED! WAIT OUT!'

I get to them, unsure of what I'm going to find. Squeak and

McD are stunned, momentarily incoherent, their faces drawn white. But they are OK. I move on. The cloud has dissipated, only the earthly smell lingering. A large crater is blown out of the path where they knelt. Speedy is OK. Caylie is OK. Joe Bog is OK. They're all OK. Miracle.

I knew it.

A command wire daisy chain IED is designed to kill or maim as many of us as possible. It is a string of IEDs wired together to explode either simultaneously or sequentially. This trap was simultaneous and could have killed five of us. But it didn't. Because the numbers didn't add up. Only the middle part of the deadly trap initiated, five feet from kneeling Joe Bog, while both ends, where Caylie and Speedy were actually sitting on buried shells, did not.

Why not? Let's roll the dice . . .

Chance.

We unearth the buried wire in the fading light and see it leads towards a compound. Locals. Someone in this village dug and then initiated this.

I return to the mullah, who barely reacted when the explosion rocked his mosque.

He knew.

My rage builds again. They nearly killed my men. These people knew it was there; it was in their field.

'We know nothing.' Usual response.

Fuck you. You'd know something if I stuck my rifle in your face. Blew your fucking brains out. Then you'd know, you stupid impassive bastards, wouldn't you?

Betrayed yet powerless, I discuss the mosque improvements with the friend of my enemy. Eventually, in the darkness of his prayer room, away from prying eyes, greed prevails and we settle a fee by candlelight.

Bitter and angry, I leave.

Radio traffic says the Taliban are west. We go east.

Manpower is becoming a problem. Since the daisy chain, Joe Bog is temporarily deaf, Squeak's been evacuated to the rear with an eye injury, another one has gone back with battle stress and we have Mark still hanging in there. McD and Speedy were on their first patrol since returning from their injuries inflicted by that IED. Then there's the constant trickle of R and R. Then there are the ones who won't come back. It's getting tight.

We patrol through the green maize stalks that tower above us, wide leaves brushing our arms, over our shades. Entering a corn-field, our world shrinks to the three feet between us and the next man; the pure unending greenness, the swish of the leaves, the blue above us, the brown below us, the heat. The plant life draws it in, sucking it, moisture and us into a stifling, still, silent jungle that we both love and hate. Hate because pockets of humid heat blast our faces. Hate because visibility is three feet. Hate because we could literally bump into Taliban in this maze. Love because we are hidden. Love because we are covert. Love because there are no IEDs.

The point men creep forward nervously, machine guns on hips, safety catches off, ready in an instant to unload into anything that moves. Behind them, their section commander, bayonet fixed, safety off, is ready to kill a drug-addled Taliban that the bul-lets have failed to stop. Dead men's lessons.

We are ejected out of the greenness into the dirt, trees and streams. Sopping wet, red-faced. Men start vomiting, heaving breakfast on to the paths as their buddies watch the fields and waterways. The electronic equipment breaks down in the heat. We are fixed. The boss gets frustrated. Speedy gets frustrated. H,

Mac and an EOD soldier go down with heat exhaustion. The sergeant major collects them in his quad. We return to base.

We'll try again tomorrow.

This time the company forces itself south. Long lines of helmets and aerials move down the dusty canal path, snaking through the fields with the British EOD team in tow. As the search team move cautiously down the track, sweeping, stopping, digging, sweeping again, a young boy in a brown dishdash brushes past. He mutters something in Pashto and is gone.

'Sir,' says our interpreter, 'there is an IED just up there.'

'Davy, Naf, STOP! STOP! Move back now!'

We move away and the EOD specialists come forward to deal with it. Unlike with Gunny, it is a long, deliberate process that is all the more painful in the forty-five-degree heat. We sit in an orchard while the local kids swarm around and annoy us.

A flurry of small hands extend hopefully.

'Kalaam, kalaam. Bic, Bic.'

'Biscood, biscood.'

'Choclaid, choclaid.'

Their requests reverberate around our tired heads until we distribute some pens and biscuits. They are appeased. Temporarily.

We wait and wait, slumped in the shade as the sentries rotate through short periods of over-watch on the baking flat roofs above.

More kids come begging again. They wear my helmet and we share a joke as they use sticks to play soldiers. I take a photo. They go.

As I sit in the doorway of a compound, a woman, face exposed, appears from within. She distributes packets of spicy, claw-shaped crisps and sweets in coloured wrappers to the kids, just like back home. Cupples and I are astonished.

'This place never fails to surprise ya, boss, does it?'

I laugh and look at him. He is leaning back on his heavy radio pack contentedly.

'It sure doesn't, Ranger Cupples . . . It sure doesn't. You know what? I'm gonna write a book about this some day,' I reply thoughtfully, as if the idea just came to me.

'Really, boss?'

He's interested.

'. . . And what would ya call it?'

'Oh . . . I don't know . . . *Five Months of Violence* or something like that . . .'

'Naaww, boss,' he drawls confidently, like he's letting me in on a big secret, 'ya gotta call it *Callsign Hades*.'

Maybe he was.

Meanwhile, not so surprisingly, the boy who tipped us off now tries to rob my patrol camera, slyly unzipping my daysack as I sit and chat.

Eventually, there is a boom that signifies the device has been cleared: another daisy chain that Davy was five metres from. It would have been carnage, and it's obvious the threat is evolving. Now they watch how we react to these devices when we find them and try to blow us up on the cordon. Just like the IRA at Warrenpoint. We are caught in the middle of a battle of wits, of technological measure and counter-measure, of drill and counter-drill, where one lapse of concentration can be fatal. And despite all the technology, our eyeballs remain our best defence.

The IED team move on. Another device is found, another daisy chain, right where we were blown up yesterday. Another wait in the sweltering, salty heat. It too is cleared.

And so it goes for ten hours. *We're going to get ambushed.* We know it. We know it is dangerous to stay on the ground for so long, but we'd all rather face Taliban bullets and RPGs than the hidden IEDs. We find five IEDs within two hundred square metres, the final one twenty kilos of home-made explosive packed into a booby-trapped motorbike outside a mosque. Right where we could have set up our cordon, as a mosque is hallowed turf. Not so. A massive bang echoes through the fields, sending shards of motorbike screaming through the air and raining down on us 250 metres away.

7 Platoon start to collapse back through the fields, avoiding the canal path. That is what saves us.

The five-year-old boy leaves the brightness as he runs through the door. Inside is dark coolness. The man sits on a red prayer mat.

Pashto. 'The British are out; they are near the canal. They have found our bomb near the bridge. They have been there for a while.'

He strokes his beard thoughtfully and stands up.

'Good . . . well done, little man. Your brother would be proud. Go back and watch them. Tell me if they move.'

He leaves his compound and sees US Marines patrolling below in the bazaar. Confidently, he moves through the alleyways to another compound. This is his town.

'The infidels are at the canal where we placed the bombs. They are finding them. We will kill them. Get the others. Do not use the radios.'

It takes hours to collect their group. But they have time. Slowly, they form in a safe compound in the Green Zone, while outside children watch the alleyways. He looks at his group. Most are younger than him, some teenagers. He knows only three of them are motivated by jihad. Some by the legends of the muja-hedin. The rest want money, status, wealth, adventure. He can provide all.

He knows their positions. He has sent forward scouts. They

have watched for hours as the infidels have found and destroyed every bomb they have laid for them, including the trap by the mosque. He is angry.

He tells them the infidels have found their bombs. He tells them they will ambush them from the other side of the canal. He tells them to collect their weapons, bring the rockets and to be careful: there are other infidel patrols out. He tells four to attack the traitors' base when they hear his group firing. He tells them to keep them busy for a few minutes. That that will allow them to escape. And he tells them to leave the motorbikes at the blue mosque for them. Go now. Allah Akbar.

He moves his band through the alleyways to the field that over-looks the canal. Locals see him and leave the fields. Women clutch children to their chests and swirl inside their compound doors, burkas blowing behind them. Old men eye them coldly. He stares back until they walk away.

They move sprightly, along the wall enclosing the wheat field, quickly picking their way over the small ditches. Only two men carry exposed rockets; the others hide their weapons under their dishdashes. They get to the high, thick mud wall. Perfect cover. Perfect view. Below, in the field, they see an infidel platoon moving back towards the DC.

'Set up . . . Use the holes in the wall to fire through. Do not fire at that patrol; they are too far away.'

Those with the RPGs move to either end of their short line. He places the belt-fed machine gun in the middle, just as he was taught. The others draw their AKs and wait behind the wall.

He stares through a small crack. The first patrol and a smaller group have passed. But another is coming up the canal path.

'Get ready,' he whispers as he moves to one of the RPG men. 'Wait for my command . . .'

Machine-gun fire erupts in front of and behind the section, impacting inches above their helmets. The canal bank roars as the ambush is sprung. An RPG screams from the undergrowth across the canal and explodes on the compound wall to their left, showering the last man in dust and shrapnel as he instinctively ducks down. Another RPG whizzes harmlessly away into the empty blue sky.

The section is stuck. They have a wall to their left and the canal to their right. Past that, in the undergrowth, is what threatens to kill them all. They are smack in the middle of a well-prepared Taliban ambush.

Chunks of earth explode around them. Bullets zip at their feet, over their heads, into the wall behind them. Somehow none find their target.

The section has no option but to manoeuvre through and out of this killing area, bullets splattering all around them. But they have survived these first crucial seconds. Now they are moving, now they are thinking, now they are firing. The rest of their platoon joins them. Bullets and grenade launchers smash the Taliban positions behind the wall, spraying them blindly, wildly, with a raw fury that catches them off guard.

The second I hear the firing my heart stops. I am scared. For the first time fear nearly freezes me. Because this time I know what we're going into.

It's not at us . . . but it's close. In an instant I have moved the platoon behind the wall of a bombed-out compound. Into safety, into all-round defence.

The boss is in a ditch by the canal, firing back and screaming for me. I watch him for a second from behind the wall, not wanting to run up the exposed track towards him. Frightened. More frightened than ever before. Frightened that I'm frightened. *Don't run please don't run don't do it you're going you're going GO!*

I run and dive into a ditch in which the shocked EOD are crouching and ducking at every bullet that whines over us. *Halfway. See . . . it's not so bad once you get going.* Another sprint gets me to the boss's boots. He has no clue how scared I am.

One of them is hit.

He lies in the field, writhing in agony and his rapidly reddening dishdash.

Pashto: 'Break off! Break off! Get him and let's go! Let's go!'

They sling their weapons, dragging their wounded comrade quickly through the field. A boy observes them from around a mud corner, watching as they pull him to the track.

'Can you walk? Can you walk? We need to get out of here now.'

'Yes, Ah . . . yes . . . I think so.'

Two of them place his arms over their shoulders to support him and begin walking hurriedly. Up front a youngster with an AK clears the way. Few locals are out, but behind cloth doors, through mud slits and rusted keyholes, they gaze at the wounded fighter. They have seen him before. Maybe they know him. Off to the east they hear another base being attacked.

The fighters get to the mosque.

'You three, take the weapons and hide them . . .' he says as he jumps on the kick-start and the engine bursts into life. 'We'll take him to the doctor; he'll be OK. Umshallah . . . well done . . . Go . . . Go . . .'

They disperse. The motorbikes tear off, heading south out of town. The Marines can see them. They know it's them. But they can't intercept them.

The gunfire is still raging.

'Right . . . Paddy . . . PADDY!'

'Yessir.'

'I want you to get your guys across the bridge and clear south on the eastern side of the canal. Go now.'

'Roger.'

The platoon is lined up in the ditch right behind me, ready to go. I give them a quick brief. Then Naf's men charge past me and run over the exposed bridge. They make it. Then Cupples and myself, then Matt's section. It goes quiet.

We peel into the humid field, Matt's men sloshing in the stream to our left, Naf's men fanned out in front. The other platoon guides us on.

'That wall above you now: that's where they fired from.'

'Roger. We'll check it out.'

Carefully, we do. We find bullet cases, blood. Nothing else. By the time we get to the wall, they are long gone.

Overhead, our might is collecting in the air.

'Hades Four One . . . Standby for low show of force in figures two.'

'Roger.'

Twenty minutes after we need it, a jet roars low over the canal to show how powerful we are.

Vanished, it just reminds us of how powerful they are.

As night falls we return to camp. Suddenly, a luminous green beam from above illuminates us on the canal bank. My heart jolts again.

'Whatthehellwasthat?'

'Sir, that's just the jet marking our position.'

'Oh . . . right . . . Nearly gave me a heart attack.'

This is getting harder.

While we were out, more IEDs have been found near Armagh and Wishtan.

That night we learn one of the EOD team has had a nervous

breakdown. Your first day, forty-five-degree heat, five complex IEDs and an ambush will do that to you.

We laugh. Because he is soft.

The next day, by chance more than anything, we find an IED that we can barely detect. It is designed to explode when our metal detectors sweep over it. Now we realize it is a matter of time, of when, not if. The migration of the IED threat, coupled with their increasing complexity, has changed our mindset. Gone are the quick attacks on Brecon hills, the exhilarating symphonies of violence, replaced by careful shuffles through dusty alleyways and constant wall climbs to avoid them. Now, when we are shot at and look for a safe ditch or wall, we dismiss it as too obvious, too likely to hide a bomb. We second-guess everything. Our only hope of staying alive lies with our brains.

Days are now numbers to get through. Empty, meaningless dates that decide if we are on patrol or not, if we are to be blown up or not. People say war is fun. I know Steve and other officers are enjoying their time in Musa Qaleh, giving out aid and interacting with the locals. *Maybe Sangin is worse than other places?* Because this is not enjoyable. This is not fun. It is far too serious for that.

It is war.

'So what do you think about PB Armagh, sir?'

'I think we're fixed, sergeant major, and I think we'll lose blokes down there to an IED any day now . . . It's just a matter of time . . . Y'know, we've been there a month . . . It worked for ten days or so, but it's not working now, and the boys are questioning it again.'

'Yeah, and most of the intelligence we're gettin' out of there now is bollocks. They're just shoppin' their neighbours to us.

We're down there tearin' the place apart to see the 611 and I reckon we're going to take a casualty and then leave. It'll look like defeat.'

Patrol Base Armagh is becoming a contentious issue. Paul, the sergeant major and I think it should be abandoned, that it's past its sell-by date. The boss doesn't. He thinks that with more resources, more men, it can still work well. Both are valid arguments, but what we are really divided over is not Armagh but survival. The boss has his mission, and he still fiercely believes in it. He is motivated by it, enthused by it, and he is very, very good at professionally executing it. He spends hours in planning, sifting through intelligence reports, thinking of new ways to get the upper hand. Unlike us, he is solely responsible for delivering the mission, but that is not his only responsibility. Like any commander, he also has to be prepared to lose men to complete the mission. That pressure of responsibility for 120 lives in such an unsure and changing environment must be immense. Lately, the strain is starting to show. Five months in and reluctant to leave the company in the thick of it, he still hasn't taken his R and R. Some of his decisions, once so carefully planned and executed, seem to be becoming more emotive, more reactionary. The decision to stay in PB Armagh, we think, is one of these.

Our mission is vague compared with the good old wars. We are not storming trenches or defeating Russians, or even taking ground. We are expanding the influence of the Government of the Islamic Republic of Afghanistan. The corrupt government that most of us would hate if we lived here. We're warriors and we accept risk and death, but we need a good reason. Out here, where's the reason? Where's the reward? What's the point in taking risk? Exposing ourselves? For what? What's worth a life? Or five? Children going to Sangin's school? A more secure bazaar? Women's rights? Worker's Registration Day? A safer Britain? The real difference between us and the boss is that we don't believe in the mission any more. Not enough to risk our lives for it. Too much reality has eroded our convictions. We don't have the deep commitment of some of the Americans. We just want to bring everyone home alive. Fuck this place. I don't care about the kids going to school or goddamned women's rights. If the people in Sangin want them, then why aren't they fighting for them? And I don't see any Al Qaeda here, just a load of poppies being farmed and sold and us doing nothing about it. We are being corroded, eaten by this hard place. And now, because we are staring at our own deaths, and because the locals are often complicit in it, I resent the very people we came to save. We eye everyone like they are a suicide bomber. That cold, hating stare is now mutual. The compassion we once held eroded. It's too dangerous. So fuck hearts. And fuck minds. And fuck PB Armagh, because if we stay down there we'll die. For nothing.

We just want to survive. We're all tentatively counting the days, hoping we're not tempting fate. And it feels like the boss is trying to kill us. To expose us to more risk.

But the boss gets it. Gets it at a higher level, and under his wise direction Ranger Company take calculated risks to try to improve Sangin. What I really don't understand until much later is that to make any progress in these wars among the people the infantry have to be exposed to more risk. We can't hide behind our hesco walls; we have to get out and into the communities, win over the people and gain intelligence exactly when the risk is highest to us. And that is very hard to accept when you are the one taking the increased risks and when you are the one who has to keep smiling while you do it. Would you? Is it worth your face, your leg, your life?

Because that is our only chance of winning. And it is a small chance.

Despite our growing differences, life in Sangin goes on. I watch as two pristine black Hungarian AK74s are wrapped in clear cellophane bags, having been found under the dishdashes of two captured locals. They are so new they have never been fired. Echo Company conducts another search. We detain locals at PB Armagh. One of them turns out to be the nephew of a mid-level Taliban commander. He talks. The intelligence cell goes into overdrive. We will launch a raid tonight. I am sceptical, knowing I wouldn't hang around if my nephew was arrested. In the night we cordon the quiet compound. Gunny blows the door in, the ANCOP follow. Right compound. Wrong night.

In reply, the next morning Armagh is hit again.

As I sit safe inside the DC and listen to the rattle of the contact, I think about my impending departure from the platoon. I am short-toured, a deserter, with ten days to push. But I'm not sure if I'll even make it to then. No one is. The selfish voice inside me is thankful. The honourable voice has offered twice to stay on. Both are relieved when the offer is declined.

Outside, the boys talk excitedly about the prank they are going to play on the new platoon commander, due to arrive today. I know it will be hard to hand over 7 Platoon after two years of commanding them. For a month before I have been preparing myself, but it's not making it any easier. It dawns on me that I know these men intimately. I know if they have financial problems, if their marriage is in difficulty. I know their pasts and their hopes. I have shared shell scrapes and bus journeys with them from Kenya to Cape Wrath. I have sweated and bled with them, cursed and laughed. People have tried to take our lives and together we have taken life. I feel traces of it now, but later I will realize there is a bond, an unspoken, intangible magnetic bind that holds us together and apart from civilians. Of shared experiences, shared tests, of danger and death, which no one else can understand or even wants to. A closeness that is rarely equalled outside these circles. A mutual understanding, an affirmation of manhood. The strange emotion, magnetism, that pulls you across the street to chat to them. Or that sees them hover in my office months after we've returned.

But I will discover all this later, for now I have an ambush to plan.

That night, after 7 Platoon's new officer, Drew, has arrived from Bastion, I give my orders in the briefing room. He will shadow me, like I did Tom five months and a lifetime ago. We will leave in the early hours of the morning. Afterwards, the platoon stands up from the ops room benches and stretch and yawn. Ronnie, H and Matt close in around the map and gently coach Drew. They disperse.

I run to the accommodation.

'Get your kit! Get your kit! Change of plan: we're out now, out now!' I try to convey my panic.

There is pandemonium as the platoon pull themselves out of their cots in the dark.

Shouting.

'Quick! Quick! Close in for a brief! Close in for a brief!' I roar.

They start to settle down outside the accommodation. I catch some conceited smiles.

'Right, change of plan, change of plan, lads. We're going out now. They've seen some Taliban down the canal path and we're going to get them. I know we're all scared, lads, but don't worry, don't worry. It'll be fine . . . See anything that moves, waste it, just waste it. Ask questions later. Got grenades? Throw a few of them too. Remember: STAY CALM, LADS! STAY CALM! Any questions?'

Silence. Smiles. Only Drew is looking at me in wide-eyed wonder.

'. . . Good. Platoon sergeant, take over.'

Davy steps up.

'Right, sir. I'm the 7 Platoon sergeant. Davy's me name and ducking's me game . . .' He shakes Drew's hand. 'Now listen in, you pack of spanners. We're going light. No med kit, one mag, that's it. Any questions?'

Caylie shyly raises her hand. 'I don't want to go on this one.'

'No worries, pet, you don't have to. We won't need a medic anyhow. Anyone else?'

'Yes, Sergeant Dave. I've got a bad feeling. I've got a real bad feeling about this one,' says Matt.

'OK, you can stay here . . . Let's go, quick.'

We run to the gate in a jumbled mess of shorts, flip-flops, bare chests, weapons and helmets. Only Drew is fully dressed, as Mowgs, disguised as an Afghan local, hounds him in broken Pashto.

'Boss, I forgot the electrical equipment!'

'We don't need it.'

'Boss, what about my helmet?'

'OK, you need that. You can stay here.'

We line up by the canal. Alarmed, the Rangers murmur: 'Where are we going? What's going on?'

'Listen in: load.'

From down the line comes a nervous, 'Boss, I forgot my weapon.'

'You won't need it.'

'And I can't find the metal detectors.'

'No problem. We'll do what we always do. T, Naf, you know the drill. Quickquicklet'sgo!'

We move down a hesco wall, just outside camp, a nervous, bunched-up line of comedic idiots watching in the darkness as the point men stamp their feet with gusto in every step, trying to clear imaginary mines. Someone laughs. I look at Drew. He looks concerned. I offer my hand and smile. The platoon erupts in laughter.

I shake his wary hand.

'Welcome to 7 Platoon!'

That night we are a different platoon.

We swing out of camp on to the shale of the Helmand and head south, Ronnie leading the way. It is utterly black. *Good.*

Ronnie guides our bobbing line of helmets, silently, expertly through the high black cornfields. We stop, kneel and whisper.

'RV [Rendezvous] 2.'

The next man nods and turns to pass it back. We stand up and are stalking again. No dogs hear us. No dogs smell us. Just the light breeze shaking the cornfields. *We are experts now.*

We move towards the final rendezvous, that little mosque in Monkey which that fat mullah should be redecorating. Nothing stirs. Ronnie stops. An orange-gold glow lights the track around it. Someone has installed a new street lamp. It will blow our cover.

Whispers: 'See that, boss? Whaddaya wanna do?'

'Yeah. Bastard. We'll have to drop back behind it, but I guarantee the dogs'll start barking.'

'You know it, boss.' He smiles.

We drop off Speedy and our protection group nearby. With him is Mark. He has refused to go back to Bastion, to leave the platoon, and has forced himself to come out with us tonight, despite all his fear, his terror. I remember what the sergeant major said today when he saw him before we left: 'See that fella, sir, that fella is the bravest lad in the whole company, bar none.' Thucydides' ancient words flared in my mind: *'the bravest are surely those who have the clearest vision of what is before them, glory and danger alike, and yet not withstanding go out to meet it'* . . . I watch him nervously twitch and scan, but endure. It was pure courage, the very essence of it. The triumph of will over fear, and it was humbling and inspiring to witness. *Greater love hath no man* . . .

The dogs start their howling, but quieten quickly. We move off, towards the objective.

The objective is an IED. Someone has told us there is one just outside Monkey, on that prominent bridge at Green 1 2 we use often. That's why it's there. But the intel seems good. We are looking for a command wire buried along the edge of the track. We want to find it, follow it to its firing point, and then sit and wait. When morning dawns and the bomber comes to check it, we will end his life.

But we can't find it. In the dark we use hands to scrape back dust, to claw along the base of walls, to scrabble through an orchard. It takes hours and is infuriating. But we can't find it. And it's getting light.

Decision time. I leave Matt in Monkey to over-watch the bridge from a treeline, then move the rest of the platoon forward into a high-walled field beside Green 1 2. *We'll try to find the device and take it from there.*

Dawn breaks, and Sangin slowly stirs into its usual rhythm of locals, motorbikes and prayers. We stop a local man. He says the IED is in the field in front of Matt's men. Unsure and frustrated, we move to investigate, but first I tell Ronnie to check the track near the bridge. As the point men move off, Davy taps both legs with a hand and smiles.

'You're coming back with me today.'

Then he picks up the metal detector and steps on to the track.

I watch Ronnie watching Davy sweep, quietly questioning him, directing him. He follows a yard behind him. Leadership. By following. By sharing. As search team commander he is the best-trained IED spotter in Sangin. Now he notices something. He is about to earn his fifty pounds today.

'Lads, hold on . . . Pull back.'

They do. He slings his weapon and lies flat on the earth, extending his arm out in front as far as it will go. Gently, carefully, he brushes back the dust. He scrapes lightly with his fingers.

He shuffles back on his elbows, then turns and stands up. As he brushes past me I sense his nervousness. He quickly searches for a cigarette and draws deep.

'That's a fucking IED, all right. Reckon it's a mortar shell . . . That was close.' He shakes his head, contemplating his brush with death, with chance.

We check the other side of the wall we have been sitting behind and, in the daylight, find a black coil burrowed through it and leading off to the orchard. The intel was right.

I call in the IED to the ops room and we keep the locals away. Gunny and the US EOD will be down soon. We are tense. It could be radio-controlled. We scan for dickers. A small boy is popping his head up over the lip of a roof on the other side of the canal, watching us.

'Move back, move back!' I order. There is a fluster as the men run to increase their distance from the safe side of the wall.

The boy pops his head up again.

I raise my crosshairs. I see his fair hair, his blue dishdash. His head.

I snatch on the trigger.

The bullet kicks the lip in front of him. A small mushroom cloud of orange dust slowly rises up. *Hopefully that splinters his eyes.* The report cascades down the canal in the morning stillness.

The radio chatters in my ear. I turn to the man next to me.

'If he does that again, kill him.'

And I move behind the wall to speak into the radio. Somewhere inside a little whimper of conscience begs what have I become.

Numb.

The Marines arrive disconcertingly quickly. They have come down the five hundred metres of canal path in fifteen minutes. It would take us an hour to sweep. One of them has his weapon slung on his shoulder like he is on a route march. Ronnie looks at me and shakes his head.

'They won't last long like that, boss.'

'I know . . .'

Gunny goes to work. There is that heavy, tense silence again. We stay alert, scanning the rooftops and bushes.

'Keep watchin' out. This one's dangerous . . .' Gunny shouts.

Silence.

He walks back to us. Behind his dark shades he is more talkative than usual.

'That was a close one. I saw it and thought, hell, same ol' shit, and nearly just cut the wires. But then I thought, screw it, do it right, just in case. Lucky I did. We got us a collapsing circuit daisy chain IED there, boys. Three-eighty-mill shells six feet from a one-oh-five. Woulda ended my day mighty fine.'

It would've ended Ronnie's and Davy's day too, blowing them in pieces into the canal, but it was designed especially to kill the EOD team when Gunny cut the wires.

The battle of wits is still escalating.

One IED down, three more to go.

The other reported bombs are on the far side of the canal, as well as the one in the field Matt is watching. I decide to break the cardinal dead man's lesson: I split the callsign both sides of the canal, reasoning that now we have enough Marines with us to fight independently on either side. We do.

We sweep forward slowly through deserted dusty alleys and warily check the reported spot. Nothing. Below us, near a telegraph pole, the Marines report the same.

Beside the treeline at the edge of Monkey, Matt and H are discussing developments when an RPG tears between them and explodes against a mud wall five feet behind. The force flings them both straight into a deep mud ditch and showers them in torn green branches and clay. They are stunned as the crash of small-arms fire explodes around them. The Rangers dive for the ditch as scythes of noise slash over their heads. Lines of mud rapidly erupt and explode into the air, mini-volcano manifestations of the hurtling copper impacting around them. Clarkey dives on McD to avoid them, pinning him into the mud like locked lovers. Ally is flattened by two locals who jump on him. The ambusher's initial burst of fire is so heavy that no one can do anything but cower in the ditch and hope, as soil and twigs and leaves rain down on them.

Matt starts to come round. He lifts his rifle over the ditch with one hand and sprays wildly in their general direction. Then Delaney pops up with his Jimpy and starts chewing into his belted brass bullets. Ally has pushed the civilians away and starts lobbing grenade rounds behind the attackers, who are only fifty metres away. Clarkey and McD are back in, laughing at their mishap and firing wildly. The rest start firing. H fires an LASM into a small outhouse where a gunman has raked them from, taking the building's roof down around him. Joe Bog has the fifty-one going now, arching mortar bombs behind them to cut off their escape. We have won the firefight. The attackers cannot match this enormous weight of fire. They break off. As we rush across the canal and link up with them, the noise is inspiring.

It dies down. The contact lasted only three minutes but it was close, intense violence. It proves our observation that if you survive the first thirty seconds out here, the chances are you will survive the whole contact.

We consolidate around the ditch and then move off to clear the firing points. We kick in doors to compounds, and a crying woman wails at us. They have been firing from her roof, but she won't talk. We find a small blood trail. We sweep into the green jungle of cornfields and move back up the canal towards the Marines. No IED found.

Later, it's confirmed we killed one. It is a good, wholesome feeling.

That night news comes in that the well water in Armagh is infected with tiny red bloodworms. This development forces our differences into the open.

The sergeant major sits on a table in a room adjacent to the ops room. A half-finished Ranger Company mural of a caubeen-wearing vampire skull stands behind him. I am perched on another table. Paul stands next to me, the boss in the doorway. He is loath to collapse the PB, but with no drinkable water we will have to resupply it every day. That means a convoy, that means setting patterns, that means IEDs and that means less chance of survival.

The boss searches for alternatives, but in reality there aren't any.

It goes quiet as we all think. The sergeant major, Paul and I are waiting for one of us to speak up.

Screw it. I've nothing to lose.

'Sir, I think Armagh has had its day . . .'

The sergeant major and Paul don't let my words linger.

'So do I.'

'So do I.'

They immediately back me up.

We all launch into our reasons: the way the intelligence seems to have dried up, the IEDs, the attacks on Armagh, the violence engulfing Sangin again, the fact that it will be collapsed when we are relieved anyway.

The boss looks at us all silently. We know he sees Armagh in a different light from us. He seems hurt, like we've ganged up on him, betrayed him. And in a way we have, but it is what we believe is the right thing to do.

'Well, how come the Americans can do it up in Wishtan and we can't do it down in Armagh?'

Paul says gently: 'Because, sir, their area is easier than ours.'

The boss looks at us all. He is hurt.

'You aren't supporting me . . .' He trails off, gazes down the corridor, out to the night sky, and walks off.

We look at each other.

I feel guilty but relieved.

We patrol to Armagh the next morning, and at last light Ronnie's section, Drew and I patrol the peaceful, beautiful orchard. As night comes, a campfire is lit, chips cut and shallow-fried as a battered iPod plays 'Brothers in Arms' and we huddle around. Amid occasional warning shots from the sentries above, we talk about the war. It's the first time I have done so with the section commanders.

'I don't know, boss. The town's a lot busier here since last time . . . But I don't think a helluva lot of it is to do with us, y'know?'

'Yeah, and the civvies, they don't really care, do they?'

'Sir, this place is too fucked up. It's just about getting through it, about digging in together and getting the boys back home alive. That's it. We came here to do our job, and we'll do it though . . .'

'Yeah . . . but, boss, d'you hear they found a dead Taliban with an Aston Villa tattoo a while back . . .'

'And someone told me they heard the Taliban switchin' into Brummie accents when it started to hit the fan.'

'Sir, you know what I would do with this place?' an engineer, another huge Spartan, asks me.

'What's that?'

'I'd blow the Kajaki dam and flood the place,' he says with profound finality.

There is silence as we picture washing away Sangin in a tidal wave of clear blue water.

'I don't know, lads, I don't know . . . I s'ppose all we know out here is that we've got each other's backs . . . and really that's what's important in the end, that's our mission.'

'You're bang on there, boss, bang on.'

The men laugh, goading their favourite terp, the Rock, who plays up to their jibes that he's gay by trying to kiss them. He is a small, gregarious man, so full of life he leaves an impression like a fine golden dust on everyone he meets.

That night I lie awake and realize how much I love these men now. My conscience battles with my loyalty to them and my own self-preservation.

It's my time to move on . . .

In the morning one of the locals hired to cut the trees between Armagh and the 611 tells us that eight Taliban are lying in ambush near the orchard.

I decide to patrol to the 611, away from the orchard, rather than give battle on their terms. But they are waiting there also.

We sweep slowly past the torn, splayed tree trunks lying

forlornly in the dirt, the stumps, the knocked-down walls, the dried-up river the Taliban have diverted to force us out. The once beautiful glade has been ruined. *World War 1*.

Out into Tank Park, a burial ground for unexploded bombs, we sweep. Reports suggest they are all the work of a team of two sixteen-year-olds. Up ahead, on the dusty 611, an ANA Ford pickup whizzes by, Afghan flags fluttering. One of the occupants waves at us. We wave back.

Seconds later an explosion shakes the walls we kneel beneath. A plume of smoke slowly rises up near the 611.

Back in Armagh, Matt runs to the radio.

'Hades Four One Alpha, are you OK, are you OK?' he demands with dread.

'Roger. We're all OK. Think that was an IED on an ANA truck. We're going to check it out.'

Excruciatingly slowly, we have to sweep and pick our way over the dirt field, but we are still the first on the scene. The pickup is a mangled wreck of metal, shattered glass and blood. Bodies are strewn in uncanny forms on the road. A torn beret. Deep crimson pools of warm blood quickly being absorbed by the fine brown dirt. Flesh. A scalp. I turn away. There's not much we can do.

Some ANA arrive from the nearby base and commandeer a white Corolla, shoving the dead and injured in and tearing off towards the DC. A mutilated, faceless body, like a pulped raspberry, is left in the road.

The world and his dog arrive. Added to us there are ANA, OMLT and US Marines. Massive fleets of expensive and robust American vehicles line up on the 611. Overhead, a drone circles, and the usual fifteen minutes later a jet swoops down the 611 to scare away anyone who even thought about sticking around. But they hadn't. They were gone. And we know it as we search the compounds nearby and eye every local like they are the bomber. Because one of them was.

That jet costs fifteen thousand dollars a minute to fly. Look at all this equipment. All this power. Yet a four-dollar IED fired by an old man has just killed three ANA commanders . . .

I knew then.

The next morning we find out that three Marines have been killed and another seriously injured when their vehicle hit a pressure plate IED in Wishtan yesterday. It hits us all hard, even though we didn't know them. That day another platoon finds another IED outside Monkey and gets hit in another ambush. The day after that the Marines have a lucky escape when an IED explodes near the rickety bridge we know so well. It blows the whole track into the canal, injuring two. The wire runs across the torrent this time. They are watching us and learning. Maybe that boy on the roof told them about our drills. Another escalation in the battle of wits. Another counter-measure conceived.

But we also hear heartening news. A resupply that screeched into Tank Park last night has, by pure chance, caught two young men laying IEDs. They match the descriptions the locals have given us. One of them has a long list of Taliban names written on his trouser leg. We reckon we've got them. Delight.

But the ANP don't reckon we have. And we can't arrest them on our own. We know they're the ones, but the ANP are adamant they are going to be released. We are furious. The sergeant major lobbies for their detention. He wins. They are extracted to Lashkar Gar for questioning. Later, they are released because there is no prison to put them in.

Dawn comes quickly, the sun burning off the night's coolness with rapid intensity. In the morning's quiet, a relaxed atmosphere lingers in Patrol Base Armagh like a pink morphine dream. Only the sentries behind their sandbags and the watchkeepers in the radio room stir. Birdsong glides around the battlements.

A series of dull thuds to the north confirm FOB Inkerman is in its usual morning routine of contact. An ANA patrol hits an IED, the shock wave passing through our chests as we lie on our mats. A garbled, panicked message drifts over the radio as a Nabi patrol desperately tries to call in a fire mission.

Outside Armagh's high walls we pick up Taliban radio chatter: 'Be careful of the batteries and wires.' 'Meet me in the orchard. Bring the things on your bike; it is less suspicious.'

Nothing out of the ordinary.

We leave Armagh for the DC the same day we find out it is to be collapsed, which, ironically, is the same day we finally clear arcs out to the 611. We are relieved.

Choosing the safest option, Drew leads the platoon back up the 611. I have told him everything I know about the platoon and about survival, every tool, every tactic, every trick. I know he'll be fine. So now I shadow him. It is slow and cautious and I don't enjoy this threatening, tempting of fate and chance my last patrol demands. *Now I understand how those Royals felt.*

One last clearance of the 611, one last walk through the bazaar, one last nostril full and it's gone. I make it to the DC alive.

The next day I address the small gaggle of gnarled, thin men outside the accommodation. Most of them are on guard. For once I keep it short. I tell them how much of an honour it has been to serve with them and tell them to continue sticking together, to support Speedy and the new boss.

Matt says I've come a long way since Kenya and we all laugh.

I hand over my pouches, bags, backpacks, shades and knee pads to the men who will need them. I pack my bags.

I walk to the ops room. Outside I meet Speedy.

'Thanks for all your support, Speedy . . . Keep the boys together . . . Look after them and look after yourself . . .' I shake his hand.

'Will do, sir, will do . . . And sir . . . thanks . . . thanks for everything.' His look says more than we ever could.

Inside the ops room the boss and Paul tease that the chopper isn't coming, that I'm going nowhere. We laugh, and the boss thanks me, which means a lot.

The sergeant major offers his hand.

'So I suppose you're feckin' off now, sir, are yeh? That course just couldn't wait, no?' He smiles.

'I wouldn't want to stay around here and get stuck in your hair in the ops room, now would I?' I tease.

I shake his hand.

'No, you're damn right. Get out while you can. You lucky bollix . . .'

'I'll keep in touch . . . You haven't got long to push . . . Good luck.'

It is awkward. I have survived and they have another six weeks to endure. I sense that jealousy I felt when P.J. left. I was so happy he had survived, made it out, but still a nagging inner voice was jealous. *You lucky bastard, you've survived.*

I wait until I hear the whocka-whocka of the Chinook and then run to collect my bags. I avoid the quickest route, through the covered, unused area of cables and makeshift wooden stretcher tables beside the ops room where we keep the filled body bags, just as I have avoided it for the whole tour.

I pass Cardwell and Cupples, ambling along in conversation near the helipad.

'Take it easy, guys. Good luck.'

Out here, good luck is about all you can say to someone

when you say goodbye. We really mean it, understand it. We live it.

'Will do, boss, will do . . . And look after yourself, boss,' Cupples says confidently, caringly, in a tone that instantly catches me, makes me wonder: *I'm the one escaping here, not you.*

It is the last thing he ever says to me.

In the army, there comes a time to move on, to make way for those coming in behind you, and now it is my turn to move on. I tell myself this as a blackened Sangin drops away below and alone, in thought, I soar into the Helmand night sky.

Still, it feels like desertion.

Part 5

THE
LONGEST
MONTH

WARMINSTER

It is only the dead who have seen the end of war.

Plato

The rear ramp of the Chinook spits me into the cooler, dark calmness of Bastion. I walk alone with my kit to the accommodation, a sense of alienation pervading. My mind spins with thoughts of the platoon, my belly light with a tingling, electric feeling. I walk to the white phone booths. Rectangles of white light occasionally leap out of their swinging doorways.

I dial the number and listen to the crackling distant tone. It stops.

'Hello?'

'Hello . . . It's me . . . I'm out . . . I'm safe.'

Seven thousand miles away I can clearly hear the emotion break in my mother's voice.

That's when I realize how selfish I have been.

The next evening I stand in the queue for food. Behind me, REMFs joke and laugh. It annoys me. A fat major is complaining to his doting troops.

'I suppose it's steak or chilli chicken again,' he says dolefully.

He has just taken a mallet to the anger meter inside me. It's gone through the bell at the top. *You fat jack bastard.*

I want to turn around and tell him he should be ashamed of himself, ashamed to be talking like that in front of his troops when there are real soldiers on the front line who haven't had fresh food in months.

But I catch myself. The army is a small world and I am just a lieutenant. *What's the point?*

A friendly Para colour sergeant organizes our flight home. As we climb out of Kandahar in our ageing jet, darkness evaporates as the cabin lights flick on.

'Ladies and gentlemen, you can now remove your body armour and helmets.'

There is a small cheer, really just a small, collective acknowledgement of our own individual survival. It feels wholesome, relieved, hopeful, but it is tainted.

Tainted by my thoughts. Thoughts that I really don't want to deal with now but which scream silently at me as we fly through the skies. It is almost as strange as flying into war, nearly as daunting, this flying out of it. *Scooped out of danger and deposited home in forty-eight hours. What is this, this war of the medieval and the modern? What is it all for? What is our legacy?* The word dangled around my neck like a recently loosened noose. It probably haunted our commanders more, as they searched for direction and meaning in the maze of madness. Because in the military, all this violence, suffering and death had to be for something. We wanted tangible proof. We wanted, no, we were obsessed with success, progress. We were dying for it. Desperate. *Desperate for some legacy, some reason, some pride.* But where were the battles to be studied at Staff College? The sweeping manoeuvres pitting our strengths against their weaknesses? The tangible victories of yesterday? They were none, as irrelevant and as futile in Afghanistan as trying to eat soup with a knife. No one would study or even remember our little skirmishes, our battles, except those who had lost their friends and their youth in the ditches and alleyways. They would all be forgotten, overtaken, surpassed. So what had we achieved?

Maybe the Kajaki turbine operation was the flagship of our progress and success, but deep down we know the new turbine will sit unused for a long time because it isn't safe enough to install it. Despite all our efforts, all our goodwill, all our risk taking, our money, our sweat and our blood, Sangin was no safer than when we found it. In fact, it was more dangerous and getting even more so.

Was Britain safer? I couldn't tell. The notion was too convoluted, too intangible for us on the ground to ever know. I hadn't seen any Al Qaeda. But I'd heard about the Aston Villa tattoos. So who knew? Maybe you never could. Maybe that was the beauty of it. The beauty of buying time with lives to shore up a crumbling neighbour with nuclear weapons.

I wanted proof. A reason. Not schools, or women's rights or even democracy. A reason.

And honesty.

What had I achieved? I don't know. I know I have survived, that that in itself is a kind of victory.

I have endured, and in doing so I have both gained and lost much.

A few days later, having seen my family, I start my captain's course in sleepy, green Warminster in rural England. A pilot, confident and blasé, comes in to talk to us about the effects of his weapons systems. He proudly shows murky black-and-white footage of explosions like he's showing us pictures of his children. He punctuates each with a throwaway line:

'Getta load of that, ha ha.'

'And then we give him the good news!'

'That'll ruin your day!'

Does he have any idea? The answer is he doesn't. Sitting miles above his target, he plays a desensitizing computer game that keeps his conscience removed from the realities we face.

I feel in limbo, my mind and soul in Sangin, my body stuck in this weird wet world of Warminster. Of lecture theatres and plans and statistics. Of safety.

Meanwhile, that constant foreboding, that feeling that something is going to happen to 7 Platoon, lingers.

I ring through to the ops room. Speedy answers on the other side of the globe.

'Alright, boss, how's it going?'

'Not too bad . . . How you guys gettin' on?'

'OK, boss, OK . . .'

'Is it busy?' I hope it's not, *hope I'm not missing anything.*

'It's OK, boss, OK. The platoon are doing well . . . Mr Ward's doing fine. He's the new boss; you're the old one now! We're doing OK, boss . . .'

'Good stuff. Not long to push now. Hang in there and send my best to the lads.'

I am relieved.

Maybe they will make it through. Maybe I was wrong . . .

At night, in my Cold War-era room, I dream of Afghanistan. Dozens of women in our desert uniforms but with their heads wrapped in black hijabs agilely leap over the walls of Armagh and start slashing the platoon with silver scimitars as they try desperately to fight them off the battlements. We are being overrun. I am below, in a dark room, scrabbling for my helmet, my body armour, trying to get out and help. I can't find them. I am helpless.

The light-green trees sway gently over the high orange-brown dirt walls of Armagh. A mortar attack. But these are no ordinary mortars. They are huge, car-sized, rusted bombs, just like the ones we find buried in the tracks, and they are hurtling, spinning down on us, crushing and exploding against the platoon. Safe inside, I search with dread turning to terror for my rifle. Powerless. Redundant.

When I realize what my subconscious is screaming, they dissipate.

Another weak line relays Speedy's voice with the usual awkward delay.

'How is it?'

'Boss . . .' He sighs. 'It's fucking mental . . . There's IEDs everywhere. It's a joke . . . They've gone through the roof.'

'Jesus . . . You serious?'

'Yes, boss . . . Dunno what happened, but they're everywhere now. It's a nightmare. The other platoon found four within a hundred metres yesterday. We're ringed in . . . They're sending in another company of Paras to help us try to clear them . . . It's madness.'

'Shit! Take care . . . take care . . . Not long to go now, Speedy, not long. Tell the boys I'm thinking of them.'

'Will do, sir, will do.'

It is the worst possible news.

And it is true.

7 Platoon awake in the darkness. It's cooler now. They are nearly there. They gulp their last litres of water, prep their kit and place it on their shoulders, their backs and their heads. In the coolness they walk to the gate. They line up. They load. They check their radios one last time. They step out of the gate. Speedy counts them out. They move to the first IED. They find it. They confirm

it. They move on. To the second IED. They find that too. They confirm it. They move on. To the third IED. They find it. They confirm it. They turn for base. It is morning. The heat is rising. Like it always does.

They patrol through the alleyways, the always dusty and suspicious alleyways, along the edge of the Green Zone. They move cautiously, as always, sweeping in front of them. T and Davy are on point, as always, the platoon spaced out behind them. Drew walks near the front with Cupples and the Rock, Speedy at the back with Bog and Caylie. As always.

They don't find the fourth IED.

Until it goes off.

The explosion kills Ranger Justin Cupples. It badly wounds the Rock, scarring his face for life. Drew, by chance, escapes.

It was aimed at the platoon commander's group and, after so many failed attempts, they succeeded.

That is all you need to know.

You don't need to know about the smoke, the pain, the blood, the terror, the panic, the tears and the bravery.

And you can forget about the revenge.

Just like, sometimes, you forget about the war.

Telecommunication cables carry the message silently. First to headquarters. Then to 1 Royal Irish. Then to the notifying officer. Then to Cupples's family. Lithuania. America. Ireland. Britain. Then to the media.

I sit on a weights bench in the red and white gym in Warminster. The local radio is relaying the news. Second item:

'Another British soldier has been killed in Afghanistan. The soldier, from the First Battalion, the Royal Irish Regiment, was serving in . . .'

No. No. No.

'. . . Sangin District Centre with the Second Battalion, the Parachute Regiment. Next of kin have been . . .'

I sprint out of the gym and up the wet tarmac road to my room.

I don't know why I run. I already know.

NoNoNo. IknewitIknewitIknewit.

I open the door and grab my phone. It rings.

'Sean, I just heard we lost someone. Who is it?'

'Paddy, I'm sorry. It's one of yours . . . Cupples, this morning, an IED . . .'

'Fuck! . . . Fuck! . . . Fuck!'

Each emotional curse, each breath, sucks the reality down into my being. It seems the only word to describe everything. And nothing.

Sean pauses. '. . . I'm sorry no one phoned you. It's been pretty busy here trying to sort things out.'

'Yeah . . . I fuckin' knew it, fuckin' knew it.'

'I'm sorry, man.'

'Ahhhh . . . yeah . . . thanks . . . anyway . . . I'll be in touch.'

I hang up.

And then I cry.

Another phone call.

'P.J., did you hear?'

'Yes, boss, I did . . . It's shit, isn't it?'

'I knew it, I knew it . . .'

'Boss, we all knew it could happen . . .'

'I was just starting to think they'd make it through . . .'

'. . . yeah, so was I . . . What can you do . . .?'

'I dunno . . . I shouldn't have left . . . I shouldn't have left . . .'

'Boss, what the fuck were you gonna do? It was an IED . . .

You weren't going to stop that . . . You'd probably have just got yourself killed . . . There is nothing you could have done, so don't beat yourself up about it, y'hear?'

'. . . I suppose . . . I dunno . . . Are you going to the funeral?'

'I'd like to, but we'll see what the arrangements are. It may be abroad.'

'Yeah . . . I'm gonna go whatever, so at least there'll be someone from 7 Platoon there. The lads will appreciate that.'

'They will. I was talking to Speedy . . . They're hangin' in there.'

'I'll try and ring them tomorrow . . . . I'll be in touch about the funeral.'

'Roger, boss. Take it handy.'

7 Platoon have a couple of days to recuperate. Morale slumps.

Then they are back out.

They occupy a new compound, PB Cupples, overlooking that nemesis of ours, Green 12. They get hit. And hit hard. Joe Bog's sentry position evaporates around him, completely destroyed by an RPG. By chance, he survives. And they fight them off.

A bearer party is chosen from 7 Platoon for Cupples's repatriation service in Bastion. A thick square of desert uniforms, caubeens and assorted berets stand to attention in the desert's evening heat. The padre says his prayers. The piper plays the lament, the bugler the last post. The pall-bearers carry the Union Jack-draped coffin slowly on to the waiting Globemaster. The ramp goes up. The plane taxis and takes off, banking over the still-solemn square, tipping its wing mournfully in a final salute, firing its flares, and then slowly, reluctantly, adjusting its course for Lyneham.

WOOTTON BASSETT

Here dead we lie
Because we did not choose
To live and shame the land
From which we sprung.

'Here Dead We Lie'
A.E. Housman

We see the black Globemaster approach in the grey sky and steel ourselves. It swoops low and silently past us and RAF Lyneham in salute, then turns, lands and begins to taxi towards the wide expanse of black tarmac. We move to our spots in our khaki jackets and black crossbelts, caubeens and sticks. His family and the Royal Irish pall-bearers sit behind us.

Today there is only one. But he is one of mine.

The bearer party move to the waiting ramp with the pristine black hearse. Slowly, they emerge with the coffin. Our short line sharply snaps their black leather gloves to their green caubeens in salute. Behind me I hear tears. The piper starts. *Thank God we did a rehearsal or I couldn't handle this.* The coffin is loaded on to the hearse. It drives towards us slowly, a man in a top hat and cane leading the way. More tears. It drives past.

We drop our salute, glance worriedly at each other and turn to the family.

In a quiet, dignified room, with boxes of Kleenex and white plates of cut sandwiches resting on old oak tables, we share the reality of war. This is the silent, grieving coalface. The black seam that runs under everything. The real, living, enduring hurt caused by that instantaneous, momentary pain on the other side of the world. I meet his kind, kind family, and it is so hard. So hard. In a way I feel responsible for their pain, simply because I share the uniform that has taken their son, their brother. *But that was his choice, as it was mine.* Having sat so many long Sangin nights with him, walked so many patrols with him at my shoulder, now I see his personal traits in those of his hitherto unknown family. It is touching. I look to the positives, reasoning that is what Cupples would've wanted, because that was his nature. I hope my being there gives them solace, some personal connection in the impersonal blur of uniforms. I look at the generals and colonels. *It must be hard for them.* They don't know Justin, yet they pay their respects just the same, with sensitivity and dignity, and a little unease. It's part of the warrior calling.

What we hadn't rehearsed is the procession through the small town of Wootton Bassett, whose high street runs between Lyneham and the road to the coroner's, and of which I know nothing.

We arrive before the hearse. The shops are closing. Old veterans, in blue blazers adorned with gold medals, ribbons of yellows, whites, reds, khaki, green and black berets sitting loosely on their greying heads, line the road. As do women and children. Three deep in places. Old colours dip in unison and shake slightly as old hands proudly hold them. *At least they appreciate us. At least they are proud of us.* It pulls at my emotions. I fight, fight the tears.

I lose.

An old boy comes up to me, his SAS badge distinctive on his ageing beret.

'Hello, sir. You with the Royal Irish?'

'I am . . . yes.' He drags me away from my thoughts.

'Did you know him?'

'I did. I did . . . He was my signaller.'

'I'm sorry . . . It's just terrible, terrible.'

'Thanks . . . thanks . . . How long have you been doing this?' I eye the parade. 'It's inspiring.'

'Oh, about six months now . . . We started to realize there were lots of hearses coming through and we found out why. Since then, we've been closing the businesses and lining the streets every time someone comes back. We all turn out from the Legion . . . There's just so many coming back now . . .'

'I know . . . I know . . .'

'Still, we'll keep doing it, pay our respects . . . It's all we can do, really . . .'

'You don't know how much this matters to us. It's . . . really touching. It's like someone actually cares, someone understands . . .'

'Well, I don't know what Afghanistan is like, but I do know what war is like, and you boys need all the support you can get, if you ask me.'

'Yes . . . Thank you . . . thank you . . . It means a lot.'

'An honour, sir, an honour.'

He walks away.

VILNIUS

Life, to be sure,
Is nothing much to lose,
But young men think it is,
And we were young.

'Here Dead We Lie'
A. E. Housman

Another aeroplane disgorges us into the airport. Outside in the wet night, a Lithuanian sergeant major in crisp green camouflage greets us and drives us to the barracks. Huge concrete Soviet-era barrack blocks loom over a large, lonely parade square. We meet the bearer party in our basic dorm room of greys and browns, of metal lockers, spring beds and a single full-length mirror. *Just like every other barracks . . .*

A grey dawn breaks as we dust uniforms, polish crossbelts, buff shoes. The bearer party have a final practice at the graveside. We meet the British military attaché, the unfortunate man who was tasked with telling Justin's wife, Vilma, that he was dead. And his family in America.

I meet a colonel whose duty it is to go to every funeral from our brigade. Still, he has had to miss some. Too many.

289

Then US Marines, in smart navy-blue uniforms, golden buttons and white peaked caps, usher us into the church. In my piper greens and khaki jacket I read the eulogy from the altar with that detached sense that I'm watching myself in a film. I try to honour him as best I can, to give it all some purpose. *Be positive.*

It is hard.

'. . . To Don, Kathleen and Vilma, know that we too have lost one of our family, our family of 7 Platoon. To Ciaran and Adrianna, know that we too have lost a brother . . .'

A distraught woman, Vilma's mother, tears rolling down her red cheeks, speaks to me in Lithuanian. A young man interprets her words for me. Her husband and others watch on.

'I want you to know that we really loved him . . .'

Her eyes search my face. There is painful accusation in her voice.

'We loved him so much . . . We loved him as a son . . . We really loved him,' she sobs.

In the graveyard it is grey. The lines of the Lithuanian honour guard, in their grey tunics and white gloves, sharply punch their rifles outward in salute. The pallbearers slide past in that mournful, measured, respectful slow march as they bear the weight of the draped coffin. A lonely caubeen sits on top. They move up, through the rows of white and grey flagstones. The pipes play. Tears behind us. As they approach our single row of varied British, American and Lithuanian dress uniforms, we salute.

They lower the coffin slowly, with difficulty, into the ground. Beside the grave sit dozens of quiet bouquets of white flowers and prayer cards. It rains.

Silence.

We hold the final salute as the bugle sounds the last post.

The Union Jack is folded neatly and solemnly presented with his caubeen to his family.

The last post stops.

Further down the row of headstones, the Lithuanians shoulder their rifles.

A command.

Report.

Command.

Report.

Command.

Report.

Our arms snap to our sides.

We turn to our side.

And exhale.

I stare at the rows of flagstones standing grey against the brown autumn leaves. Shadows fall in places. In other places sunlight kisses the stones. Chance has played its part here also.

SANGIN

I saw the danger, and I passed
Along the enchanted way,
And I said let grief be a fallen leaf,
At the dawning of the day.

'Raglan Road'
Patrick Kavanagh,

In the seven months Ranger Company served in Sangin, many
good people died. The company dealt with 110 IEDs and 122 contacts. The sergeant major personally put forty dead people into
body bags. But numbers do not describe nor qualify experiences.
I was lucky to survive with all my limbs, as were many, many
others. Today, I live, while others do not. In the time since I have
left Sangin, the US Marines have also left, and fifty-eight British
soldiers have died there. On current ratios, three times that
number will have been amputated, half *that* number wounded. I
don't know about Afghan civilians. Use your imagination.

I don't know if Sangin has improved, though I think of it often.
I do know the governor was removed for corruption. There have
been two others since.

I don't know about post-traumatic stress disorder. But I do

know about not sleeping in case I get shot in the head. I do know about nightmares. I do know about gory images flicking before my eyes. About violent fantasies. About burning rage.

Thankfully, since writing this they have dissipated.

But I am not a victim. I knew the consequences. I saw the danger, and I passed along the enchanted way. I am proud of my experiences. Proud I served with these fine men in this corrosive war. Proud I learned a lot, of myself and of human nature. For that I am thankful. Though I doubt I would be if I hadn't returned intact.

When we did return, many members of Ranger Company were highly commended for their bravery and leadership, including the boss and Matt. It was widely acknowledged, by both military command and the press, that the company had acted in an exemplary manner with restraint and intellect throughout the dangers they were subjected to. In terms of IEDs, this was *twice* the number of devices than the next highest location. A fact that proves Ronnie, T, Davy, Naf, the whole of that seven-man search team, were some of the bravest men deployed that summer. The crucial area of Sangin was and remains the most lethal place in which to be deployed as a British soldier.

7 Platoon, that team of individuals chance threw together for that summer in Sangin, is no more. Like all things, they have moved on, been scattered to the winds. Some, like myself, have left the army; most still serve. Some will not return to Afghanistan; most will. For some of those who do, their mothers, wives and children will endure their third tour of Afghanistan as much as they will.

You can only roll the dice so often.

Warriors accept this, as they accept this is their war.

But these are your warriors.

And this is your war.

IN MEMORIAM

Sangin's Fallen

March–September 2008

They that fought so well – in death are warriors still;
Stubborn and steadfast to the end, they could not be
    dishonoured.
Their bodies perished in the fight; but the magic of
    their souls lives on –
Captains among the ghosts, heroes among the Dead!

Chinese 'Hymn to the Fallen'

Marine Dale Gostick, 3 Troop, Armoured Support Group, Royal
    Marines, 25 May 2008
Private Nathan Cuthbertson, 2nd Battalion, The Parachute
    Regiment, 8 June 2008
Private David Murray, 2nd Battalion, The Parachute Regiment,
    8 June 2008
Private Daniel Gamble, 2nd Battalion, The Parachute Regiment,
    8 June 2008
Warrant Officer Class 2 Michael Williams, 2nd Battalion, The
    Parachute Regiment, 24 June 2008

Private Joe Whittaker, 2nd Battalion, The Parachute Regiment, 24 June 2008

Lance Corporal Kenneth Rowe, Army Veterinary Corps, 24 July 2008

Private Peter Cowton, 2nd Battalion, The Parachute Regiment, 27 July 2008

Corporal Anthony Mihalo, Echo Company, 2nd Battalion, 7th Regiment, USMC, 14 August 2008

Lance Corporal Jacob Toves, Echo Company, 2nd Battalion, 7th Regiment, USMC, 14 August 2008

Lance Corporal Juan Lopez Casteneda, Echo Company, 2nd Battalion, 7th Regiment, USMC, 14 August 2008

Ranger Justin Cupples, Ranger Company, 1st Battalion, The Royal Irish Regiment, 4 September 2008

And to the more than sixty British soldiers who have been killed there since . . .

RANK STRUCTURE

CO – Commanding Officer. In infantry regiments this is usually a Lieutenant Colonel, an officer with nearly 20 years' experience, who commands a battalion of about 500 infantrymen.

OC – Officer Commanding; aka '*The* boss'. Holding the rank of Major, he typically commands a company of 5 officers and over 100 infantrymen, organised into 3 combat platoons, often reinforced with other attachments such as Forward Air Controllers (FACs), Forward Observation Officers (FOOs) and numerous supporting rear troops such as Vehicle Mechanics (VMs) and chefs.

2iC – aka Company Second in Command. Usually a Captain with four to five years' experience, he is responsible for enabling the OC's plans by aiding and executing orders and maintaining company headquarters, aka the operations centre. In peacetime he is responsible for all training.

CSM – Company Sergeant Major; aka Sergeant Major. The senior non-commissioned soldier in a company who supports the OC in running it. In Ranger Company he has almost twenty years of experience and has worked his way up the rank structure the hard way. In charge of all discipline, logistics and the medical evacuation of casualties, he also mentors young officers and his Junior Non-Commissioned Officers (JNCOs).

Platoon Commander – Referred to as 'boss' in 7 Platoon. Usually a 2nd Lieutenant or Lieutenant, with up to two years of experience. In Ranger Company there were three, of which the author was the most senior. They are accountable and responsible for over thirty soldiers each, including attached personnel, and their actions.

Sergeant – Like the Sergeant Major is to *The* boss, the Platoon Sergeant supports, but also mentors, the Platoon Commander, his boss. He is also in charge of discipline, all logistics and casualty evacuation for the platoon. A Sergeant normally has eight to ten years' experience. P.J., then Speedy, were 7 Platoon's excellent Sergeants.

Cpl – Corporal; a Non-Commissioned Officer with five to eight years' experience. In 7 Platoon there were three: H, Matt and Ronnie. They command Sections of six to eight men, three of which, plus the Platoon Commander's and Platoon Sergeant's Group, make a Platoon deployed tactically for operations. They report directly to the Platoon Commander.

Lance Corporal – aka Lance Jack. Each Corporal has one or two of these JNCOs in their Section. These are soldiers with usually two to four years' experience and work directly to the Platoon Sergeant. Ake, Ally, Dev and Naf were 7 Platoon's Lance Jacks. Casualties and R and R mean each soldier, from Ranger to 2iC, must be willing and able to 'step up' and do the job of his commander.

Ranger – title given to all private soldiers in the Royal Irish Regiment, continuing the history of one of their antecedent regiments, The Connaught Rangers, disbanded in 1922 on formation of *Saor Stat na hEireann* (the Irish Republic).

DS – Directing Staff. Usually experienced Captains or Colour Sergeants from the top ten per cent of the infantry, who have been selected to train the next generation of young officers.

NCO – Any ranks of Corporal, through Sergeant, Colour Sergeant and Sergeant Major, to the highest, the Regimental Sergeant Major, who is the most senior soldier who does not hold the Queen's Commission in a battalion.

SANGIN GLOSSARY

AGAI – Army General Administrative Instruction. The official army discipline system.

ANA – Afghan National Army. Consists of mainly Tajiks from northern Afghanistan, who are generally brave and, most important, respected by the Pashtuns in Sangin.

ANCOP – Afghan National Civil Order Police. Mainly tough Tajiks from the north, they are akin to a heavily armed gendarmerie with an anti-corruption mandate. They hate the Pashtun ANP.

ANP – Afghan National Police. Usually corrupt and unreliable police force, often drawn from local areas. Hated by the locals for their extortion and power plays.

AO – Area of Operations.

EOD – Explosive Ordnance Disposal. Engineer teams that destroy IEDs. Increasingly crucial as the situation in Sangin deteriorates.

Faugh a Ballagh – 'Clear the way.' The motto of the Royal Irish Regiment.

FLET – Forward Line of Enemy Troops. Always changing, malleable, and in Sangin in summer 2008 encroaching on us.

FOB – Forward Operating Base. Typically semi-converted large Afghan compounds that ISAF forces operate from throughout

Afghanistan. The 'DC' is Ranger Company's FOB in the centre of Sangin town.

FSG – Fire Support Group. Consists of about twelve Paras armed with GPMGs and Javelin missile launchers to enable the assault group to manoeuvre. Unknown to the author at the time, it is commanded by a hugely respected Para Sergeant Major.

IRT – Incident Response Team. A Chinook helicopter with full surgical team that is used to extract both ISAF and civilian casualties to the field hospital in Camp Bastion.

ISAF – International Security Assistance Force. Almost all foreign soldiers in Afghanistan are serving in this UN-mandated force. Some Americans are not.

JDAM – Joint Direct Attack Munition.

NGO – Non Governmental Organization. Usually a charity, in Sangin there is evidence of past projects, but now it is too dangerous for almost all NGO activity.

NDS – National Directorate of Security. Afghanistan's domestic intelligence service.

OMLT – Operational Mentor and Liaison Teams. Small teams of isolated British soldiers that live with, train and guide the ANA on operations. Although they provide the basis for the exit strategy in Afghanistan, most infantry soldiers would initially prefer to be deployed as a company group, as Ranger Company was.

OP – Observation Patrol. Usually a concealed, static patrol location from which enemy movement can be observed.

PKM – Soviet belt-fed machine gun, firing 7.62-millimetre bullets. Similar to our GPMG. Along with the AK-47 and rocket-propelled grenade, a favoured weapon for Taliban ambushes.

Tabbing – Derives from 'tactical advance to battle' and describes infantry covering large amounts of ground in full pack.

USMC – United States Marine Corps.

Zap numbers – The first two letters and last four numbers of a person's regimental number, used to ID them quickly in emergency situations.

9 Liner – The casualty report that gives the concise, relevant information for medevac.